Regional Fictions

CULTURE AND IDENTITY IN NINETEENTH-CENTURY AMERICAN LITERATURE

Stephanie Foote

The University of Wisconsin Press

The University of Wisconsin Press
2537 Daniels Street
Madison, Wisconsin 53718

3 Henrietta Street
London WC2E 8LU, England

1   3   5   4   2

Printed in the United States of America

Library of Congress Cataloging-in-Publication Data
Foote, Stephanie.
Regional fictions : culture and identity in
nineteenth-century American literature / Stephanie Foote.
224 pp.   cm.
Includes bibliographical references and index.
ISBN 0-299-17110-8 (alk. paper)
ISBN 0-299-17114-0 (pbk.: alk. paper)
1. American literature—19th century—History and criticism.
2. Regionalism in literature.
3. Nationalism—United States—History—19th century.
4. National characteristics, American, in literature.
5. United States—Civilization—19th century.
6. Local color in literature.
7. Nationalism in literature.   I. Title.
PS217.R44 F66   2001
810.9'32—dc21   00-010613

Publication of this book has been made possible in part
by the generous support of the Anonymous Fund of the
University of Wisconsin–Madison.

Contents

Acknowledgments

Many people read this book as I was writing it. Kenneth Dauber, Neil Schmitz, Roy Roussel, William Patrick Day, and Sandra Zagarell read all or part of the manuscript in its earliest stages and helped me imagine it as a book. My colleagues at the University of Illinois have been remarkably generous with their time. I would particularly like to thank Nina Baym, Leon Chai, Bruce Michelson, Cary Nelson, and Robert Dale Parker. I also thank the Research Board at the University of Illinois for released time from teaching. My students have patiently let me work out these ideas in seminars, and I am grateful to them. My friends and co-conspirators Janet Sorensen, Simon Joyce, Joseph Valente, and Joanne Slutsky (all of whom shoot a mean game of eight ball), Eva Cherniavsky, and Priscilla Wald provided critical advice and conversation when I most needed them. Peter, Deby, Zachary, Krystina, Don, and Pat supplied regional distractions that were decidedly nonacademic and therefore doubly valuable to me as I was (not) writing. I also thank the staff at the University of Wisconsin Press, especially Raphael Kadushin and Sheila McMahon. Finally, I thank Cris Mayo. Her sharp intellect made every page of this book better, and her presence charmed all the hours it claimed.

Chapter 1 first appeared in *Arizona Quarterly* 52.2 (1996) and is reprinted by permission of the Regents of the University of Arizona. The first half of chapter 2 previously appeared in *Studies in American Fiction* 27.2 (fall 1999) and is reprinted by permission.

Regional Fictions

Introduction

What Difference Does Regional Writing Make?

Regional Fictions studies the late nineteenth century through regional fiction, one of its most important but most short-lived literary forms.[1] Regional fiction is best remembered today for its nostalgic portraits of preindustrial rural communities and people. Although regional texts focused almost exclusively on rural concerns, their nostalgic tone shows them to have been profoundly shaped by an awareness of the globalizing and standardizing tendencies of urbanization and industrialization. Regional fiction's most recognizable formal characteristic was its use of dialect to render the speech of regional speakers. But the juxtaposition of local accents with the standard English of most narrators of regional fiction shows that while the subject of the texts was rural life, their readers were nonetheless urban inhabitants. Regional fiction's appeal was its presentation of people and places that seemed to have "escaped" the dubious improvements of a stronger and more integrated urban economy. As I explain, these textual features inspired the contemporary admirers of regional fiction as well as its first critics to define regional writing as a "minor" literature, concerned only with eluding the potential ravages of modernity. I challenge that interpretation by suggesting that regional writing developed strategies to transform rather than to passively resist the meaning of the social and economic developments of late-nineteenth-century urban life.

In the following chapters, I examine regional texts for what they can tell literary critics about the late nineteenth century's anxieties about national identity and citizenship in an era marked by social and political upheaval. I also look at the texts to see what the nineteenth century can tell twentieth-century literary critics about the sources of their current interest in the formation of national identity. The global ambition of the late-twentieth-century United States bears a striking resemblance to its late-nineteenth-century incarnation; it has been variously characterized as, among other things, the age of greed, the end of history, the triumph of capitalism, the dissolution of the nation-state, or, if the idealists are to be believed, the dawn of an informed cosmopolitanism.

Despite the totalizing claims made in its name, the contemporary United States has inherited from the nineteenth century its preoccupation with more minute matters—specifically the legal and social status of gendered, raced, and ethnic identities in a nation that presumptively is politically unified. Like the nineteenth century, the twentieth is troubled by claims for recognition and representation by marginal people. Because it is a form that works to preserve local customs, local accents, and local communities, regional writing is a form *about* the representation of difference. As such, it offers critics a way to analyze one of the nineteenth century's most effective literary strategies for managing the conflict between local and national identities. An analysis of regional writing's literary strategies becomes even more important when we realize how many of our contemporary ideas about the value and status of a particularized cultural (or local) identity are derived from regional writing's strategy of protecting local identities by preserving them in literature.

The regional fiction with which I am concerned in this book had a brief but influential reign in American letters. Its privileged position in periodicals like the *Atlantic Monthly*, the *Century*, *Harper's*, and *Scribner's* (the era's most respected and elite periodicals) spanned roughly the thirty years between 1870 and 1900.[2] Although fiction about unassimilated territory or dialect speakers had been produced before the Civil War, its popularity and development as an elite periodical form are post–Civil War phenomena. Even in this manifestation, though, the "origins" of regional fiction are still occasionally debated, with its beginning as a genteel periodical genre often attributed to, for instance, the runaway national popularity of Bret Harte's 1867 *The Luck of Roaring Camp*.

I am less interested in the development of the form than I am in how the regional fiction that was marketed in national venues represented various sections of the consolidating nation to an audience that was conscious of itself as a national elite.[3] The appearance of regional fiction in periodicals like the *Atlantic Monthly* ensured that its primary reading audience was already concerned with national affairs and national politics. Such an audience could afford to travel, and if its members did not think of themselves as exactly worldly, they probably did not think of themselves as provincial either. The relationship of this audience to a genre that was, on its face, dedicated to elucidating and even celebrating provincial mores is compelling; it suggests that the representation of provinces served the needs of a group of readers whose freedom from the constraints of provincial communities made them vulnerable to the isolation and alienation of urban life at the turn of the century.

Ideas about how regional writing served the needs of a particular audience have generally concentrated on the conditions of its consumption. For instance, regional writing has been thoroughly examined in relation to the urban middle-class reader's sense of alienation, with critics pointing to the chaos of turn-of-the-century life. For example, although the late nineteenth century's rapid changes promised unparalleled physical mobility, they also threatened psychic dislocation, or what T. J. Jackson Lears famously called a sense of "weightlessness" in everyday life (1981:45). Weightlessness, or the sense that no experience was quite real, is symptomatic alienation, or self-estrangement, and it sought its cure, according to Lears, in a search for some experience or place more real or more "authentic" than the conditions of modern life. Regional writing's careful, thick descriptions of the rhythms of rural life and provincial communities embodied a formal or technical commitment to fidelity. It therefore fulfilled the substantive requirement for "real" experience largely *because* of this formal commitment to descriptive fidelity. Its nostalgia met an ironically modern need for urban readers. Indeed, many of the regional novels I analyze include passing but pointed remarks about the tendency of Easterners to rejuvenate themselves by visiting (and sometimes spoiling) previously pristine regions. Along similar lines, Richard Brodhead (1993) argues that regional writing appeals to (and participates in) a tourist economy that is itself driven by a desire to collect new experiences to help combat the sense that "real" experience was harder and harder to come by in everyday life.

Although regional writing's popularity was sustained by its ability to fill an imagined need in its urban readers, we need to supplement a consideration of the conditions of its consumption with some of the historical conditions of its production. That is, we must consider that the interest in producing and consuming regional "folk" occurred in an era that witnessed steadily increasing waves of immigration. A more pointed way of saying this is that regional writing gave strangers with accents literary recognition at exactly the same moment that accented strangers in the form of immigrants were clamoring for recognition and representation in the political arena.4 Literature's role in establishing and mediating the "average" urban citizen's sense of self-estrangement in a world filled with increasing numbers of strangers has been the topic of much recent work in American literature, especially in the genre of realism. But it seems clear that depictions of regional life were uniquely suited to reconciling urban dwellers' endemic feelings of self-estrangement and their various (often fearful) responses to strangers.

By depicting a rural folk, regional writing constructs a common national past for readers concerned with national matters. Historians and critics of the development of national identity have noted that the imaginative representation of a "folk" who seemed to represent a pre-modern past is a common feature of consolidating nations. Eric Hobsbawm writes, for example, that "where the supremacy of state nationality and state-language were not an issue, the major nation could cherish and foster the dialects . . . within it" (1990:35). Ernest Gellner argues, "Nationalist ideology suffers from a false consciousness. It claims to defend folk culture even while it invents high culture" (1983:124).5 Susan Gillman agrees, adding that "the point of constructing a more harmonious, 'imaginary' past is to look both away from and toward the disturbing present. Similarly Janus-faced is the category of regionalism itself, which constructs region as both separate from and engaged with nation" (1994:115).

In presenting provincial persons who speak in an accented English as the temporal equivalents of its readers (regional characters are characters who live now) as well as spatially distant from them (they are far enough away to have escaped or been bypassed by industrialization), regional writing creates a circuit between its "standard" readers and its provincial characters. First, regional folk are distinctly American—they inhabit, after all, American territories and thus are droll likenesses of regular Americans. They might even be images of the ancestors of middle-class urban dwellers, emblems of an earlier, generative community. But in creating the folk as specimens marked by their folkways, their accents, and their reliance on older notions of community, regional writing also creates the folk as doubles of foreigners, or immigrants. Regionalism's most interesting ideological strategy, then, is exactly counter to its narrative strategy. Rather than depicting a familiar, timeless, and shared agrarian past, regional writing *defamiliarizes* narratives about the origins of national identity in the United States. Regional writing's dissemination in high cultural venues, its appearance in the late nineteenth century (a moment when the newly reunited states were becoming not just a powerful nation but also a powerful imperial force), and its substantive preoccupation with dialect as the formal corollary of something like ethnic self-expression combined to make it a genre uniquely suited to imagine a homogeneous past for a heterogeneous nation.

My reading of the culture that the literary form of regional writing imagined is similar to the interpretation given to it by its greatest fan. Regional writing's depiction of local customs, its vision of the value of ordinary rural lives, made it, for writers like William Dean Howells, an antidote to the psychic ravages of modernity as well as a model of assimilative democracy. In *The Social Construction of American Realism*, Amy Kaplan casts William Dean Howells as the standard bearer in the battle over realism; it is not surprising that he also brokers the triumph of regionalism in the literary market. In his capacity as the editor of *Harper's Monthly* magazine, Howells championed not only regionalist writers but also the *idea* of regionalism. Howells devoted column after editorial column to elaborating regional writing's connection with the idea of a strong, democratic national identity. But in doing so, he also asserted that it allegorized the emergence of such a national identity.

One of regional writing's staunchest backers and most powerful brokers, Howells worked to ensure the circulation of regional writing and to solidify its reputation. To writers like Sarah Orne Jewett, Howells offered professional support and encouragement. Others writers, like Hamlin Garland and Gertrude Atherton, thought of Howells as an ambivalent symbol of the literary establishment's power in creating fame and fortune for a certain kind of literature. Howells's criteria for good writing were as well known as his reputation as an editor. His program for regionalism was at once strict and romantic; his editorial columns and his individual advice to writers reveal that he tended to focus on the mimetic qualities of regional writing, on its promise to be "true" to life. Howells's interest in the mimetic quality of regional fiction underwrites his estimation of its literary merit as well as its social value. In championing the local, and the local-color story, Howells directly yokes the project of regional writing to the project of democracy. In perhaps the most famous passage from his monthly column, Howells wrote in May 1887:

Let fiction cease to lie about life; let it portray men and women as they are, actuated by the motives and the passions in the measure we all know; let it leave off painting dolls and working them by springs and wires; let it show the different interests in their true proportions; let it forbear to preach pride and revenge, folly and insanity, egotism and prejudice, but frankly own these for what they are, in whatever figures and occasions they appear; let it not put on fine literary airs; let it speak the dialect, the language, that most Americans know—the language of unaffected people everywhere—and we believe that even its masterpieces will find a response in all readers. (1983:81)

This often-quoted passage allows Howells to make an interesting double gesture. He becomes both the editor who controls the production of representations of "most Americans" and the representative of "most Americans."[6] Pleading for fiction to represent people as they "really" are is a democratic appeal, as it asks literary representation to bear the symbolic responsibility of democratic representation. But such a unitary image of "most Americans" collides with the rhetoric of "different interests," and Howells's manifesto exposes problems in literature's relation to democracy, as well as the local's (different interests) relation to the national ("we all know").

In September 1887, Howells repeated his formulation that "real" or ordinary life could be elevated to an aesthetic standard and a political principle:

The pride of caste is becoming the pride of taste; but as before, it is averse to the mass of men; it consents to know them only in some conventionalized and artificial guise. It seeks to withdraw itself, to stand aloof; to be distinguished, and not to be identified. Democracy in literature is the reverse of all this. It wishes to know and to tell the truth, confident that consolation and delight are there; it does not care to paint the marvellous and impossible for the vulgar many, or to sentimentalize and falsify that actual for the vulgar few. Men are more like than unlike one another: let us make them know one another better, that they may be all humbled and strengthened with a sense of their fraternity. (1983:96)

Howells's assertion that democracy in literature shows men to be more like than unlike one another hints at what he believed to be one of the most important elements of regional writing. By faithfully depicting specific local cultures, regionalism adheres to a standard of fidelity, of accuracy in representing the content and contours of regional life. This fidelity also extends the narrative strategy of individual regional texts, as it promises the reader that out of all of the writing about distinctly different regions, a single national type can be discerned. Likewise, Howells extends his analogy of making people "known" to one another to making them "like" one another by observing,

It is true that no one writer, no one book, represents [America] for that is not possible, our social and political decentralization forbids this, and may forever forbid it. But a great number of very good writers are instinctively striving to make each part of the country and each phase of our civilization known to all the other parts; and their work is not narrow in any feeble or vicious sense. (1983:98)

Howells specifies regional writing's role in transforming cultural variation into national identity in his July 1891 column. Reviewing H. H. Boyesen's *The Mammon of Unrighteousness*, Howells praises the novel for its scope but cautions,

Of course he has not got America all in. America will never be all got in till the great American novel is conceived in an encyclopedical form, with a force of novelists proportioned upon the basis of our Congressional representation, and working under one editorial direction. . . . We are cynically selfish, we are magnanimously generous; the antagonism felt in each is expressed on a continually widening scale from the citizen up through the town meeting to the government of the whole republic. (1983:326)

Amy Kaplan has examined Howells's editorial persona, reading his nationalizing rhetoric through his conflicted relationship to the emerging mass market that threatened (rather than promised) to supersede fiction's role in "introducing" citizens to one another by making citizens just like one another. According to this interpretation, Howells is not only an arbiter of realism but also of the real itself. Howells's attention to the genre of dialect fiction and his elevation and theorization of the meaning of the local short story reveal him as the first reader to be seduced by regionalism's impossible claims to represent accurately the real.

In his July 1891 column, Howells comes the closest to shifting the debate over regionalism's role as a democratic literature to regionalism as democracy. His rhetoric about the local's relation to the national conflates the differences between literary and political representation, establishing writers as congressional representatives and himself, presumably, as president. Yet in his faith in the ability of dialect writers to construct versions of local culture that can coexist peacefully in a single political entity, Howells conceals, as regionalism itself will, the absence of certain kinds of local cultures, identities, and accents in the democratic republic. His interest in occluding the ways in which local accents resemble but replace foreign accents is apparent in his oddly myopic September 1890 review of *A Japanese Boy*:

The curious autobiography of *A Japanese Boy*, which has lately come into our hand, testifies to the fact of human equality, and there is . . . pleasure in . . . recognizing the Japanese boy's identity in essentials with the American boy. . . . It is all very queer, outwardly; but inwardly the life is like our own, with the same affections, the same emotions, the same ambitions, the same ideals of rectitude and kindness and purity. We value the book not only for the pleasure, the sincere and graphic life-pictures given it, but for the contribution to man's knowledge of himself which it makes. It will help to clear away the delusion that the quality, the essence of human nature is varied by condition, or creed, or climate, or color; and to teach the truth of our solidarity which we are so long a-learning. (1983:276)

This review envisions a singularly coherent idea of the local. External difference, masking an internal similarity, establishes regional writing's democratic promise. Pointing out that something transcends ethnicity, showing an "us" the truth of "our solidarity" echoes Howells's desire for fiction that shows men that they are like one another. Although Howells's review of *A Japanese Boy* accords with his belief in the social value of regional writing, it does not seem to recognize that the autobiography is not that of a "regional" American. Rather, the truth of national solidarity exists only when it covers over real political or ethnic differences, relegating them to the abstract and paradoxically focusing on the "interior" of characters and subjects. Howells's interest in interiority also paradoxically confounds regional writing's "lesson" that cultural difference is an infinitely exchangeable commodity.

Although Howells is the most famous champion of regional writing's social possibilities, other contemporary critics joined him in his advocacy. In the *Century*'s monthly column "The Topics of the Time," in a subsection entitled "Our Obligations to Dialect," another reviewer writes that

> it is not unusual to hear the remark, "I never read stories with dialect," and every now and then this personal attitude finds expression in the press in the shape of a savage ban against this form of composition in prose or verse, as thought it were a sort of literary heresy. The impression is sometimes given that dialect is an invention of the modern magazine.

The columnist counters the readers' exhaustion with dialect writing by pointing out that

> could one put into practice the anathema against dialect with *ex post facto* effect, the variety and flavor of democracy would largely disappear from fiction and the color would almost fade out of it, while the gaiety of nations would well-nigh be eclipsed. It would not be the abolition of dialect, but the extinction of a large measure of literature. To object to dialect is to object to the types it represents, and to deny them the right to speak in their natural voices.

He goes on to make the point that figures in local-color stories who are represented in dialect "compose a gallery of American characters so various as to accentuate the political homogeneity of a land that holds them all" ("Topics of the Time" 1902:635–636).

The *Century* commentator asserts that local-color writing gives "nations" the right to speak in their "natural" voices, assuming that local color is the authentic expression of the people depicted in it—as though only Tennesseans wrote about Tennessee and only New Englanders wrote about New England. Although the commentator protests the notion that dialect is the invention of magazines, seeming to uphold the idea that dialect is the authentic expression of the folk and that dialect writing is their authentic literature, he was not entirely accurate. Regional literature's popularization of dialect had no necessary relationship to the way that people "really" spoke, nor did the high cultural status assigned to regional writing's dialect translate into an equivalent political or social respect for provincial or rustic dialect speakers. If dialect were seen to be the true representation of regional folk, it also, in the terms of genteel regional writing, concealed the voice of the folk by mimicking, however carefully, their speech. It is necessary to remind ourselves that many people in the United States at the end of the nineteenth century spoke with an accent or participated in or were shaped by a local culture that seemed, in the lived experience of everyday life, very remote from standard national culture.

Regional writing's project of valorizing local dialect maintained that a speaker's accent should not exclude her from the standard culture but, rather, that accents measured a speaker's relationship to the standard culture. Its formal concern with assigning to different kinds of people a place in relation to the standard, national culture demonstrates that regional writing was a powerful method of understanding not just the "place" where certain people lived but also the "place" they inhabited in a social hierarchy. In this capacity, regional writing could often be remarkably progressive. As Howells noted in his December 1888 "Editor's Study," "We need not remind the reader of the Study how little it cares for literature except as the language of life; and how always it is the Study's aim to include all accents rather than to exclude any" (1983:170).

That *A Japanese Boy*—about a member of an ethnic group that, along with the Chinese, most puzzled the American public—could be evaluated in the same terms as, for example, a short story by Mary Wilkins Freeman tells us at least as much about the function of magazine fiction in the imaginative democratic republic of letters as it does about regional fiction. While the *Century* reviewer mistakes the idea that the popularity of dialect was not an invention of the literary magazine, Howells does not. In February 1887, he reflects on the causes for the abundance of short stories in American fiction, deciding that their success is due to the

success of American magazines, which is nothing less than prodigious, [and] only commensurate with their excellence. . . . By another operation of the same law, which political economists have more recently taken account of, the demand follows the supply, and short stories are sought for because there is a proven ability to furnish them, and people read them willingly because they are usually very good. The art of writing them is now so disciplined and diffused with us that there is no lack either for the magazines or for the newspaper "syndicates" which deal in them almost to the exclusion of the serials. (1983:66)

Here Howells is, in effect, announcing a market formula for the distribution of the fiction that he will champion from his editor's column, but his use of the rhetoric of supply and demand does not, for example, anticipate problems in marketing local color in the future. Although Howells seemed to rely a great deal on metaphors of participatory democracy in his trumpeting of local forms, his democracy strongly resembles the operations of a consumer market. That is, although William Dean Howells believed that regional writing served to create a unified national identity, he was less aware of how relying on market indicators of regional writing's value served the nineteenth century's "wholesale commercialization of life" (Ziff 1979:14). Therefore, he was unable to see that one of the effects of advocating the national importance of regional writing was the paradoxical evacuation of individual regional specificity. No specificity, no market. Indeed, regional fiction did not endure long past the turn of the century. But clearly, its ubiquitous appearance in late-nineteenth-century periodicals and its extraordinary popularity with the upper-middle-class reading public testify to the cultural and literary ground it covered.

One of the finest critiques of regional or agrarian writing, Raymond Williams's *The Country and the City,* charges the disappearance of rural culture to the account of expanding urban centers. Williams argues that nostalgia for the idealized country becomes nostalgia for the idealized past.

A willing, lulling illusion of old country life [pays] its political dividends. A natural country ease is contrasted with an unnatural urban unrest. The "modern world," both in its suffering and, crucially, in its protest against suffering, is mediated by reference to a lost condition which is better than both and which can place both: a condition imagined out of a landscape and a selective observation and memory. (Williams 1973:180)

But even when yearning for an idealized landscape, market considerations intervene. The relationship between nostalgia and a market economy reminds us that even the innocent rhetoric of yearning for the region—a rhetoric that invokes "loss" and "dear" memories—is also the rhetoric of the marketplace.

The "lost condition" that Williams describes relies on a vision of the folk-as-family and of the family as the site of lost wholeness. Susan Stewart argues that "distressed genres" like regional writing and other forms of folklore elicit and feed a kind of nostalgia that "is not a nostalgia for artifacts for their own sake; rather it is a nostalgia for context, for the heroic past, for moral order, for childhood and the collective experiences of pre-industrial life." She goes on to say that "the closely guarded thematics of distressed genres—heroism, paternity, the domestic past, the rural/agrarian, the tribal/communal, the 'primitive,' and the child—are radically separated from their mechanical reproduction" (1991:91, 93). The inscription of the "nation" as "family" is a pervasive trope of regionalism, but it also was a crucial factor in the recovery of its reputation.

Feminist critics like Josephine Donovan, Sandra Zagarell, Elizabeth Ammons, and Marjorie Pryse led the recovery of regional texts by critiquing some of its most important elements—nostalgia, the figuration of the region as the "haven" of the urban nation, and, finally, the persistent devaluation of regional writing as "feminine" or "feminized" by the first generation of twentieth-century critics who studied and classified works of nineteenth-century literature.[7] Feminist critics have claimed that regional writing was especially hospitable to women writers, a judgment with which it is difficult not to agree, as most of the most popular writers of regional fiction were women and nearly all the regional writers we study now are women.[8] But the pioneering work of feminist critics also tended to establish women as the most important regional writers because, in reclaiming the implicit derogation of previous definitions of the "domestic" or "feminine" content of regional writing, they usually ignored the work of middle-class white male writers of regionalism. Although my analysis does not directly continue the feminist project of recovering regional writing, it overlaps with and is indebted to it. Feminist critics have provided an object lesson in how and why scholars need to attend to the processes by which women's writing has been systematically (and institutionally) devalued.

Like feminist critics, I see regionalism in its broadest terms as a critique of the universal subject. Judith Fetterley believes, for example, that using the evaluative category of "unAmerican" to describe regionalism underscores its role in representing marginal lives and marginal voices: "In regionalism I find a literature that models a subjectivity attained by standing up for others not on them. Invoking the concept of 'unAmerican' thus helps focus attention on the significance of which texts by minority males and women we choose to include [in the canon]" (1994:878). The project of mining regional writing for its representation of the "foreign" or the "unAmerican" suggests that one of the most important functions of regional writing was to rectify exclusion.

My own analyses use regional writing less to identify the terms under which regional writers were excluded from the canon than to examine the exclusions they depicted as constituting the individual region. A close textual analysis of regional writing shows us that contrary to even the most current reevaluations, regional writing does not depict internally homogeneous regions. This is particularly important because it shifts the grounds on which we can critically reevaluate regionalism. It is no longer possible to regard regional writing as representing a common national past; rather, we must see it as helping construct a common past in the face of, and out of the raw material of, the increasing immigration and imperialism of the nineteenth century. This means that regional writing was responsive to the nationalizing demands of the era that produced it and that its depiction of regions showed them all to be heterogeneous, founded on the differences that regional writing was assumed to eradicate. Regionalism, therefore, did not merely attempt to mediate national concerns about the relationship of strangers and natives; it also indicated that at the core of every representation of the native was a foreigner.

My assertions build on the work of literary critics concerned with the formal expression of cultural change and those who have considered the specific political implications of regional writing. Amy Kaplan and June Howard have examined the relation of the major genres of realism and naturalism to their contemporary social fields. Eric Sundquist and Richard Brodhead have uncovered the social components underwriting regionalism's form (see Howard 1986; Kaplan 1988; Sundquist 1988).[9] Yet even in the important work of contemporary critics like Brodhead, Nancy Glazener, and Michael Davitt Bell, the minor status of regional writing is reinforced by its appearance only in the final chapter in books about realism. My own concern is not to show that regionalism may or may not be a genre apart from realism. I don't, for example, believe that it can be valorized only by elevating it as a freestanding genre that is like, but not part of, realism. If it were still possible to describe realism apart from its publication history or from its authors' relationship to the profession of writing or from its attempt to imagine an interior life for people—that is, if it were possible to identify what realism "is" rather than what it does— it might be important to distinguish regional writing from realism. But my own analysis of regional writing finds that regionalism was less a coherent genre than a remarkably coherent system of ordering and presenting places and characters who were, when measured against a standard middle-class identity, distinctly foreign.

Because my argument is predicated on understanding regionalism as a literary strategy, I cover more ground in my analyses than regionalism has traditionally been assigned. Recovering regional writing's cultural work has allowed me to reread texts like Gertrude Atherton's *The Californians* (1898) or George Washington Cable's *The Grandissimes* (1880), which have fallen out of favor (or occasionally even out of print) largely because there has been no available model through which to understand them. In selecting the texts for this book, I had to exclude a number of novels that I might easily have incorporated. I made my selection based on three factors. First, the texts had to have literary aspirations—that is, because genteel literary regionalism was marketed to an urban elite audience, the authors I chose had to understand the literary market and aspire to a particular place in it. Second, the novels had to indicate that they considered and understood the conventions of nineteenth-century writing; they had to discuss and evaluate the relation of literary techniques, or even literary status, to their own form. Finally, all the texts had to be set in partially unassimilated or unstandardized territories, and they had to develop their characters as similarly nonstandard. Any number of books might have fit these criteria. But I particularly wanted to test the idea that regional writing was less a genre than a strategy by selecting novels set in unlikely or unexpected locations.

This book is organized to advance my critiques cumulatively. Thus each section has two chapters, and each section makes a single broad argument on which the following sections depend. In the first two chapters, I argue against conventional readings of regionalism as an antidote to the

trauma of urban life. For regional writing to succeed in restoring wholeness to the fragmented urban reader by offering "authentic" experiences,
it must be read as a static repository of the nation's past. It must portray
regional communities as simple and complete, structured by face-to-face
(rather than market) transactions. But when we look closely at regional
conventions, we see that the binaries that are assumed to constitute
regional writing (rural/urban, native/stranger, simplicity/chaos, nostalgia/
modernity) cannot hold up under the pressures of late-nineteenth-century
anxieties about how to represent strangers. The exotic yet familiar regional
types populating small towns are uncannily similar to the foreigners and
immigrants in the city, and the solidity of the simple "primitive" folk of
the region is not an antidote to, but instead the alibi for, alienation and
self-estrangement.[10]

In my first chapter, I look at Sarah Orne Jewett's *The Country of the
Pointed Firs* (1896) and her short story "The Foreigner" (1900). Jewett's
text is a logical beginning for a book that reconsiders the cultural work of
regionalism; it is Jewett whom nearly all critics of American literature
seem to agree (for different reasons) was the apogee of regional writing;
and it is Jewett who provided the touchstone for most of the recent critics
of regionalism. In using Jewett to reveal the hidden histories of foreignness
underpinning the notion of a national identity, I lay the groundwork to
look closely at the strategic failure of regional conventions to develop a coherent or homogeneous source of national identity. Chapter 2 examines
Hamlin Garland's short stories (all written and published in the 1890s,
although finally redacted in 1917) and Harold Frederic's *The Damnation
of Theron Ware* (1896). In each author's work, I look at depictions of the
region's relationship to an urban center, as each writer critiques the ro-
manticization of the "unchanging" region and its inhabitants. Specifically,
each writer turns the tables on regional conventions, demonstrating the
symbolic violence that regional representation imposes on "real" regional
inhabitants. In the case of Hamlin Garland, regional literary conventions
give him a way of entering a national literary marketplace, but only at the
price of what he sees as the commodification of his "real" regional identity. Harold Frederic's novel makes a similar critique of regional conventions. The "damnation" of the eponymous Theron Ware is precipitated by
his rebellion against being seen as a rustic innocent by the leading citizens
of the town.

Chapters 3 and 4 build on my analysis of regional writing's ambivalent depiction of regional figures and the audiences that consume them. In
the third chapter I examine Gertrude Atherton's 1898 novel *The Californians,* and in the fourth, I consider *The Grandissimes,* George Washington Cable's 1880 novel of New Orleans. Having contended in the first
two chapters that regional writing's strategy places the "native" and the

"foreign" in tension, I show how novels written from and about half-assimilated or colonial U.S. territories attempted to represent "realistic" foreigners. Each novel regionalizes its foreign characters, describing them as if they were local-color characters and thus representing potentially problematic political differences as cultural differences. The novels thus turn on the successful conversion of a Spanish American woman into a Californian and a French Creole into a Louisianan. But as I demonstrate, the gesture of assimilating a newly made cultural identity depends on the exclusion of its racial components. Together, these two chapters argue that regional writing gives us a way to read some of the nineteenth century's anxieties about race and ethnicity, producing still-familiar and functional definitions of racial and ethnic subjectivity.

In the third and last section, I rely on the second section's argument that regional writing produced a familiar, workable model of ethnicity. Chapter 5, which discusses Jacob Riis's *How the Other Half Lives*, and chapter 6, which analyzes novels about Tammany Hall, claim that regionalism's rhetorical practice of making an analogy between regional and ethnic characters also structures texts about the urban areas that regional writing has often been assumed to resist. I build on a twinned notion of regional representation, asking how urban subjects are produced regionally and how regional identities become "vested" identities in a contentious public sphere. In closing with a consideration of how local identity resembles what we might consider vested identity, I hope that *Regional Fictions* will help reconceptualize current critical conversations about the invention and meaning of race and ethnicity. If we look closely at regional writing's practice of representing individuals who are analogues of foreignness, as well as communities that are underwritten by racial or ethnic mixing, we will see, I believe, that regionalism's careful presentation of specific and local character still haunts our own definitions and evaluations of identities.

1

"I Feared to Find Myself a Foreigner"

Sarah Orne Jewett's *The Country of the Pointed Firs*

There is a kind of justice in the current critical rediscovery of nineteenth-century American regional fiction. Traditional critiques of regional writing tend to feminize and diminish this "minor" genre, appreciating its aesthetic dimensions while noting its childish, although perhaps charming, inability to come to terms with its contemporary conditions of mature capitalism, urban unrest, and expanding immigration and imperialism. Louis Renza argues that according to this view, "regionalism amounted to a kind of genteel evasion of realities of the more complex if not sordid social aspects of American society" (1984:44). Many critics of American literature now point out that regionalism must be approached as a genre that participates in and responds to the very social discourses in the late nineteenth century from which it ostensibly turns away.[1] Its elaborate, lyrical construction of a pristine, imaginary national past testifies to its investment in conflicted public conversations about immigration, alienation, and the effects of capitalism on private life.

Susan Gillman observed that in regional literature, "the point of constructing a more harmonious, 'imaginary' past is to look both away from and toward the disturbing present. Similarly Janus-faced is the category of regionalism itself, which constructs region as both separate from and engaged with nation" (1994:115).[2] In this chapter, I contend that regional writing's formal attempt to imagine a homogeneous rural past is countered by its substantive inability to imagine a past not already animated by a heterogeneous population. Although critics have provided the background for understanding how depictions of regions in literature combine to produce a larger representation of a heterogeneous democratic nation, my own argument is that even ostensibly coherent regions are the products of suppressed relationships between natives and strangers. Those suppressed relationships are themselves modulated interventions in a more general concern over origins and nativity. Regionalism's role in mediating the relationship of strangers and natives is thematized through its displacement of political difference onto the field of the social and the local. Regional writing expresses immanent political differences enabled by globalizing capital as cultural differences between geographic locations. But even if the cumulative effect of a standardized difference is a nation hospitable to cultural variation, we must not assume that regionalism's depictions of local culture are always coherent. Although regional writing is largely set in villages and rural areas, it is a homeopathic genre and seeks to counteract the ills of the urban with an antidote whose medicinal qualities are derived from the very poison it is supposed to counteract.

In this first chapter, I use a single regionalist text, Sarah Orne Jewett's *The Country of the Pointed Firs* (1896), to examine how regionalism rehearses historical and cultural issues concerning identity, community, and citizenship. Specifically, I look at how representations in *The Country of the Pointed Firs* of folk and folk community thwart its ostensible project of constructing a culturally homogeneous region as the source of the nation's childhood. I focus in particular on the character of the narrator, examining how her desire to become a real and authentic resident of Dunnet Landing contradicts her desire to construct as strange and foreign the population of Dunnet Landing. Because this narrator/stranger disrupts the fabric of community, even by the act of observing it, she opens the text and the region it represents to the pressures of the outer or other world from which she comes. She thus serves as a center around which the historical moment of regionalism's production and consumption can enter the text. The textual stranger in regional fiction is, like the reader, peripheral to and fascinated by the miniature of the self-contained world of the region and frames an observation of the "natives," the figures of regional interest, as both exotic (they represent a type that city folk think of as charmingly rustic) and homelike (they also represent the communities that urban industrialization threatens). The narrator, a stranger among more conventional strangers, is a tourist, not an adventurer, and only briefly escapes urban life. Thus rather than discovering, this participant-observer-narrator rediscovers regional figures in the leisure time that urban capital allows.

The narrator of *The Country of the Pointed Firs* has aesthetic advantages from her apparent class position, and she presents the curios of the region like photos, timeless artifacts for readers' contemplation. Concentrating on how the text is framed, how its occupants are set apart by the urban narrator, reveals that regionalism and the communities it narrates are not, as they initially seem, innocent. Traces of history and conflict score their narrative surface. Through the narrator, the hostile conditions of the material world that regionalism turns away from and yet responds to become apparent. I look at the narrator's fascination with regional characters' stories of the "other" spirit world, reading that fascination as Jewett's complex recoding of the outer world beyond and outside the text that threatens to supersede the values and communities that village life—the "other" world of the tourist narrator—celebrates.

My larger aim is to show that regionalism does not provide neat and predictable transactions between what is foreign and what is native. Such a predictable transaction might be typified, for example, in the way that regional texts routinely note that the city often comes to seem fractured and strange to urban visitors after a stay in the country. By the same logic, regionalism cannot be considered simply a received body of literature that must be accepted more or less as a whole and subjected to different interpretations at different historical moments, although there are certainly ways to show how *The Country of the Pointed Firs* can be used to measure the changing attitudes of the literary establishment toward the value of regionalism. Regionalism negotiates and only momentarily fixes the always shifting identity of "the stranger" and "the native." Its instability in fixing these terms is, in fact, the defining textual economy of regionalism, as it was of other kinds of cultural work in the late nineteenth century to which regionalism bears some similarity. Regional fiction shares, as Richard Brodhead pointed out, bourgeois tastes for the exotic encoded by such cultural practices as tourism, ethnography, and anthropology. Brodhead argues that

the post-bellum elite and its adherents made other ways of life the objects of their admiration and desire, objects which they then felt free to annex; the upper class vacation, thus, entails crossing out of one's own culture into another culture (not just place) to the end of living another way of life. Regionalism can be guessed to have ministered especially effectively to the imagination of acquisitiveness. (1993:133)

Regionalism is a genre, then, that is responsive to the market and to bourgeois readers' desires for experience, a desire that finds its most pointed expression in the fascination with the other.

Because its topic is the preservation of (and its tactic the construction of) peoples and communities that appear to be fading away, regionalism also participates in that instability that Emmanuel Wallerstein found as constitutive of any definition of a people: "Peoplehood is not merely a construct but one which, in each particular instance, has constantly changing boundaries. Maybe a people is something that is supposed to be inconstant in form" (Balibar and Wallerstein 1991:77). Regionalism is a set of narrative strategies that privileges an ongoing and conflicted relationship regarding the nature of peoplehood and the ongoing constructedness of stranger and foreign, in both the imaginary past of U.S. history and its own conflicted present. Regionalism, then, must be finally understood here as a strategy for constructing the terms of membership in various communities.

In *Camera Lucida*, his essay on photography and memory, Roland Barthes writes that "each photograph is read as the private appearance of its referent: the age of Photography corresponds precisely to the explosion of the private into the public, or rather . . . the explosion of a new social value, which is the publicity of the private" (1974:98). The publicity of the private explains both the appeal of regional texts in the late nineteenth century and the economic conditions that underwrote the vogue for regionalist magazine fiction. Any personal response to the fictional region registered in the literary marketplace as a common kind of public acclaim for the genre of regionalism itself. That is, it was a textual effect of regional fiction to provoke that feeling of intensely personalized and individual response as a way of creating a community of readers. This textual reinvention of a national past is epitomized by the rediscovery of a domestic geographical territory that is made slightly exotic and slightly foreign in the regionalist text. This rediscovery, I suggest, is in turn occasioned by both the "discovery" of the vast lands of the West and the emergence of very different regions in American cities—such as ethnic enclaves and ghettos in the eastern cities. Within this context, the conditions of regional fiction's production also influence its consumption. Against these two such solidly historical and future-oriented material territories, regionalism reterritorializes and privatizes a safe and homelike geographic space. In its fullest flowering and at its most lyrical, regionalism always asks its readers to read outside history—that is, to recollect.[3]

Perhaps more than other regional writers, Jewett amplifies the traditionally valued concerns of regionalism. This amplification comes from the text's overt nostalgia, its persistent, though veiled, gestures toward an outer world that may be read as the embodiment of nineteenth-century history threatening to destroy the world of Dunnet Landing. Amid even the slow cadences of life in the village, the narrator manages to impart a sense of urgency about her own project of collecting and arranging folklore and folkways. This urgency is not simply a result of the knowledge of village decline that readers bring to regionalist fiction—any reader might note that nostalgia is already a factor in Dunnet Landing's citizens' perception of themselves. Instead, charting the path of the stranger—here the narrator—demonstrates various kinds of estrangement by showing that a regional American may be a foreigner, an exotic curio, *and* a safe regional type. Her desire to inhabit the position of village resident is a map for the terms under which one can become a member or an inhabitant of other communities. In the uncollected chapter of the text, "The Foreigner," Jewett returns to Dunnet Landing's "exotics." The figure of the foreigner who tests the boundaries of membership in Dunnet Landing is a narrative flashpoint around which larger issues of citizenship and community gather, but she is also a test case for the limits of regionalism's ability to adjudicate belonging and exile.

The nameless, faceless, female narrator who spends her summers writing and living in Dunnet Landing with Mrs. Todd is the most difficult and most important stranger in the text. She is the reader's link between her own progressing urban world and the quaint coastal village of Dunnet Landing. Her changing position in the village marks the place and measures the possibility of psychic movement for a stranger in Dunnet Landing. Her estrangement from herself shifts in direct proportion to her ability to believe that she has overcome her difference from the regional folk by exteriorizing her desire for self-identity as one of *their* inherent qualities. The narrator, though, is not a completely estranged subject, for part of her success is derived from her sympathetic curiosity. She is not an ordinary tourist and so is neither obviously nor offensively enamored of the quaint. In short, she works hard to fit into her newfound community. Work is an operative term here. The sign that she is too comfortable as a resident is her childish happiness in selling an herbal remedy while her landlady is away. Holding the money in her hand, she tells herself that she must return to her real job as a writer, that her action as a regional inhabitant is interrupting the project that brought her there in the first place.

Her landlady Almira Todd, the arbiter of life in Dunnet Landing, also grants her the position of intimate, saying, "Yes'm, old friends is always best, 'less you can catch a new one that's fit to make an old one out of" (Jewett 1981:62) and trusts her with secrets of the townsfolk and even some of the secrets of her mysterious herbs. The narrator scores a kind of coup with other characters as well. William, Mrs. Todd's reclusive brother, immediately takes her into his confidence. Captain Littlepage and Elijah Tilley, two elderly sea captains, also take her into their confidence, each privately telling her his own story of loss and estrangement from this world. Her success in joining the community is ratified at her departure; her farewell gift from Mrs. Todd is the coral pin originally intended for poor Joanna, the long dead hermit of Shell Heap Island. This souvenir makes the narrator a kind of honorary exile, paradoxically commemorating the idea of estrangement and exile while also affirming the narrator's final transcendence of them.

The narrator, unobtrusive and sympathetic, acts as a guide to the closed world of Dunnet Landing, collecting and arranging voices and people, and she is also the sign of self-estrangement that this story tries to counteract for its reading public. The structure of the story demonstrates the region's *and* the regional narrative's ability to help the alienated subject. Although most of *The Country of the Pointed Firs* is written in the first person, the first chapter, "The Return," is written in the third person and explains the narrator's relationship to Dunnet Landing. An omniscient narrator opens:

> After a brief visit made two or three summers before in the course of a yachting cruise, a lover of Dunnet Landing returned to find the unchanged shores of the pointed firs, the same quaintness of the village with its elaborate conventionalities; all that mixture of remoteness, and childish certainty of being the center of civilization of which her affectionate dreams had told. (Jewett 1981:2)

By the time this lover of Dunnet Landing begins her own account in the second chapter, she has already established herself in the household and in herself, and the text moves easily into the first person.

The first omniscient narrator frames but also distances readers from the village, suggesting exactly that kind of reading-as-remembering that I have identified as a quality of regional writing. Roland Barthes writes in *S/Z* that a commodity culture discourages rereading, instead forcing readers into purchasing yet another book and experience (1981:15, 16). It is exactly this commodity culture that the first-person narrator is escaping when she comes to Dunnet Landing. Not surprisingly, then, the opening chapter—"The Return"—indicates that the narrator herself is coming back to "reread" the text she only skimmed once and also that she is reversing the trend of modernization and the forward motion of an endlessly circulating capital economy by reentering the "quaint" village that she had seen earlier only from the deck of a pleasure yacht. This notion of return also gives readers a way to begin reading as rereading, since they are invited to "return" too, to this unchanging shoreline, to linger in a house whose herb garden "roused a dim sense and remembrance of something in the forgotten past" (1981:3, 4). This sense of remembrance sets up a kind of cycle of returns that structures both the position of the narrator in the book as a whole and the position of the readers, who also can return at will.

Initially, the narrator cannot implicate herself in her report; she must simply watch herself mounting the hill to Mrs. Todd's, detached and distant from her own experience of Dunnet Landing. On another, later visit, for example, the narrator writes that "the hurry of life in a large town, the constant putting aside of preference to yield to a most unsatisfactory activity, began to vex me" and that she set out to Dunnet Landing to cure herself, to make herself "feel solid and definite again, instead of a poor, incoherent being." She makes "a return to happiness" (1981:213). Her initial visit, in the third person, thus dramatizes this narrative estrangement from herself which, with her later sense that urban life makes her "incoherent" or fragmented, points to the worst of subject positions in industrial America—reification.4 Even the windows of the town appear to be looking at her when first she arrives, rather than she at them and their inhabitants. It is only by returning to the scene, by moving *backward*, that the narrator can overcome her alienation and begin to claim an "I" in the process of narrating her region by collecting other stories of loss and estrangement. Not coincidentally, the stories that interest her most are analogous to her own sense of alienation.

Part of the way she begins to feel that she is not a stranger to herself is to make curios of the residents of this town. The narrator approaches many of the characters with a keen photographic eye, and her careful arrangement of her collected vignettes makes clear her archival, nearly anthropological interests. The narrator's relationship with the two sea captains, Elijah Tilley and Captain Littlepage, for example, culminates in two narratives of loss and estrangement. The two men are not major characters, however, but are peripheral to both the village and the narrator's visit. Captain Littlepage seems to snap in and out of the present when he talks to the narrator about his "other world," and Elijah Tilley lives in a static moment of the loss of his wife, "poor dear." In her report, the narrator creates these men as exotic specimens lost in the steady march of history, although it is certainly instructive that in each man's plaintive anticipation of the "other word," the spirit world intrudes on the narrative. More important, traces of the *other* other world press in— the *outer* world of commerce, of shipping and trade, both of which seem equally ephemeral.

As she sits in Tilley's little house, which he has carefully preserved for the memory of his lost wife, the narrator remarks that in the face of the overwhelming temporal event of his wife's death, he has elected to make each day an exact replica of the next: "Folks all kep' repeatin' that time would ease me, but I can't find it does. No, I miss her just the same every day" (1981:121). In mourning, time appears to freeze, an observation that might apply also to regionalism's nostalgia (or mourning) for the past. But Tilley's lament shows us a time in the past when he was able to imagine a future. When Tilley shows the narrator his sitting room, he explains that each precious piece was purchased from the larger sea towns or imported from faraway places. This sitting room is a memorial to society, a tribute to his wife and to the idea of the welcome stranger. It also is a reminder of a time when Dunnet Landing had contact with the other, outer world of commodities and shipping.

Captain Littlepage ties together the "outer" and "other" world even more clearly. Discussing the fate of Dunnet Landing since industrialization moved the centers of shipping and commerce away from the villages, he explains,

In the old days, a good part o' the best men here knew a hundred ports and something of the way folks lived in them. They saw the world for themselves, and like's not their wives and children saw it with them . . . they were some acquainted with foreign lands an' their laws, an' could see outside the battle for town clerk here in Dunnet; . . . shipping's a terrible loss to this part o' New England from a social point of view. (1981:20)

Each of these men indicates a time when the interests of the quaint town were more worldly, referencing the narrator's busy urban world, which does not mimic but *extends* this previous age. Littlepage's recollection of this busy time and its connection to another world is echoed in his reverential telling of the strange events after the crash of the *Minerva*. It is important to note the narrator's position during Littlepage's visit to her. She is in an empty schoolhouse, trying to work on her mysterious but all absorbing writing, watching a funeral procession go by, and knowing that not joining in the funeral march has jeopardized her position in Dunnet Landing: "I had now made myself and my friends remember that I did not really belong to Dunnet Landing," she remarks sadly (1981:15). As she notes her difference from the community, she looks out of the window, which presents the jarring image of seeing the narrator framed rather than framing.

The image of the window, so much associated in criticism of late nineteenth-century literature with urban displays of commodities, is telling here. In a reading that seems particularly apt to the relation between rural and urban in this novel, Philip Fisher writes that

the window substitutes for the porch, enabling one to see the street as a spectacle, a performance. . . . A window theatricalizes experience both for the one rocking on the inside as well as for the passerby who glances up and sees the "pretty scene" of a young lady wistfully rocking at the window. (1987:156; see also Bowlby 1985)

The exhibition space of the window and the street allows Fisher to uncover the conventions of the rural in the midst of the urban, and it here echoes the narrator's urban identity in the midst of the rural. Her citizenship in the world of Dunnet Landing is momentarily destabilized.

The combined scene of mourning and writing crystallizes the narrator's sense of separateness from the Landing and also her hunger for it. Just as she remembers her separation and begins wishing for "a companion and for news from the outer world" (1981:15), she is interrupted by Captain Littlepage, who tells her a story that reflects her own estrangement. Rather than news from the outer world of contemporary urban life, the narrator gets news from the shadowy other world of the spirits.

Relating the tale of the *Minerva*, Littlepage tells the narrator that there is a town "two degrees farther north than ships had ever been" and that it is

a place where there was neither living nor dead. They [the sailors] could see the place when they were approaching it by sea pretty near like any town, and thick with habitations; but all at once they lost sight of it altogether, and when they got close inshore they could see the shapes of folks, but they never could get near them. (1981:25)

He describes it as "a kind of waiting-place between this world and the next" (27). Certainly, the town of Dunnet Landing functions for the narrator as a friendlier version of this polar spirit world that Littlepage talks to her about, and there even are echoes of the same language of distance in the description of the two. For example, as she leaves Dunnet Landing at summer's end, the narrator writes,

The little town, with the tall masts of its disabled schooners in the inner bay, stood above the flat sea for a few minutes then it sank back into the uniformity of the coast, and became indistinguishable from the other towns that looked as if they were crumbled on the furzy-green stoniness of the shore. (132)

Her final look reveals that "Dunnet Landing and all its coasts were lost to sight" (132). The ghostly inhabitants who appear to populate the village at the pole are akin to the wasted old men and women who inhabit Dunnet Landing—they, too, are between two worlds, living in a sort of waiting place. But it is interesting that the facts of the other, material world's loss are also narrated by Captain Littlepage and that he seems to feel the same way about the past of Dunnet Landing as he does about the polar village— that he isn't quite sure if it were ever there. Was Dunnet Landing ever a bustling town filled with strange inhabitants going about their business? That past recedes with each passing year, and without such industry, Dunnet Landing seems like an undiscovered village waiting out its own life, a small pocket of antiquity in the modern world. Indeed, when she goes to the Bowden family reunion, the narrator describes Littlepage in his accustomed place, but she also trades places with him, saying that she sees "Captain Littlepage . . . sitting behind his closed window . . . there was a patient look on the old man's face, as if the world were a great mistake and he had nobody with whom to speak his own language" (88).

Captain Littlepage's sense that the inhabitants of Dunnet Landing have receded from the world and sunk into a morass of isolation and ignorance is echoed by Susan Fosdick's comment, "What a lot o' queer folks there used to be about here, anyway. . . . Everybody's just like everybody else, now; nobody to laugh about, and nobody to cry about" (64). These sentiments, though, are not shared by the narrator, who thinks to herself "that there were peculiarities of character in the region of Dunnet Landing yet" (64). Her careful investigation of the exotic and her equally careful entry into this habitual way of life force her to preserve the peculiarities and pull them out of time. But in order to counteract the flow of the book, to keep herself from occupying the position of the fearful but curious shipmates who see the ghost town at the pole, the narrator must give substance to the peculiarities and make a series of living connections out of the many narratives of estrangement that seem to pervade the lives of the villagers. The most powerful instance of this is when the narrator participates in one of the key episodes of the text—the Bowden family reunion. As she tries to fit into and chronicle the reunion, the narrator works to keep in motion the exchanges between the categories of stranger and family, native and foreign.

The reunion is central to this text, but its centrality stems more from the fact that it reverses the trend of the text than it does from its place as the culmination of the text's events. Although the annual reunion commemorates tradition, it is also a space in which the knowable order of regional life is overturned. As a reunion, this episode commemorates the idea of community and family. But the reunion flickers between times and, in so doing, elicits strange behavior. It is, for example, the only time that Mrs. Todd behaves badly, when she expresses her hatred of a relative. As the gathering, led by a "Major" who was denied duty during the Civil War, progresses, the narrator thinks to herself, "I already knew some of Mrs. Todd's friends and kindred, and felt like an adopted Bowden in this happy moment" (1981:99). But because the narrator is in fact a foreigner, an outsider, her position at this reunion is precarious. The text has already presented a character who has come to the Bowden family reunion even though she does not belong to the Bowden family anymore, and the scorn with which Mrs. Todd refers to this woman is surely indicative of the tenuous relationships that the narrator herself must sustain.

In order to feel like a Bowden, the narrator must absorb the ethos of the reunion and enlarge her experience by refiguring the terms of being a stranger. She must extend "this happy moment" past the confines of her own life—through which the outside world presses in—and past the confines of the reunion itself, celebrating the region but also forcing the region to fold in protectively on itself:

We might have been a company of ancient Greeks going to celebrate a victory, or to worship the god of harvests, in the grove above. It was strangely moving to see this and to make part of it. The sky, the sea, have watched poor humanity at its rites so long; we were no more a New England family celebrating its own existence and simple progress; we carried the tokens and inheritance of all such households from which this had descended, and were only the latest of our line. We possessed the instincts of a far, forgotten childhood; I found myself thinking that we ought to be carrying green branches and singing as we went. (1981:100)

The narrator occupies a double position as both foreigner and family, observer and participant. Her use of "we," except in her final meditation in which she makes a tableau of the scene, indicates her shifting perspective, and her observation "It was strangely moving to see this and to make part of it" indicates her precarious social position. Her desire to chronicle the moment as she participates in it is revealed in the double meaning of the phrase "make part of it." She maintains her tenuous position as member and outsider by erasing regional time ("we were no longer a New England family") and national time (they are not regional folk, but "poor humanity" at its rites). She advances her narrative project by comparing the festivities with those of the Greeks. This gesture toward timelessness is not isolated. It is part of her larger strategy to "make" the world of Dunnet Landing into a kind of timeless frieze and to include her own guide and hostess as its center: "She might have been Antigone alone on a Theban plain," for example, is not a typical description of Mrs. Todd. Language like this calms—it stops the progress of nationalizing time and erases sectional or regional characteristics. But the compromise of times cannot last, and the world presses in.

Temporality bursts in on the narrator and contextualizes and historicizes her fancy: "Perhaps it is the great national anniversaries which our country has lately kept, and the soldiers' meetings that take place everywhere, which had made reunions of every sort the fashion" (1981:110). Although the Bowden family reunion is quickly set apart from these national reunions—"it is an instinct of the heart" (110)—the reunion does have a national and nationalizing function, especially when read against this brief mention of the Civil War. Similarly, although nationalized or regional identity is subsumed beneath the narrator's descriptive use of the Greek procession, the text is also devoted to a commemoration of foreignness. "Somebody observed once that you could pick out the likeness of 'most every sort of a foreigner when you looked about you in our parish" (103), one of the Bowdens remarks. As if reminded of the temporal and spatial proximity of foreign identities her own descriptive fancy bears within itself, the narrator abruptly concludes:

It was not the first time that I was full of wonder at the waste of human ability in this world, as a botanist wonders at the wastefulness of nature, the thousand seeds that die, the unused provision of every sort. The reserve force of society grows more and more amazing to one's thought. More than one face among the Bowdens showed that only opportunity and stimulus were lacking—a narrow set of circumstances had caged a fine able character and held it captive. One sees exactly the same types in a country gathering as in the most brilliant city company. (107)

It is perhaps most interesting that whereas the narrator usually attempts to remark the likeness of regional folk to generalized foreigners temporally—thus protecting regional folk by creating them as ancestors—she here remarks their likeness to contemporary urban inhabitants.[5] Her rhetoric moves the narrator closer to the voice of Mrs. Todd, but it also echoes the complaints of the older residents of Dunnet Landing by recognizing the impersonal waste of ability that characterizes capitalism's assimilation of country and city residents alike. In this way, she may be seen as joining in a bond of sympathy with the citizens of Dunnet Landing. But this reunion, the apotheosis of the region, also inspires the first comparison with the narrator's "real" life in the city. This is one of the only extended observations of the community as a whole, and as the narrator stands back from it in order to view it, she is struck not by the hidden riches of the regional personalities but by the waste of those riches. What she has said about the "reserve force" of society might have been more appropriately applied to those other regions with which the narrator, as an urbanite, must have been familiar. Clearly, the "reserve force" of society is more applicable to the "reserve army of labor" (a term much in vogue in the newspapers of the time to refer to the urban poor). The narrator represses the parallel between a rural reserve force and an urban reserve army, writing at the end of the reunion that she is rich with a "new remembrance." The narrator's conclusion that her experience at the reunion has given her a precious new memory allow her to convert her anxiety about her own complicity in the decline of the region into nostalgia for its inhabitants.

Although the narrator's participation in the Bowden family reunion is the expression of her adoption by the "family" of the region, it also exposes her inability to reconcile herself to that family's various contemporary struggles. Indeed, she seems preoccupied with exiles. This leads her to visit the house of poor Joanna, to imagine the shape of Joanna's solitary life, and to narrate it as an allegory of her own condition.

In the life of each of us, I said to myself, there is a place remote and islanded, and given to endless regret or secret happiness; we are each the uncompanioned hermit and recluse of an hour or a day; we understand our fellow of the cell to whatever age of history they may belong. (1981:82)

This echoes her feeling on Green Island when she looks at Mrs. Todd:

There was something lonely and solitary about her great determined shape. She might have been Antigone alone on the Theban plain. It is not often given in a noisy world to come to the places of great grief and silence. An absolute, archaic grief possessed this countrywoman; she seemed like a renewal of some historic soul, with her sorrows and the remoteness of a daily life busied with rustic simplicities. (49)

These "silent spaces" are the times and places of the narrator's deepest connection to the regional figure. Her readings of the regional figure drive her not only to connect with her new friends but to classify them as well. She yearns to belong, but when she leaves, she begins to modify her image of Dunnet Landing. Unwilling to leave, she writes, "At last I had to say good-by to all my Dunnet Landing friends and my home-like place in the little house, and return to the world in which I feared to find myself a foreigner" (129). It is precisely that part of her that she fears to find foreign that comes closest to being "a true Bowden" (110). She remarks as she leaves, "So we die before our own eyes" (131).

Perhaps it is this metaphor of dying that connects the world of folk myths and spirits to the other, outer world of industrial America. Certainly this metaphor was at work in both Tilley's and Littlepage's stories. It also becomes the source of a more perverse relationship in the text, that between the "foreign" narrator, who dies before her own eyes as she leaves the town, and Miz Cap'n Tolland, known in the expanded collection as "the foreigner," who dies in Dunnet Landing as unassimilated as when she first arrived. Mrs. Captain Tolland is a character in whom almost all previous mentions of foreignness meet. Although her story is not officially a part of the text of *The Country of the Pointed Firs*, having been written in 1900, some four years after the novella, it is appropriate, I think, to look at it as a gloss on its parent text. I see it as the most explicit way in which Jewett returns to her region in order to disturb the assumed homogeneity of the region. Jewett's use of "the foreigner" as the sign under which she revisited Dunnet Landing reveals that the regions assumed to be the *source* of an imaginatively unified past bear within themselves heterogeneous histories.

Against the assurance from Captain Littlepage that Dunnet Landing has fallen into decline because it lacks the invigorating influences of the wider world comes the disruptive presence of the foreigner. In fact, the very influences from the "outside" that Captain Littlepage mourns in *The Country of the Pointed Firs* seem to be roughly contemporaneous with Mrs. Captain Tolland's arrival in Dunnet in "The Foreigner."

Mrs. Todd tells the story of Mrs. Tolland's life by beginning, "It was all of thirty, or maybe some forty, year ago" the foreigner arrived in Dunnet (1981:161). On a voyage to Jamaica, the bachelor sea captain Tolland meets a desperate young widow. Because she is defenseless, he agrees to take her aboard his ship. Sometime in the journey, they fall in love, and he brings her to Dunnet Landing, marries her, and leaves her a widow again when he later dies at sea. The new widow never manages to fit into Dunnet Landing and dies shortly after her husband does. Her effects, however, illuminate *The Country of the Pointed Firs*. The fact that she is "carried back" to the community by way of a sea voyage echoes both the sea captains' laments about the loss of foreign influences and the narrator's arrival in town as a stranger. Mrs. Captain Tolland's arrival also resonates with an even more disturbing textual point. As Susan Gillman pointed out, in Jewett's narrative "the foreign has been reduced to the status of 'best things' displayed in 'best room' cabinets, remnants of the international trade of the past. Thus we hear a string of exotic place names . . . all associated with the 'outlandish things' " (1994:110). The story of Mrs. Captain Tolland, then, appended to the main text of *The Country of the Pointed Firs* is the story of how one of those "outlandish" mementos was brought home. But Mrs. Captain Tolland's life and, more important, her death change the terms under which the region can be equated with "home." Mrs. Todd remarks that the story of Mrs. Tolland is a ghost story. Indeed, Mrs. Tolland haunts the text, revealing how the community negotiates repressed social, cultural, and ethnic differences.

It is remarkable how many times in the short narrative of Mrs. Tolland's life that Mrs. Todd uses the word *strange*. Mrs. Tolland's first visit to the church finds her feeling "homesick and strange" (1981:167), and her person strikes Mrs. Todd as at once both beautiful and strange. Mrs. Todd explains, "I never knew her maiden name; if I ever heard it, I've gone an' forgot; 'twould mean nothing to me. . . . She was a foreigner. . . . She was French born, an' her first husband was a Portugee, or somethin' " (1981:161–162).

Mrs. Todd's disregard for the particulars of this woman's experience is also apparent throughout her description of Mrs. Captain Tolland's life. Striking in Mrs. Todd's imperfect recollection of the woman is her isolation of "French-born." The region that Sarah Orne Jewett depicted contained a large population of French Canadian factory workers and farmers, and the text itself favorably describes other characters' French features. Mrs. Todd's dismissal of Mrs. Tolland's French heritage thus seems even more interesting when read next to Mrs. Todd's confession to the narrator in *The Country of the Pointed Firs* that "they used to say in old times . . . that our family came of very high folks in France, and one of 'em was a great general in some o' the old wars" (102). The fact that the common past of Frenchness does not unite Mrs. Tolland with her new community demonstrates how easily the fictions of the past are deployed to construct the present—that "pastness" itself is a fiction that becomes cultural or natural in different circumstances.

This unsteady line between the cultural and the natural also underwrites Mrs. Todd's invocation of childhood and sacrifice to describe Mrs. Tolland. Mrs. Tolland is an accomplished singer, guitar player, and dancer. Mrs. Todd notes of her performance at the social circle in the meeting house that Mrs. Tolland was "just as light and pleasant as a child. You couldn't help seein' how pretty 'twas; . . . 'twas so catchin', an' seemed so natural to her" (167). Mrs. Tolland also "took on dreadful" when her husband went to sea, in contrast to the inhabitants of Dunnet Landing who "ain't so much accustomed to show their feelings" (168). Mrs. Todd describes Mrs. Tolland's behavior as lovely and girlish, or pretty and graceful, adding that "you often felt as if you was dealin' with a child's mind" (172), perhaps because "she spoke very broken English, no better than a child" (168). Mrs. Todd's rhetoric conjures up a spontaneous girl, a charming exotic misplaced among a taciturn New England community.

But this impression is in contrast to Mrs. Todd's other descriptions of Mrs. Tolland, which are figured in terms that present Mrs. Tolland as duplicitous and indecipherable. Mrs. Todd remarks that Mrs. Tolland had a very "singular expression: she wore a fixed smile that wa'n't a smile; there wa'n't no light behind it, same's a lamp can't shine if it ain't lit. I don't know just how to express it, 'twas a sort of made countenance" (171). She echoes this sentiment when she muses that although Mrs. Tolland "made me imagine new things . . . you couldn't get no affectionateness with her. I used to blame me sometimes; we used to be real good comrades goin' off for an afternoon, but I never give her a kiss till the day she laid in her coffin" (172). Even when Mrs. Tolland is on her deathbed, Mrs. Todd confesses to conflicting feelings. She explains that "there was always times when she wore a look that made her seem a stranger you'd never set eyes on before." Even Mrs. Todd's attempt to comfort Mrs. Tolland on her deathbed by telling her "You're one of the stray ones, poor creature" (183) manages to exclude Mrs. Tolland before it soothes her.

Sandra Zagarell has argued that there are strong textual hints that Mrs. Captain Tolland was of mixed race: "The possibility that she is a creole in no way diminishes the legitimacy of her claim to membership in the Dunnet community." Furthermore, the text as a whole "seems to call into question the nationalism and Nordicism that, as we have seen, inform and help shape the earlier narrative" (Zagarell 1994:55). Indeed, there is a reference to Mrs. Tolland's "cast" and to the "dark" face of her mother's ghost. But in my reading, the question is not how "legitimate" Mrs. Tolland's claims on Dunnet Landing are. Nor can we use Mrs. Tolland's "race" to argue that *The Country of the Pointed Firs* casts out its others. I argue that we must see Mrs. Tolland's creolized identity as underwriting Dunnet Landing, paradoxically activating the region's conversion of strangers into natives. Mrs. Tolland is not, as we will see, cast out, she is ultimately embraced in the terms in which regionalism encodes difference.

Mrs. Captain Tolland is physically and culturally in transition between nations and countries—she has not lived in France since she was six years old, she tells Mrs. Todd, but was on her way back to France from the French colonies when she was rescued by Captain Tolland. She appears to have spent most of her life in the creole and colonial society of Jamaica, where keeping pure her cultural identity, if not her racial identity, would have been impossible. I have been arguing that traces of the foreign underwrite and constitute local color, making it a genre most suited to negotiate various kinds or orders of cultural difference. The story of "The Foreigner" exemplifies that dialectic in *The Country of the Pointed Firs*. The narratives about "the foreign" that underwrite the market demand for local-color fiction are distorted and rewritten in the story's reference to Jamaica. The captains are retracing a slave route; the sugar that Captain Tolland moves to make room to bring home Mrs. Captain Tolland is a reference to the equivalence in slave economy between Mrs. Captain Tolland's body and slave bodies. As Mrs. Todd speculates,

Oh yes, there was something very strange about her, and she hadn't been brought up in high circles nor nothing o' that kind. I think she'd been really pleased to have the cap'n marry her an' give her a good home, after all she'd passed through, and leave her free with his money an' all that. (1981:171)

The rhetoric of distress is placed in racial terms—is the captain leaving her free to spend money, or is he *making* her free and giving her money? Within this context, images of Mrs. Tolland's simple, childlike singing are reminiscent of late-nineteenth-century stereotypes of African Americans derived from the images of minstrel shows. Like Mrs. Tolland's alternately "happy" and "made" countenances, minstrel performers displaced tensions in the national imagination concerning race and otherness (see esp. Lott 1993:chap. 2). Similarly, Mrs. Todd's remark to Mrs. Tolland that she is "one of the stray creatures" emphasizes inferiority and difference. Mrs. Captain Tolland's coldness or "made"ness are somehow offered as "personal" reasons for the community's decision to exclude her. Yet it is precisely her artifice that gives Mrs. Tolland a passport into the region's ideological economy because it frees Mrs. *Todd* from her community's constraints.

When Mrs. Todd befriends Mrs. Captain Tolland, she receives in return the knowledge that has so persuasively argued for her inclusion in the pantheon of great female characters in American literature—the "natural" knowledge of herbs and medicine:

"She taught me a sight o' things about herbs I never knew before nor since; she was well acquainted with the virtues o' plants. She'd act awful secret about some things too, an' used to work charms for herself sometimes . . . 'twas she that first led me to discern mushrooms; an' she went right down on her knees in my garden here when she saw I had my different officious herbs. Yes, 'twas she that learned me the proper use of parsley too." (1981:170)

It is Mrs. Todd's secret relationship with the soil and plants of her region, her pivotal role in her community as an herbalist and healer that allows the nameless narrator of *The Country of Pointed Firs* to use Mrs. Todd as a sign of the particularity of Dunnet Landing. It also allowed her to extract Mrs. Todd from the world of Dunnet Landing and make her a type of the timeless regional woman, "mateless and appealing." Mrs. Todd's knowledge is *not,* however, regional or local knowledge. Mrs. Todd's regional specificity depends on foreign knowledge. The secret at the heart of Mrs. Todd's fetishized, autocthonous identity relocates the center of the text away from the unified region and into the late nineteenth century's debates about cultural difference.

Although Mrs. Captain Tolland "come a foreigner and . . . went a foreigner, and never was anything but a stranger among our folks" (170), she gives the region its final connection with the wider world—and unlike the curios on every seafaring family's mantelpiece, it is a vital connection. The mysterious things that Mrs. Tolland knows, the "new things" Mrs. Todd imagines because of Mrs. Tolland, and the images of Mrs. Todd as a kind of witch (exactly as Mrs. Captain Tolland appeared to be a witch thirty or forty years earlier) are crucial to the urban narrator's fantasies about Mrs. Todd's identity. The narrator's occasional sense that Mrs. Todd has become "a sybill" or "a priestess" reinvoke Mrs. Tolland's foreignness. Like Mrs. Tolland, Mrs. Todd becomes "strange" despite being familiar.

Once again, that "other" outer world laps at the margins of the text in the same way that the stories of Littlepage and Tilley do; it comes to Dunnet Landing under the cover of the spirit world. Mrs. Todd shares with the text's narrator Mrs. Tolland's dying vision. On her deathbed, Mrs. Tolland sees the ghost of her mother beckoning Mrs. Tolland toward the other world. Mrs. Todd also sees this ghost, saying finally to Mrs. Tolland, " '*You ain't never goin' to feel strange an' lonesome no more*' " (186, emphasis in original).

In the face of the two worlds that Mrs. Tolland stands between, Mrs. Todd is moved to reconcile the outer material world and the other spirit world, paving the way for the privileged position that the narrator/stranger comes to occupy in Dunnet Landing. "There's somethin' beyond this world; the doors stand wide open. There's somethin' of us that must still live on; we've got to join both worlds together an' live in one but for the other' " (187). Perhaps because the young woman known as "the foreigner" could not join the two worlds together, Mrs. Todd is able to penetrate the center of her own community and to welcome the invigorating influence that the narrator, from the "other" world of the city and the nation, represents. After all, what Mrs. Todd tells the narrator, the most recent stranger, is that she became interested in "watching" Mrs. Tolland, exactly as the narrator became interested in watching Mrs. Todd.

The fact that Mrs. Tolland and the narrator have occupied the same subject position does not mean that they are the same person, of course, but it does reaffirm the tension between native and stranger at the heart of regionalism by elaborating it on the body of the foreigner. Mrs. Todd calls her story a "ghost story," and the tale ends with the death of Mrs. Captain Tolland, with an odd detour in the middle in which Mrs. Todd reveals that she was the heir to the Tollands' "fortune."

The two meanings of the inheritance that the foreigner leaves to Mrs. Todd are made explicit here. But the economic dimension of Mrs. Tolland's gesture to Mrs. Todd cannot be correlated with the "spiritual" dimension of the text as if the two somehow complete each other. That is, the text is not suggesting that the "secret" of the communities on the Maine coast is that they were funded by the slave trade. Rather, it suggests that Jewett's stories were not just *valuable* but also *profitable*.

Accordingly, after having been made the heir to the estate of Mr. and Mrs. Tolland, Mrs. Todd does not actually inherit the chest of gold that others in the town believe must be hidden somewhere in their house. In fact, the house is burned down accidentally by one of Mrs. Todd's relatives who is searching for the money in the cellar. The absence of actual money—the lack of a commonly recognized standard against which to measure the value of the foreigner—questions other standards of value in the text. In this context, it might be argued that watching the exotic, the foreign, and the odd was good business, that it paid off. The advice that Mrs. Todd's mother gives Mrs. Todd, to "neighbor" with the poor creature because it might be "you" who was "a stranger in a strange land," was not just a formal strategy of Jewett's work but a strategy that determined the content of the work. The stories, then, become the inheritance on which Jewett's Mrs. Todd and, through her, Jewett herself capitalize.

Second, and perhaps equally important, the foreigner's inheritance might be traced back to her racial composition. A racial theory based on eugenics, the science of biological inheritances, became popular in the late nineteenth century. Mrs. Tolland's racial composition—so difficult to pinpoint in the text—hints that the financial inheritance left to Mrs. Todd might be "tainted" or "colored" by race. But like Mrs. Captain Tolland, who is circulated through reputation while she is alive, through Mrs. Todd's story when dead, and through the marketplace by Jewett, money has no immediately discernible social history. We might similarly understand the shifting, mysterious, and occulted value of the foreign in Jewett's work.

Even though regional texts like Sarah Orne Jewett's *The Country of the Pointed Firs* create imaginative social spaces of privacy and memory for readers, those careful recollections should not erase the function of history and memory in the construction of the present. In *The Country of the Pointed Firs* Jewett writes in regard to solitary life on Shell Heap Island that "it seems an awfully small place to make a world of" and then, as if to create space in the diminished world of the region, later has her tourist-narrator say that "we all have a Dunnet Landing of our own," moving the historical location of Dunnet Landing out of geographical space and into the murkier terrain of memory and nostalgia. Through such direct appeals to an audience, the narrator of *The Country of the Pointed Firs* solidifies the meaning of Dunnet Landing for a nation that seems to be moving away from the kind of community that the village represents. She also personalizes the region for those individuals who will carry it around, or at least carry around the memory of a place just like it. The representation of Dunnet Landing is meant to be marked with the user's own imprint, to appear to have a private and intimate meaning.

The double act of textual substitution (public into private historical memory, compounded by the readers' supplying a missing private memory by purchasing this now doubly "dear" narrative of someone else's memories in a public market) is one of the ways that regionalism blurs the boundaries between self and other and foreign and native in the marketplace.[6] Indeed, the construction of the region as a place in which one can buy public memories bears out T. J. Jackson Lears's claim that the cultural preoccupation with "authenticity" and experience in the late nineteenth century might be read as one of many "therapeutic quests for self-realization, easily accommodated to the dominant culture of our bureaucratic corporate state" (1981:xvii). More pointedly, Susan Stewart contends that "distressed genres" like regional writing and other forms of folklore elicit and feed a kind of nostalgia that

is not a nostalgia for artifacts for their own sake; rather it is a nostalgia for context, for the heroic past, for moral order, for childhood and the collective experiences of preindustrial life. . . . The closely guarded thematics of distressed genres—heroism, paternity, the domestic past, the rural/agrarian, the tribal/communal, the "primitive," and the child—are radically separated from their mechanical reproduction. (1991:91, 93)

Since so much regional writing in the late nineteenth century is constructed around the poles of nostalgia that Stewart identifies, it is interesting to use them to analyze the kinds of subjectivity that might also be located between these poles. Although *The Country of the Pointed Firs* shows that local color is interested in constructing types, or objects of consumption, that will function without any dangerous or realistic pretensions to a conflicted interior life precisely because regional subjects are imputed a unitary and unified subjectivity, regionalism provides a wedge into the social conflicts of the late nineteenth century. A recontextualization and a repoliticization of regionalism bring into focus those textual conventions that we most need to interrogate in the context of the nineteenth century's industrial and territorial expansion, rising capital and corporate economies, and expanding immigration. Regionalism displaces cultural anxiety about strangers, as well as paradoxically demonstrating that anyone may become an alien, an exotic fetish, through the smooth functioning of a commodity culture. Its figuration of "the stranger" suggests that regionalism highlights and affirms bourgeois, urban visitors' cultural authority to represent and interpret the inhabitants of a region. Accordingly, the representation of regional characters allows us to look at how genres negotiated which persons would be granted character, personhood, status, and individuality.

Frederic Jameson argues that people increasingly imagine and represent their class privileges—and thus their separation from the other or the stranger—to themselves "in spatial terms: privacy, empty rooms, silence, walling other people out, protection against crowds and other bodies" (1989:525). An ideological notion of personal privacy highlights regional fiction's investment in notions of identity and community within its novels as well as its more general interest in imagined citizenship within a social organization. Ideas of privacy and space press closely on the late nineteenth century's figuration of the problems of urban life—increased immigration, the massive growth of capital, the widening schism between rich and poor, and the issues of alienated labor and self-alienation—and they also press closely on its invocation of the rural as an antidote to these problems. Raymond Williams writes that "most novels are in some sense knowable communities" but that

this is not the whole story, and once again, in realising the new fact of the city, we must be careful not to idealise the old and new facts of the country. For what is knowable is not only a function of objects—of what is there to be known. It is also a function of subjects, of observers—of what is desired and what needs to be known. And what we have then to see, as throughout, in the country writing, is not only the reality of the rural community; it is the observer's position in and towards it; a position which is part of the community being known. (1973:166)

Williams's study offers a way to evaluate the ways in which the problems of the urban are resolved by selective acts of commemoration and remembering. Such commemoration details far more about the observer than it does about the object under consideration. Furthermore, it constructs an imagined heritage, available to be "reclaimed" at the moment of its creation. Williams's critique also demonstrates, in this instance, that the problem of the foreigner allows the narrator to see what is not visible at first in the community of Dunnet Landing. She finds that the foreign constitutes all she holds dear about the origins and intrinsic value of Dunnet Landing, pushing her to include in her descriptions of the region assorted exiles and foreigners who share similarities with her own fears about whether or not she "belongs." The community, in other words, is much more heterogeneous than it might at first appear, and it has a strong, although partially veiled, method of legislating and assigning citizenship. The narrator, for example, never finds out why poor Joanna decided to leave the mainland to live on an island by herself, nor does she find out why so many of the members of the community have chosen to live in exile or apart from one another. The exile on which the narrator focuses as easily allegorizes the kind of urban solitude she wishes to escape as it does the kind of subjectivity she discovers in the putative "wholeness" of regional community.

I have used *The Country of the Pointed Firs* to show that the foreign constitutes what seems most comfortably homelike in the region and have argued that foreignness is analogous to the reification and alienation of urban observers. The problems of citizenship in the supposedly homogeneous region have strong implications for much of New England women's regionalism generally. A brief look at Mary Wilkins Freeman's short stories, for example, reveals her belief in the necessity of community and also the variations in many characters' local or individual relations with a normative community. Even though community may be ideationally privileged in these stories, a certain withdrawal from normative public life sustains many of the main characters. This withdrawal paradoxically provides the fullness of experience enjoyed by Louisa Ellis in "A New England Nun" or provokes the rebellion of the caustic Hetty Fifield, who moves into the meeting house because she has neither family nor home of her own. Many of the women in Freeman's stories are considered to be or are named as artists. Their devotion to and cultivation of their art appear to be not just a rejection of the domestic, but a total reappropriation of the space of the domestic as thoroughly private. They cultivate the domestic as an art—sewing, distilling flowers, writing poetry, developing vocal ability become secret but public vocations (Freeman 1983).[7]

The "knowable community," organized by "face-to-face relations," becomes elastic and susceptible to radical realignment as it tries to keep track of and normalize the relations of the many different private citizens from whose will it supposedly is produced. While Sarah Orne Jewett especially amplifies what I consider to be the cultural work of late-nineteenth-century regionalism, the thematic possibilities I have developed operate in more or less similar ways in other regional writing. The relationships between urban and rural, native and foreigner, and participant and observer therefore also appear in the next chapter, in which I examine what the traces of foreignness demonstrate about the self-construction of the observer.

2

The Region of the Repressed and the Return of the Region

Hamlin Garland and Harold Frederic

As I argued in my first chapter, pastoral regionalism, like Sarah Orne Jewett's *The Country of the Pointed Firs*, constructs regional folk as figures of a receding past. By narrating the distance between reader and regional figure as temporal, regional writing can posit the spatially distant region as "ahistorical" and outside the time of industrial development. The regional folk themselves become the standard of, rather than participants in, regionalism's adjudication of a fantasized unity of national identity because they are described as outside the problem of the reified subject and its relationship to capital. Such narratives of the region are nostalgic and cover up the questions of ethnicity and nativism that arise when the half-hidden histories of regions intrude into the present as likenesses of contemporary crises in immigration, capital, and the normative subject's felt lack of solidity. Such likenesses acknowledge that regional writing's dialectic between native and stranger (figured through the marketplace) are activated by contested contemporary definitions of strangers and foreigners.

The Country of the Pointed Firs generates the likeness between stranger and native as a strategy to create a new national value for the local. To do so, it creates the region as leisure space and its folk as collectibles. The private meaning of regional fiction becomes an indication of its use value, and that use value, although it is fictitiously generated, becomes the standard of its market value. But not all genteel nineteenth-century regional fiction undergirds its market value with its problematic conversion into use value. In this chapter, I look at what happens when regional fiction's appropriation of the region decouples the relation between the region's marketability

38

and its usefulness as an object of nostalgia. What kinds of value does regional fiction generate about geographic spaces that are not picturesque? What market value can be assigned to characters who are neither quaint nor charming?

The discursive economies of regional writing that I outlined in Sarah Orne Jewett's *The Country of the Pointed Firs* generate a value for the local that has nothing to do with the labor of the regional inhabitants. In fact, it is crucial that the inhabitants have nothing to do except be themselves. In Jewett's text, all occupations were local, and labor was performed in the community and for the community.[1] In this chapter, I examine two novels set in regions that are neither tourist destinations nor untouched, self-sufficient geographic areas. In Hamlin Garland's collection *Main-Travelled Roads* and Harold Frederic's novel *The Damnation of Theron Ware*, the profession of the regional writer or the occupation of the regional observer is implicated in the text's internal representation of the labor performed by the regional figures in a nationalizing market.

Even though each form of labor in these novels aligns the region to a national economy of production and consumption, national and regional economies are in tension, since the formation of both the region and the regional folk is still incomplete. That is, the region is not yet the site of nostalgia; rather, its consolidation *as* a region reveals the difficult process of creating nostalgia. These two works, then, demonstrate how a representational literary economy and a national market economy combine first to produce a marketable idea of the local for the nation and then to enable national financial markets to exploit the local. In this argument, regionalism exists in a doubly speculative economy, first by foregrounding the narrator's observation of regional culture and second by demonstrating specific regions' vulnerability to economic interests. Literary representation and economic exploitation exist simultaneously in the regional writer's project, but in the fictions I examine, the economic value ascribed to the region cannot be renewed by or derived from the fictions constructed around it. My argument is not that these texts show us how the "real" region can be uncovered through a critique of representation itself. Instead, it asks how regionalism—a genre of writing about an elsewhere that is also a "here"—foregrounds the contest over the meaning of the real through multiple determinants of the "value" of the region.

Regional fiction about or from culturally barren regions enters the market for regional fiction on defensive terms, and so the relationship between native and stranger that I have already established is more sharply drawn than it is in New England. In the first chapter, we saw that Jewett's text contains a variety of textual strategies that seem contradictory but which finally reconcile themselves around the figure of the stranger. First, the narrator, an outsider/observer in the region, struggles out of the city that has made her an incoherent being, thus bringing the point of view of urban capital to the social organization of the region. The narrator thus battles her self-estrangement by paradoxically drawing the subjects of her observation and representation into a market economy.

Second, the outsider's perspective draws the narrator to the traces of the foreign that underwrite the community of locals, who themselves are cast as "foreign" in the text's construction of the local. Thus in a text like *The Country of the Pointed Firs*, the region becomes a microcosm of the nation even as the text acknowledges that at the level of national origins, the local traces of the foreign shape the perceived unity of the region. The double gesture of Jewett's presentation of native and stranger (through the figure of the half-assimilated narrator as well as her discovery of half-assimilated foreign elements in the community) occurs in the past, echoing New England's reputation as the origin—or national past—of the United States. Even though the creation of such regions has a spatial dimension (since one must travel to them), the creation of such communities as rustic villages ensures that even their contemporaneity with the world of the narrator might be misrecognized as temporal distance.

While such a reading of the stranger/native dialectic might provide a certain ideological smoothness to texts such as Sarah Orne Jewett's, I do not want to suggest that it can be applied uniformly to regional writing. The self-estrangement that ironically finds its antidote in a market economy operates somewhat differently in narratives in which the actual territory of the region and its population of "foreigners" still have a vital if difficult relationship to the national economy. Generically, regionalism foregrounds quaint and colorful folk who can stand in, as in Jewett's stories, for new raw materials even while acting as emblems for obsolete industries. But if New England regionalism is a "diminished" genre because of its reduced participation in a national economy, midwestern regionalism is an internally incoherent genre because it acknowledges on every level how violent the processing of raw material is and how sharply the remains of rural society measure regional differentiations within uneven capital development.[2]

In the two texts I consider in this chapter, a reconfiguration of regional material emerges. Both Hamlin Garland, a midwesterner, and Harold Frederic, an easterner, focus on regions that are hardly tourist draws. In fact, the people and places that each writer portrays seem cramped, even dour, in comparison with the lyrical descriptions of a writer like Jewett. Hamlin Garland, writing in his autobiography about life on the "middle-border," frequently and passionately rails against the sentimentalization of the region and the construction of a literary audience hungry for tales about the quaint "ahistorical" folk. Instead, in his work as well as in Harold Frederic's, we see a deliberate satirizing of the conventions of regional fiction. Whereas many critics have long celebrated Jewett's artfulness, Garland and Frederic seem to expose the artifice of regional narratives—they look behind the scenery, as one character in Frederic's novel remarks. In so doing, each connects his literary region—the middle border and upstate New York respectively—to contemporary issues in U.S. experience.

In Garland's work, for example, the tie between the region and the nation is truly one that sustains—the farmers of the Midwest produce food for the metropolis. But for Garland, the farmers' so-called local culture is nowhere apparent in national culture; rather, their lives are valued because they drive big business and capital. Similarly, whatever is "local" in their lives is always exposed as a lack. Harold Frederic constructs a similar argument about the lack of a coherent, unitary local culture. In the region about which he writes, local culture, coextensive with the acceleration of capitalism in the metropolis, can only be provincial and partial. Although Frederic's text picks up more explicitly than Garland's does the failed conversions of strangers into natives, the failure of that conversion drives their larger critiques of regional fiction's failure to convert the local into the national.

THE REGION OF THE REPRESSED: HAMLIN GARLAND'S *MAIN-TRAVELLED ROADS*

Hamlin Garland has always occupied an uneasy place in the canon of American literature. Even those who find his work historically important seem to hold it in contempt. Prolific, passionate, and sometimes absurdly polemical, Garland is best remembered for his early collection of regional stories, *Main-Travelled Roads* (1891), and for the reformist sympathies those stories seem to embody. Garland's later literary output consists almost entirely of popular romances, heartwarming narratives of his frontier childhood, and Western potboilers.

Garland's decline from the flinty realism of his early work into the domain of the popular has long puzzled critics, prompting some to regard *Main-Travelled Roads* and his collected essays, *Crumbling Idols* (1894), as foreshadowing his later fall from serious literature.[3] Bill Brown has attempted to reinterpret Garland's seeming defection from radical populist causes (and the critical disparagement that accompanied it) by returning to Garland's early attitudes toward popular culture, on the one hand, and the culture of the people, on the other. Brown argues that Garland's construction and valuation of that most charged and fantastical category, "the people," stands at a crossroads between populism's fetishization of the people (embodied in Garland's early regional work) and popular culture's perceived anesthetizing of them (exemplified by his later work). Whether or not critics follow Brown's invitation to place Garland at the center of current debates in cultural studies, it seems clear that part of Garland's literary significance is that his career announces some of the terms of the debate about the status of local authorship and experience, and national identity and value, in the late nineteenth century.[4]

Just as Garland's literary output might be used to examine the assumptions about how popular and populist fictions both inform and thwart each other, it can also be used to uncover some of the components that inform ideas about the value of regional identity and authorship in local-color fiction, the genre in which his earliest fiction self-consciously participated and that his early critical essays championed. Even Garland's supporters describe his fiction as rough and workmanlike, without subtlety or nuance. But even if we agree with such dismissals of the formal infelicities of his writing, we may still wish to reevaluate the use of the aesthetic to judge Garland's work; that is, just what does stylistic infelicity mean or do? If Garland's work is laborious or workmanlike, it is perhaps because representation in his texts is entangled in potentially irreconcilable political and aesthetic economies. Even though examining the conjuncture of politics and aesthetics in Garland's work may not rescue his critical reputation, using his work as a case study allows us to discover the histories of local identity, regional culture, and regional authorship that the "best" and most successful regional writing has helped conceal.

Crucial to our own reevaluation of Garland is an examination of his refusal to aestheticize the Midwest. Whether or not people in the late nineteenth century really took vacations not just in New England but also in the Midwest or journeyed to the Midwest, as they often did to the South, for their health, Garland's prose deliberately eschews any rhetoric that might have been even remotely connected to tourism. He "de-aestheticizes" the landscape, the lives of the farmers and townsfolk, and the culture that sustains them. The question of value here is especially interesting. How is value assigned to regions that are not picturesque or to people who are not quaint or who are in possession of some mystical, mystified knowledge city dwellers need to protect themselves from the emotional depredations of capital? How does regional fiction that deliberately disarticulates aesthetic value (the picturesque) and market value (tourism, land price) arrive at its own theory of a region's significance? How does it construct authorship and imagine and evaluate the meaning of the local?[5]

Garland's extensive, and extensively chronicled, ideas about the role of the regional writer and his position in the literary market offer an opening wedge into these questions. In *A Son of the Middle Border*, his 1914 autobiography; *Main-Travelled Roads* (1891); and *Crumbling Idols* (1894), the profession of the regional writer (or the occupation of the regional observer) is to represent his region accurately to the literary centers of the United States, to create an innovative fiction that is true to the region. But the regional writer cannot be a tourist. Local writing "will not be spectacular, it will not deal with the outside (as a tourist must do). It will deal with the people and their home dramas" (Garland 1952:25). Yet the regional writer cannot, as we shall see, be merely another local. He must be the impossible combination not only of insider and outsider but also of commodity and broker in a literary market that values the region for the very qualities that Garland disavows. Even though this dilemma may be suppressed in conventional regional writing, as I have argued earlier, it nonetheless is always present.

Regionalism foregrounds quaint and colorful folk who embody literary raw material while simultaneously indexing the national economy's supersession of local industries. Although the idea of regional writing that I use here is most relevant to New England local color, I use it because New England literary culture was something of a flash point for Garland, who tried to resolve the problematic status of midwestern literature within the east's intertwined economies of cultural and economic capital. Garland's version of regionalism acknowledges what local color normally suppresses: how sharply rural culture registers the economic violence of uneven capital development.

In the following section I examine how a representational literary economy and a national market economy combine to produce an ambivalent idea of the local. Misrepresentations of rural life play into the hands of two kinds of speculators: those who read and observe and those who invest and exploit. For Garland, both outsiders who represent and outsiders who exploit the region threaten the local culture. The challenge of Garland's fiction is that while he champions the "real" local-color novel, rather than the eastern local-color novel, the "real" local-color novel can be written only by a "native." Yet in his fiction, natives, once introduced to the values of the east, must become strangers and thus unable to represent accurately their former lives.

This contradiction, apparent in Garland's early work, is also expressed in his autobiography, *A Son of the Middle Border*. In this work, Garland verifies the "truth" of the information in *Main-Travelled Roads* by describing his boyhood life on the middle border. His autobiography repeats stories and phrases from *Main-Travelled Roads* nearly verbatim, but more important, it also replicates its tone. The two books might be seen as self-authorizing in terms of content. But in terms of form, Garland's autobiography tells the story of how a "local" boy learns to regionalize his experience at the same time he learns that his region is always in a position of economic dependence. The texts are in a complex relation of self-citation, each ratifying the claims of the other. It is Garland's tenuous self-creation as a local subject and a national author, and thus as both an arbiter and a challenger of literary value, that is of particular interest here.

Garland's attempt to separate the region from corrupt representations of it—his ambition to represent it more authentically—is one of the unifying themes of *A Son of the Middle Border*. As I have said, his memories of his boyhood are "regionalized." Garland recalls his boyhood in some of the same rhetorical terms that his midwestern stories, written some twenty years earlier, had already established and circulated. The tone of his memoir is lyrical, and his memory of the Midwest is that it is a place already disappearing. But even as he follows the lyrical tone established by the genre of regional fiction, his lyricism is counteracted by brutally realistic descriptions of the economic conditions leading to the region's disappearance. For Garland, capital both created and devoured the Midwest, establishing farmers as easily as it pushed them out or bankrupted them.

A Son of the Middle Border expresses Garland's complex relationship with the region. Garland describes his carefully tended childhood memories, and he sometimes speculates about the economic motives that drove his family westward. His authorial tone, with its odd combination of briskness and lyricism, reveals a great deal about Garland's vacillating imagination of his western past:

It all lies in the unchanging realm of the past—this land of my childhood. Its charm, its strange dominion cannot return save in the poets' reminiscent dream. No money, no railway train can take us back to it. It does not in truth exist—it was a magical world, born of the vibrant union of youth, and firelight, of music and the voice of moaning winds—a union which can never come again to you or me, father, uncle, brother, till the coulee meadows bloom again unscarred of spade or plow. (1914:67)

This passage is unremarkable, a conventional expression of childhood, loss, and nostalgia. But because Garland's autobiography is in many ways a careful detailing of how he became a writer, and particularly a regional writer, passages like these invite scrutiny. This passage is bound up with regional rhetorical conventions. It is replete with images of loss, lyricism, and a "magical world." Especially interesting is the warning that neither money nor railway can take one back to the remembered homestead, a caution that resonates with the leisure classes' pursuit of "childhood" and the unspoiled places of the nation's memory. But even more pointedly, it is money and railroad that are responsible for spoiling this tender scene. The interests of capital and the railroad itself bring the region into a more direct and exploitable relationship to "you and me." Money and railroad not only cannot bring one back, they also are responsible for destroying the remnants of that memory. Garland's rhetoric thus installs a paradox it cannot acknowledge, much less resolve. As the region he talks about becomes more spatially accessible, it recedes temporally. He can get there, but there isn't there anymore. Garland's lament for the disappearance of the region is also marked by another factor in its decline, the waves of small farmers and homesteaders who "scar" the land with "spade or plow." The invocation of big business via money and railroad gesture toward the effects of the independent homesteader, supposing an impossible region, one that could never have existed *as a region* because it would precede culture and thus the possibility of narration.

Describing one of his family's many moves, for example, Garland writes that "the bleaching white antlers of by-gone herbivora lay scattered, testifying to 'the herds of deer and buffalo' which once fed there. We were just a few years too late to see them" (1914:85). In concert with this strange blindness about having missed, rather than having helped exterminate, the buffalo and deer, Garland seems to say that in fact, it is the homesteader who precedes, even flees, capital rather than announcing it. About an early move, Garland writes, "My father again loaded our household goods into wagons, and with our small herd of cattle following, set out toward the West, bound once again to overtake the actual line of the middle border" (81). About another move,

I now perceived that our going was all of a piece with the West's elemental restlessness . . . we were bidding farewell to one cycle of emigration and entering upon another. The border line had moved on, and my indomitable Dad was moving with it. . . . From this spot we had seen the wild prairie's despair. On every hand wheat and corn and cover had taken the place of the wild oat, the hazelbush and the rose. (237)

Although in almost all instances, the general trend of farmers leaving their homesteads could be traced to the demands of big business, that history is effaced in this account. Garland dissociates small homesteaders from the machinations of capital, describing the desire to move to new land as a romantic instance of a pioneer spirit. Such a description dissociates farming from business, as either its victim or its manifestation. But as we will see, Garland's relationship to his multiple family homes is not always so lyrical.

On closer inspection, Garland's nostalgia for the experience of moving farther west is quite tempered. If in fact the autobiography's incidental descriptions of the "middle border" are enabled by his earlier immersion in a literary and regionalist sensibility—his descriptions look regional because he is an accomplished regional writer—it still is interesting to inquire where the autobiography places the origins of young Garland's aesthetic sensibility.

The autobiography changes in tone and in style once it begins to describe Garland's education. Eventually he leaves the Midwest and moves with his brother Charles to New England. About this trip he writes: "I had all the emotions of a pilgrim entering upon some storied oriental vale . . . it was the cradle of our liberty, the home of literature, the province of art—and it contained Boston" (1914:274). Everything he sees is "strange, yet familiar!" and every scene reminds the Garland brothers of pictures from books. Traveling through the New England countryside, he remarks that "the lanes made *pictures* all the time" (280). Garland's construction of himself as someone who recognizes that New England is exhausted, that it *imitates* itself, is modified in his startled but pleased note that

everything was old, delightfully old. Nothing was new,—most of the people we saw were old. The men working in the fields were bent and gray, scarcely a child appeared, though elderly women abounded (This was thirty-five years ago, before the Canadians and Italians had begun to swarm). Everywhere we detected signs of the historical, the traditional, the Yankee. (274)

Garland's recollection of New England from the vantage point of "some thirty-five years" is expressed in the images and language of a New England regionalist. It is impossible for him to arrive at a pure "view" of New England, since his view of it has been created by literary conventions.

The inescapability of seeing or reading other than through prior representations is solidified by Garland's account of his stay in New England. Describing his first visit, he labels Boston as both an "ancient city" and a "new world," forecasting his literary essays' gestures of conciliation and repudiation toward the reified literary center of "the East." These gestures are particularly important as an index to Garland's understanding of his value as a "western" author. Boston is new for him in two senses, as the site of literary and cultural capital and the source and measure of literary skill and fame.

Although his autobiography is, as I have argued, suffused with the imagery and tone of regional writing, it is Garland's introduction to the world of Boston that produces his awareness of himself as a western man. His life in Boston suggests to Garland, in other words, that he has a regional identity, which might inform his authorship and his subject matter. Returning from Boston to yet another homestead (the Garland's fourth, this time in the Dakotas) he writes that in his job tending a store counter, he seldom gossiped and conversed with his customers as a shopkeeper should. He comments that he regrets this: "A closer relationship with the settlers would have furnished me with a greater variety of fictional characters, but at the time I had no suspicion that I was missing anything" (1914:306). In his recollection, Boston—a metonym for the reified East—is the dividing line separating his unself-conscious participation in his life from his recognition that he ought to have been observing it.

If his stay in the East informs Garland's sense that his own experience is appropriate material for fiction, it also tells him that in order to get such material, he needs to be not merely a participant but also an observer in his own life. This paradox—which is at the heart of regionalism more generally—makes untenable Garland's self-appointed role as a regional spokesman. Narrating "real" experience, even one's own, demands that one extract oneself from one's life. But the concern with self-estrangement and reification that is implicit in this demand was also at the heart of contemporary debates about realism. Casting his autobiography as a narrative of the development of his newly produced regional identity thus allows Garland to stand at the heart of the late nineteenth century's struggle over legitimate personhood and cultural authority.

More prosaically, Garland's new sense of distance from his midwestern life helps him establish a schedule of self-improvement and autodidacticism. Garland writes that "I determined to go to the bottom of the laws which govern literary development, and so with an unexpurgated volume of Taine . . . I set to work to base myself profoundly in the principles which govern a nation's self-expression" (1914:306–307). To aid his memory, he plasters the walls and ceiling of his cabin with charts of his literary development, noting that "these charts were the wonder and astonishment of my neighbors whenever they chanced to enter the living room" (307). Garland's other major intellectual discovery is Henry George's *Progress and Poverty*:

Up to this moment I had never read any book or essay in which our land system had been questioned. I had been raised in the belief that this was the best of all nations in the best of all possible worlds, in the happiest of all ages. I believed (of course) that the wisdom of those who formulated our constitution was but little less than that of archangels, and that all contingencies of our progress in government had been provided for or anticipated in that inspired and deathless instrument. (313)

Garland's desire to find the "laws" governing a nation's "self-expression" and his sudden discovery that the laws of his country governing the distribution of land might be unjust open the ideological space in which he can first imagine his own relationship to literature as well as to his own experience. He creates a parallel between the way things are governed and narrated on a national level and contrasts it with the way things "really" are at the local level. In equating his desire to expose the unreality of fiction as it is practiced in the East with his desire to expose the falsity of laws that legislate and therefore attempt to narrate or describe land, Garland's autobiography presents his assumption of authorship as deeply political. In making a parallel between the unjust or corrupt laws governing the distribution of the land and the unjust literary laws governing the representation of the land, Garland also recursively initiates the argument about the representation of the folk and the genre of local color that inform the collection of stories in *Main-Travelled Roads*.

When he sells his claim in Dakota to return to Boston, Garland once and for all lays claim to his own ground of writing. Feeling that the East "was rather as a story already told, a song already sung" (1914:350), he recalls that he was not inspired to set words to paper until he began thinking of himself as far away from home. Although exhausted by Boston, the East enables him to distance himself from the place that, he will also argue, gives him his identity. Spatial distance evokes for him a romantic temporal distance:

Each season dropped a thickening veil of mist between me and the scenes of my youth, adding a poetic glamour to every rememberable form and fact. . . . I thought of the lonely days of plowing on the prairie, and the poetry and significance of those wild gray days came over me with such power that I instinctively seized my pen to write of them. (350)

At this point, Garland's desire to write about life on the middle border converges with the desire to *own* part of the middle border, as if the yearning to claim it for literature and the desire to claim it back from the unsettled wilderness were products of the same "instinctive" force. Garland notes about his early fiction that "in this my first real shot at the delineation of prairie life, I had no models. Perhaps this clear field helped me to be true" (1914:351). About his return to Dakota from Boston he writes: "I was eager to clutch my share of Uncle Sam's bounty as any of them. The world seemed beginning anew for me as well as for these aliens from the crowded eastern world. 'I am ready to stake a claim,' I said to my father" (302). His proprietary desire to "stake a claim" speaks to an imbrication of the economy of regional fiction and the economy of the regional farmer that seems to deny Garland's carefully wrought description of the political advocacy of his authorship. Later, when evaluating his literary success, Garland also casts it in terms of an imperial ethos. Aside from Eggleston, Howe, and Joseph Kirkland, he writes, "I had the middle west almost entirely to myself" (419).

Setting up New England literary culture as not only exhausted but also too mannered, too rule or law bound, Garland retreats into the rhetoric of spontaneity, which allows him to figure his return to and recording of life in the Midwest as natural and even liberating. Returning for a visit home, he feels that "the east had surfeited me with picturesqueness. It appeared that I had been living for six years amidst painted, neatly arranged pasteboard scenery. Now suddenly I dropped to the level of nature unadorned" (1914:355). Yet as he seizes instinct, truth, and the rhetoric of nature as the constitutive elements of his writing, he also falls victim to an increased sense of artificiality.

On his way back to see his parents, he stops in Osage, one of his boyhood hometown, and writes that "I wished to spend an hour or two in going about in guise of a stranger. There was something instructive as well as deliciously exciting in thus seeing old acquaintances as from behind a mask. They were at once familiar and mysterious" (1914:359). He writes, too, that he "perceived the town from the triple viewpoint of a former resident, a man from the city, and a reformer, and every minutest detail of dress, tone and gesture revealed new meaning to me" (361). Recovering the "real" life of his town forces him to make himself an outsider. In fact, it is Garland's immersion in metropolitan culture that regionalizes him, makes him on his visits home able to speak for the farmers as a man who comprehends how land is forced into an "unnatural" relationship to the metropolitan center. No longer a farmer, not yet an eastern writer, his relation to his past self is mediated by his new profession. New literary values tell him about the value of the people he has left behind. But he also is torn by his suspicion that he might be exploiting the material of his memory, in the same way that speculators seem to exploit the improvements the people make to their land.[6]

Garland's negotiation of the double identity of the speculating observer and the land speculator is uneasily concretized in the way that each position is invested in arbitrating representation and its value.

In my judgment the men and women of the south, the west and the east, are working (without knowing it) in accordance with a great principle, which is this: American literature, in order to be great, must be national, and in order to be national, must deal with conditions peculiar to our own land and climate. (1914:387)

Garland's relationship to reformism and the land is solidified when in his travels back and forth between his parents' home and his own, he begins to attend meetings of the Populist Party, which his father joined at its inception. "I took part in meetings of rebellious farmers in bare-walled Kansas school-houses, and watched protesting processions of weatherworn Nebraska Populists" (423). Eventually he begins to speak for them. He writes that "for six weeks I travelled [in the service of the People's Party], speaking nearly every day—getting back to the farms of the west and harvesting a rich fund of experiences" (427).

Garland's desire to "reap" something in speaking *as* or *for* the population foregrounds his negotiation of a doubled economy of national politics and culture and the field of literary production. Nancy Glazener reads Garland's support of Populism and the 1890 People's Party more positively, noting that many of his early essays of "literary criticism" appeared in the political journal the *Arena*. She writes that this journal's politics, in contrast to elite periodicals such as the *Atlantic*, made

it possible to read regionalism as a minor literature in a different sense: as a literature bearing special importance for a distinct minority of the population, as a literature posed against a minor literature, and as a body of fiction minor as literature but not as social representation. Hamlin Garland's strongly politicized advocacy of regionalism, which shows up in many of his early *Arena* essays, suggests that it was even possible to write regionalism as this kind of minor literature, to some extent. (Glazener 1997:214–215)

Indeed, when he speaks to William Dean Howells about his ideas of local-color fiction, Garland writes, "Once set going, I fear I went on like a political orator who doesn't know when to sit down" (1914:387). But the congruence between his identity as political orator and local-color writer—a congruence that *A Son of the Middle Border* is at pains to track—is not so easily achieved in Garland's fiction.

It is probably one of the best-known facets of Garland's writing that all his stories are drawn "from life," particularly his life. As I have demonstrated, Garland's autobiographical tendencies are no more "natural" than his "instinct" to write about his childhood regions. But if it is true that we can read his work autobiographically, such readings are possible only if we look at Garland's narrative persona, even that of his autobiography, as shaped less by any kind of psychological development than by a keen rhetorical development. His sense of literary and personal value comes only after he learns to define value as eastern forces do.

Garland's autobiography, written thirty-one years after his most famous collection, demonstrates that his version of his life was not merely fictionalized but that it was structured by a clear sense of fictional conventions. It is not, therefore, his life as a midwesterner that authorizes his autobiography but his narrative self-production through regionalism that does so. Zona Gale wrote in the *Yale Review* in 1922 that Garland's autobiography is "the story of a man who had never ceased to be identified with himself!" and that "never did anyone so hate the town that he loves as Hamlin Garland hates his beloved homestead town" (Nagel 1982: 106–107).

Hamlin Garland, author, comes to be an almost perfect embodiment of the uneven economic and cultural development that national consolidation and industrial capital produce in the region. He is the fallow region developed by eastern influence, and as such, his personal and literary growth can be narrated only in the twin modes of land value and literary value—his art is, as one anonymous reviewer from the *Overland Monthly* commented in September 1901, "a soil-fed art" (Nagel 1982:

79). As a professional observer, Garland is also a professional speculator, and as a professional speculator, his observation of the people he "values" causes him profound anxiety.

I now turn to a selection of stories from *Main-Travelled Roads* to explore the ways in which regional writing is evaluated according to the perceived "real" needs of the regional inhabitants. In *Main-Travelled Roads* (1962), Garland's stories turn on the relationship between the rural and the urban, often using a narrator who classifies the raw material of equally raw rural life. Garland's stories also critique the position of the narrator even while they sometimes appear to valorize his perceptions. In doing this, Garland aims both to critique the genre of regionalism and also to reinstall the region as an appropriate, even necessary, object of study. Garland's attempts to "correct" the standard, eastern vision of the region as a site of imagination somehow outside material economies allows us to view his vision of regionalism as one reassigning value to the region based on its real economic value rather than in contrast to it. Thus the narratives' critique of the narrator is not simply directed toward the ascribed value of the Midwest as economic fuel for the metropolis. Rather, it is directed more finely at the reader of regionalism whose ostensible site of self-recognition or identification in the text is the narrator. But as I argue, no matter how much Garland rails against and yet attempts to produce a counternarrative of the region to arrive at a more "pure" or truthful representation of it, his attempt is always framed within the narrative demands of the genre of regionalism itself. He not only is always responsive to this particular way of framing experience, the terms of his critique also are derived from it.

Nearly all the stories in *Main-Travelled Roads* deal in some way with the return of a native whose long absence has made him a stranger, and in the two about an elderly farm couple, the Ripleys, the events of the narrative are structured by Mrs. Ripley's journey to her home state of New York and by Mr. Ripley's gullibility in the face of a quasi-urban, fast-talking, patent-medicine salesman. The stories are largely explorations of the grinding life of the farmer and his wife, as well as meditations on what it means to escape from and return to such a life. Many are filled with references to banking, interest rates, elections, speculation, and taxes, all of which are seen as natural enemies of the farmer. There is then an immediate formal transaction on the level of plot between subjective experience and the objective reality of land speculation, taxes, and hard work. That so many of the stories feature a return, and usually a bitterly disappointing one, accords with the regional project, but the stories' hostility toward this project is exposed in Garland's minute descriptions of the difficulties of farm life, as well as his consistent attention to the difficulties of the native's return.7

Two of the stories articulate a divided idea about authorship and the region and about the ability of the "outsider" to narrate or imagine the region at all. "Up the Coolly" and "God's Ravens" share the narrative strategy of bringing home a former inhabitant of a particular region.[8] In "Up the Coolly," the earlier of the two stories, the main character is Howard McLane, a New York actor who has decided to return to his home in Wisconsin after an absence of ten years. As McLane rides on the train to "his West," he takes in the scenery with "dreaming eyes," feeling that it "had a certain mysterious glamour to him" (1962:45). But once he steps off the train in his tiny hometown, he notices only "an unpaved street, with walled, drab-colored, miserable, rotting wooden buildings, with the inevitable battlements; the same—only worse and more squalid—was the town" (46). His experience of the town's squalor is offset, though, by his aesthetic appreciation of the landscape at dusk, an appreciation that fills his heart "with pleasure almost like pain" (49). This aesthetic pleasure, balanced as it is against his horror at the conditions of life in the town itself, has been intensified by his absence: "in his restless life, surrounded by the glare of electric lights, painted canvas, hot colors, creak of machines, mock trees, stones, and brooks, he had not lost but gained, appreciation for the coolness, quiet, and low tones, the shyness of the wood and field" (51).

This convergence of the image of the country with its theatrical, corrupt representations is repeated when McLane, now in his squalid farmhouse room, recalls his own beautiful apartments in the city, which are decorated with a farm scene "by a master greater than Millet" (1962:58). The painting hanging on the wall of his city bedroom depicts

a farm in the valley! Over the mountains swept jagged, gray, angry, sprawling clouds, sending a freezing, thin drizzle of rain, as they passed, upon a man following a plough. The horses had a sullen and weary look, and their manes and tails streamed sidewise in the blast. The ploughman, clad in a ragged gray coat, with uncouth, muddy boots upon his feet, walked with his head inclined toward the sleet, to shield his face from the cold and sting of it. The soil rolled away black and sticky and with a dull sheen upon it. Near by, a boy with tears on his cheeks was watching cattle, a dog seated near, his back to the gale. As he looked at this picture, his heart softened. He looked down at the sleeve of his soft and fleecy night-shirt, at his white, rounded arm, muscular, yet fine as a woman's, and when he looked for the picture it was gone. (58)

McLane's ability to still take "pride in being a Western man," as the narrator tells us at the beginning of the story, is bound up with a series of representations of what it means to be a Western man. Ironically, the painting in Howard's New York apartment depicts almost exactly the work his younger brother is doing on the farm when Howard arrives for his visit.

The very excess of the description allows the reader to see that the picture McLane is recalling indeed describes "real" life on the farm. Its wealth of adjectives, its reliance on speculations about the plowman's intent—"to shield his face from the cold and sting of it"—rather than a mere cataloging of his actions, make the painting an index against which to measure Howard's inability to imagine the life of his younger brother Grant. Howard McLane's response to Grant is of interest here. He has gone to bed after a fight with his brother, who has as much as accused Howard of deserting his family. Unable to sleep, Howard charges his brother with being a brute and a savage. He relents in his judgment only after he remembers the painting of a rural laborer hanging in his city apartment. Only after going over every detail of it can he begin to sympathize with his brother's daily suffering.[9] Like the representations of country life on the sets of his plays, this painting brings Howard to a "real" sense of pity. But the nature of representation is here even more vexed. Howard has clearly placed the painting in his rooms to help him remember his former life as a Western man, and he must conjure it up, framed by the comfort of his city rooms, in order to fully return home. His reliance on dramatic representation has superseded its original function for him; his reliance on it extends to his own behavior while interacting with his family and their friends.

Drawing on metaphors of acting in order to describe Howard, Garland creates him as a man who seems to have no home. Indeed, the homestead to which he thought he was returning has been sold to a German family, and his own family has been forced to a new dwelling near, but not exactly like, the one he has cherished in his memory. This proximity, this almost-but-not-quite quality of his homecoming, might be related to his inability to coincide with himself during his visit. Coming down for breakfast one morning, he greets his family "with the manner, as he himself saw, of the returned captain in the war-dramas of the day" (1962:59). What is especially interesting in this passage is the inclusion of the phrase "as he himself saw." Howard's consciousness of his deviation from his former self drives him to more fulsome and stagy phrases. He has dressed himself in what he considers a rustic outfit, but it serves only to enrage his brother, who sees that the sheer cost of the clothes has made them unfit for the kind of outside labor for which they are ostensibly designed. Dressed as a countryman but not as a farmer, Howard can assume only the part of the actor dressed for activity that he cannot really perform. Even when he attempts to make amends with his brother, his language underscores his ability to shift between theatrical roles: "I kinder circumambiated the pond," he says in a heavy rustic accent as he sits down next to his brother, "Your barn is a good deal like that in 'The Arkansaw Traveller.' Needs a new roof, Grant" (84).

Howard atones for his guilt for leaving his mother and brother by buying back the old homestead, and he thinks to himself as he makes the transaction, "Think of it! To see his mother back in the old home, with the fireplace restored, the old furniture in the sitting room around her, and fine new things in the parlor!" (1962:65). The vision he has of making amends is quite romantic, as if he is setting the stage for the homecoming he had expected when he arrived: "He had intended to have such a happy evening of it, such a tender reunion! It was to be so bright and cheery!" (57).

Part of Howard's desire to buy back the farm is to cancel out his "debt" to his family, to repay them for letting him go to school and move away—for giving him a chance, in other words, to escape being like them. This debt gains more general meaning if we look at the way the text discusses work. When Howard casually tells his family that he can sometimes make a thousand dollars a week, they are dumbfounded, and he quickly explains that this is unusual. But gradually, he begins to feel as though he does not deserve to make this money, telling his mother that it is not his talent or hard work that has helped him succeed. "I did nothing to merit it. Everybody helps me. Anybody can succeed in that way" (1962:68). His testimony that he exists because people are *interested* in him means to his family that Howard is somehow living without working. Grant's shock at this discovery accords with the Populist or producerist critique of those who live off the labor of others, producing nothing themselves but managing to live well anyway. Indeed, Howard's invocation of the fabulous sum of one thousand dollars a week is a persuasive reminder of the Populist desire to expand the money supply. Howard's ability to make money just by talking exemplifies the imbrication of aesthetic value and financial value with which this chapter began. Those economies are juxtaposed again in a description of an impromptu homecoming party for Howard.[10]

As the guests become still to listen to a musician, the narrator says, "The magic of music sobered every face; the women looked older and more careworn, the men slouched sullenly in their chairs, or leaned back against the wall. It seemed to Howard as if the spirit of tragedy had entered this house" (1962:77). When the men talk about politics and the desperate conditions that govern their lives, their "brutally bald words made Howard thrill with emotion like the reading of some great tragic poem" (76). If Howard is the sympathetic home comer, who "ponder(s) upon the tragedy he had rediscovered in these people's lives" (78), he is also both reader and writer of them, imitator and product.

The implicit critique in the story is that even a sympathetic reading—or artistic representation—of the region is implicated in its economic trouble. Howard traffics in representation. It is the representations of his Western life that help give Howard the trustworthy personal integrity—

or character—that draws the interest of audiences and backers. Even his sympathy with the culture of the regional inhabitants separates him from them. His reading of their cultural expressions has been influenced by eastern aesthetic forms. The narrator implies that Howard needs to translate the expression of the regional folk into universal aesthetic forms before he can feel their particular sorrows. Garland thus valorizes the ability to represent the region while he is implicating representation in the economic decline of the region. That is, Garland recognizes and valorizes the economy of aesthetic representation in these stories when it appears to be the "true" expression of the people, but the kind of representation in which Howard engages is "false" representation. This conflict drives the story even while a similarly conflicted ideology of authorship as a form of populist-inflected political action drives Garland to write it.[11]

Similarly, in "God's Ravens," Garland presents the character of Robert Bloom, a Chicago newspaperman who yearns to be free of the city and to return to his native Wisconsin, where he spent his childhood summers. "As his weakness grew his ambition fell away, and his heart turned back to nature and to the things he had known in his youth, to the kindly people of the olden time" (1962:197). Bloom is also a fiction writer, and while he intends to move his family to Wisconsin to escape Chicago, he also plans to write stories about the people he meets—local-color fiction "telling about the people I meet and their queer ways, so quaint and good" (199). Here, the story nearly recapitulates a history of the genre of regionalism. Bloom, wishing to go back to the space of his youth to recapture a childhood innocence, equates the pastoral region with the innocent youth of the nation. His desire is to be at one with the "people" and also to profit by them. The irony of the story is that having moved to a small town, Bloom is repulsed by the townsfolk he had been praising to his wife. Rather than the salt of the earth he had hoped for, he sees the rural inhabitants as semi-barbarians, laborers too tired and too poor to ever be understood as poetic manifestations of the pastoral ideal: "They've saved and pinched and toiled till their souls are pinched and ground away. You're right," Bloom tells his wife, "they are caricatures" (218). His disappointment in village life is underscored by his inability to recover the health that the city destroyed. Garland writes, "He had not gained any power—he was really weaker than ever. The rain had kept him confined to the house. The joy he had anticipated of tracing out all his boyish pleasure haunts was cut off. He had relied too, upon that as a source of literary power" (207).

When Bloom anticipates his country life as a source of physical and literary health, he casts it in terms of force, or power. But rather than finding in the country the source of power, he finds instead that he is in a radically disabled position; he has become a pitiable subject rather than a narrator. Although he delights in the people's vigorous turns of phrase, he soon finds that no one wants to talk to him. While he values their speech aesthetically, in "some way his tone was not right" with his neighbors (1962:203). In fact, Bloom is "a source of great speculation with them. Some of them had gone so far as to bet he wouldn't live a year" (203). In a fairly heavy-handed inversion, it turns out that rather than being the subjects of Bloom's writing, the townsfolk have made him the subject of their conversations.

As we saw in "Up the Coolly," Garland's articulation of the aesthetic to the economic allows him to cast the outsider, even if sympathetic, as a kind of speculator. Here, as with Howard McLane, we can see that the source of personal strength—even identity—is supposed to be identification with the people of the region. But as *Crumbling Idols* is at pains to point out only a few years after this story appears, identification is not identity. "The mere fact that a writer happens to live in California or Oregon will not make him a part of that literature, any more than Stevenson's life in Samoa will make him a Samoan author" (22). Bloom *loses* power, and his inability to speculate in the lives of the people is counteracted by their speculation about him. Here, too, Garland equates economies of representation and material economies; the townspeople are wondering whether Bloom will get well and also are making bets on whether or not he will die.

Bloom finally becomes desperately ill. By the end of "God's Ravens," the townspeople have nursed Robert back to health and he learns that they're "real" people after all. When he is finally well enough, he tries to speak to one of the neighbors who "seemed never to weary in his service" (1962:210). "Oh, I understand you now. I know you all now," Bloom tells William McTurg, but the narrator immediately adds, "But William did not understand him" (211). In denying any genuine connection between William and Robert Bloom, Garland seems to forestall the possibility of genuine rapprochement between the stranger and the native. Even though this possibility is foreclosed, the story's ending is rather disquieting. Although Bloom has seen the real conditions of life in a small town, he has not been disappointed. And even though Garland seems to argue that a romantic conception of the pastoral region is not merely wrong but unhealthy as well, he seems to reestablish it by creating the regional characters as more than saintly. In fact, they seem to become the very ideals Bloom was searching for when he first moved back. Ironically, Garland's focus on the misrepresentation of the local finds its antidote in a fetishization of the regional folk.

In *Crumbling Idols*, Garland urges the project of local-color writing. But in a somewhat odd move, he defines local-color literature by defining its practitioner: "Local color ... means that the writer spontaneously reflects the life which goes on around him. It is a natural and unstrained art" (1952:52). It will, he promises, echoing William Dean Howells, democratize literature. Garland goes even further than Howells and promises that the democratization of literature will help usher in the movement of cultural and economic capital from the East to the West.[12] But as soon as he has made the argument for the public, even national, necessity of local color, Garland turns to the question of marketing.

In the chapter "The Question of Success," he writes, "but the question forced on the young writer, even when he is well disposed toward dealing with indigenous material, is Will it pay? Is there a market for me?" (1952: 33). His answer is yes, but it is important to look at the conjunction between indigenous materials and the market in Garland's philosophy. In treating the subject of regionalism as an object of exchange, Garland is trafficking blatantly and consciously in two entangled economies. But he is also mimicking the very questions that the farmers in the Midwest were themselves asking about their own products—is there a market in the East? Who is controlling consumption? How will my labor be valued in the East? Such questions, posed in the arena of aesthetics, both align and dissociate Garland with the populist/producerist rhetoric that his autobiography insists informed his desire to write fiction.

The conjunction between market economies and aesthetic economies that Garland makes in *Crumbling Idols*, although phrased positively, shows the market relations that regional fiction's creation of normative communities generally represses. But it also represses in turn the problematic nature of regional authorship. While Garland's sentiments about the value of the region are clearly expressed in *Crumbling Idols*, they are less easily practiced.[13] Garland's texts demonstrate a particularly difficult problem in regional writing. One general way to figure that problem is to consider not just how community is created in regionalism but also how membership in that community is determined. Garland's version of regional membership, for example, excludes the observer who is not "natural" or "spontaneous." But regionalism is hardly an artless genre, as Garland's extensive critique of aesthetics demonstrates.

Another way to understand the problem of regional writing produced by Garland's critique of the two economies of markets and aesthetics is to see regional authorship as an amplification of the fantasy of a coherent realist subject. In Garland's fiction, the central figure cannot achieve self-identicalness in the face of the region's simultaneous existence with the urban problems from which it is presumed to be so far removed. The uneven development of the Midwest seems to have a corresponding effect on the uneven or disjointed development of the regional subject. In highlighting these problems, Garland's fiction also highlights the tensions in even the most successful, genteel regional writing. In fact, if regional writing is, as William Dean Howells contended, the fiction of democracy that would introduce people to one another and show them that they were "more alike than unlike," it is underwritten by an assumption about the necessity of the consonance of local and national identity (Howells 1983: 96). The focus on the culture of the local, always available for identification and consumption in local-color fiction, conceals the vastly different values of national and local economies and covers over problems in the political and economic dependence of the local on the national.

THE RETURN OF THE REGION: HAROLD FREDERIC'S *THE DAMNATION OF THERON WARE*

As with Garland's stories, Harold Frederic's *The Damnation of Theron Ware* is permeated by the language and the ideology of seeing and of being seen, of being an outsider and an insider in incommensurable cultural economies.[14] As we have seen, one model of regional narration is exemplified by the narrator in Sarah Orne Jewett's *The Country of the Pointed Firs*, who performs the balancing act of observing her subjects and living among them through her strategic negotiation of local and national histories. Another model is exemplified by Hamlin Garland, who repudiates regional conventions by exposing the dismal economic conditions that regional fiction's focus on a reified notion of the local ignores.

In this section, I discuss Harold Frederic's *The Damnation of Theron Ware* (1896), the story of a young minister who takes up a new position in the Methodist church in Octavius, a small community in central New York. Released in the same year as *The Country of the Pointed Firs*, *The Damnation of Theron Ware* extends the conventions of regional fiction. Rather than comparing this text with either Jewett's or Garland's, I read Frederic's novel as a critique of the cultural economy of regionalism. *The Damnation of Theron Ware* demonstrates that regional characteristics and regionalism itself are predicated on the uneven development of capitalism, which produces a radically unbalanced cultural landscape.

The town of Octavius does not merely embody the constitutive tensions of rural and urban; it produces a tension between the "timelessness" of the pastoral (embodied here in the primitive Methodists of Wesley's persuasion) and the radically future-oriented world of modernity (embodied in the town's intellectuals: a priest, a New Woman, and a Darwinian scientist). In order to create a dialectic among these elements, the text employs the mediating figure of cultural difference embodied in various ethnic or ethnicized characters. As Theron learns more about the history of the Irish, for example, he is confronted by his belatedness as a historical actor. As he gradually comprehends the historical and social contests that have produced all the most familiar and stable elements of his world, Theron loses the ability to order his experiences and his own position in relation to them.

Frederic's depiction of regional life as a product of uneven development is not, as it was for Jewett and Garland, primarily predicated on location—the elsewhere of most regionalism—but, rather, on temporality—the elsewhere that lingers nostalgically in the fullness of the present. Like the characters in Jewett's text, Theron is caught in a transition between unevenly developed worlds, but unlike Captain Littlepage, he is at the beginning of his awareness of other worlds and has not yet become aware of their power to influence him. It is perhaps the great tragedy of this novel that Theron Ware proves to be a regional figure who does not recognize himself as such and who will not be still in the curio cabinet of this genre. He commits the unpardonable sin of pastoral regionalism: he attempts to modernize himself as he is being observed.

Frederic parodies regional writings' narrative gestures to "timeless" places and nostalgically charged spaces by creating Octavius as an unevenly developed town. In regional texts I have previously examined, the process of arriving at the region entails a backward movement, both spatial and imaginative. In order to enter the region, the reader must first remember, must take time out from the present in order to return to the metonymic region of the (national) past. In Jewett's text, this backward motion is gracefully enacted by a sympathetic narrator. Even in Garland's writing, we can see that the region bears the peculiar marks of a past that roughly corresponds to a loose rendition of "childhood." Although Garland believes that the region must not be the site of nostalgia because it exists in real time and is dependent on national financial markets, he nonetheless casts many of his stories as a kind of return to the innocence of the region, even if that innocence must be reclaimed from its misrepresentation in fictional accounts.

In *The Damnation of Theron Ware*, the psychic and geographical distance that Frederic allows both his characters and his readers from the urban experience of the late nineteenth century is almost nonexistent.[15] While privileging the temporal aspects of the region's distance, Frederic also argues that temporal and spatial distance are indissolubly linked in constructing representations of the past. Octavius, the central New York village to which Theron Ware is sent, seems to him like any other small village, but he gradually begins to realize that it is more like two villages. The first is composed of a small community of Methodists, which attempts to remain self-sufficient and transact all business and personal matters solely within the community of believers. But the burgeoning city of Octavius is also composed of strange new people: the Irish and Italian Catholic immigrants who work in the region's many mills. Standing outside and above

Octavius, Theron looks down and sees the city "at one end half-hidden in factory smoke, at the other . . . narrow bands of water gleamed upon the surface of a broad plain piled symmetrically with lumber, presenting an oddly incongruous suggestion of forest odors and the simplicity of the wilderness." It is a "jumble of primitive rusticity and urban complications" (Frederic 1960:222).

The "jumble" of Octavius confuses both the rhetoric of place and the rhetoric of temporality. The pastoral and the urban are coexistent. The community to which Theron is sent is that of a small Methodist sect that has resisted the tendency to splinter into the ever smaller doctrinal communities that characterized nineteenth-century Methodism. The text parodies this brand of Methodism as practiced by Americans who seem to have emerged from the age of Puritanism. Devoutly calling one another "Brother" and "Sister," these Methodists gesture toward America's founding belief in spiritual purity and community integrity, and they hold to the forms of fraternity that naturalize their integrity as that of the family. Frederic writes that an observer would find these Methodists to conjure up "pictures of a time when a plain and homely people had been served by a fervent and devoted clergy . . . these pictures had for their primitive accessories loghuts, rough household implements, coarse clothes, and patched old saddles which told of weary years of journeying" (1960:4–5). Frederic's use of the words *primitive* and *accessories* and especially his use of the language of pictures which, like tableaus, mark the social construction of the "original," "old," and "pure."

The members of the congregation participate in the same conflicted staging of what is primitive and what is novel. Although the Methodists are insulated from the town's modern developments—going so far as to shun the streetcars because they run on Sundays—their trustees are implacable capitalists. The aptly named Brothers Pierce and Winch run rock quarries, hold mortgages on farms and other properties, and speculate in the commodities market. Their attempt to preserve the community's homogeneity in terms of trade looks, from the angle of their professional lives, like a desire to control the market's conditions at the point of consumption.

In contrast to this sectarian Protestantism, the Catholic Church, associated throughout the book with the novelty and strangeness of European immigrants, strikes Theron as ancient and corrupt, the institution of ritual and scholasticism. Theron's inability to distinguish what is old and complete from what is partial and novel is further underscored when he nearly misses visiting the Catholic priest because he cannot figure out how to ring the modern doorbell at the rectory. Theron thinks to himself that "for custodians of a mediaeval superstition and fanaticism, the Catholic clergy seemed very much up to date" (1960:66).

The same imbrication of seemingly incommensurable modes of temporality structures Theron's relationship to the rest of the town. In fact, his "damnation" begins when he wanders outside Methodist Octavius into the population at large. He makes the acquaintance of a trio of old friends: Father Forbes, the Catholic priest; Celia Madden, daughter of a wealthy Irish immigrant and mill owner; and Dr. Ledsmar, a Darwinian scientist. They usher him into a world that seems unfathomable and dangerous as well as new and exhilarating. Each of Theron's new friends is by choice and avocation a collector, an amateur historian, and an anthropologist. They have set themselves the new task of observing Theron Ware but are so certain of the solidity of the regional type he represents that they do not imagine that he is observing them as well.

Through his contact with these three, Theron comes to believe that he has been "illuminated" and that he has learned to see himself and the world differently. But he has learned only to see himself as he believes they see him, and accordingly, he becomes a distorted version of his former self as the novel progresses. After much contact with his new friends, Theron thinks to himself that "he stood forth, so to speak, in a new skin, and looked about him, with perceptions of quite an altered kind, upon what seemed in every way a fresh existence" (1960:210). His "fresh existence" might be measured by the fact that Theron's three new friends can variously be seen as representative of what the trustees of his own church have advised him to preach against. The trustees tell Theron to "pitch into" Irish, Catholics, Italians, and especially the scientists who believe that the age of the earth can be determined by "crackin' up stones" and who believe that "our grandfathers were all monkeys" (30). Theron's new perceptions are not just borrowed but blurred with vague yearnings, as we can see when he says to Celia, "I want to get as close to you—to your ideal, that is, as I can. You open up to me a whole world that I had not even dreamed existed" (208).

This "new world" exceeds Theron's own definition of it. He thinks first that his intellectual life has been greatly expanded, but the "new world" of which his new friends seem to be longtime residents, as I will explain, also doubles for a larger world of ethnic and religious heterogeneity. Theron believes that the world that he has entered is vast and inspiring, but the text says otherwise. His initial entrance into the "new world" is not described in a way to make the reader believe that it is coherent; rather, it is delimited by a series of interiors or collections that mirror the personalities of their makers. Each character allows Theron to enter the innermost recesses of his or her home, and while he believes that it is as an equal, it becomes more and more clear that the trio enjoy his presence simply to observe him.

While Theron is busily imagining himself in the strange and exotic world of Dr. Ledsmar, Celia, and Father Forbes, they are watching him with their own delight in his exoticism. If we look at the first scene in which Theron sits at dinner with Father Forbes and Dr. Ledsmar, we cannot fail to note the text's persistent rhetoric of looking and watching. Nervous in the splendor of the rectory, puzzled by the vast quantities of gourmet food put before him, Theron is in a world of decadence and surplus. Confronted by the quality and quantity of consumable objects, he is not aware that he, too, is being consumed.

Theron innocently confides in his friends his desire to write a religious book that will approach one of his favorite stories from the Bible as if it were a real story. His ambition is to write a book about Abraham "the man" and his sayings and doings beyond those reported in the Bible. As he prattles on, he is mercifully unconscious that Forbes and Ledsmar are exchanging amused glances over his head. When Father Forbes explains to Theron that Abraham was simply a "type" and that "modern research . . . quite wipes him out as an individual" (1960:72), Theron suddenly feels an overpowering sense of danger, "that he was among sinister enemies, at the mercy of criminals" (75). His impending sense of danger is also a sense of disorientation; the church that he associates with backwardness and strange European communities suddenly seems like a vast organization with a strikingly modern knowledge of the "origins" of the Bible's meaning. As this figure of the Bible suggests, Theron's trouble lies in his inability to distinguish between appearance and reality, text and context. What initially upsets and puzzles him is that Father Forbes suggests that the natural and self-evident order of the world might be open to new possibilities, indeed, might harbor those new possibilities within its apparently ancient self.

When even the figures in the Bible begin to assume overtones of foreignness, Theron loses his sense of himself, of his own place and position in relation to texts he once thought of as inviolable and sacred. His belief that Abraham is a "real" man and not a type works in the text as a kind of symptom of his unfamiliarity with codes of representation as a whole. It is not simply that it is natural for him, as a Methodist minister, to believe that characters from sacred texts are "real"—he must, after all, interpret them in order to write sermons. Instead, it is that he is unfamiliar with the ways in which these figures announce themselves as mystified ideas carrying hidden histories and contested interpretations. Indeed, he is unaware that he *shares* that function for Father Forbes and Dr. Ledsmar while he is explaining his projected book. He represents a type or figure to his new friends and, as such, is expected to behave in a one-dimensional and charmingly naive way.

After Father Forbes has left him momentarily with Dr. Ledsmar, Theron hears Celia playing the church organ. Looking out the window toward the church, Theron sees a stained-glass image of a vibrant red-headed saint and muses that it is "very like" Celia. It is "just like her," Ledsmar says, separating the woman who is the source of the music from her likeness in the window. In mistaking or misrecognizing a likeness of Celia, Theron completes the circuit of misreading that he began with his inquiry about Abraham. In addition, Theron's misrecognitions and mis-readings are complemented by a similar meditation by Dr. Ledsmar about Theron, who becomes disturbed that "Dr. Ledsmar had turned in his seat, crossed his legs, and was contemplating him with a gravely concentrated scrutiny through his spectacles" (1960:76). The doctor, who keeps an evolutionary study of reptiles, plants, and even his "pet" Chinaman, also takes a shine to Theron as a type, a rustic, set down charmingly among them. Inviting Theron to visit him in his house, Dr. Ledsmar remarks that "I suppose you are the first man I have asked in a dozen years" (82).

The trio of characters who ultimately induct Theron into his "damna-tion" do not under any circumstances make any easier the readings they suggest. In fact, one of them, Celia Madden, the femme fatale of the novel, deliberately seeks to mystify herself, suggesting models through which to read her but failing to provide an adequate key to interpretation. She models herself after the Greeks and calls herself a pagan; discussing her relationship to the Catholic Church, this daughter of the richest entrepre-neur in Octavius says, "I'm as Pagan as—anything! Of course there are forms to be observed, and so on; I rather like them than otherwise. I can make them serve very well for my own system; for I am myself, you know, an out-and-out Greek" (1960:104). These sentences, all beginning with firm declaratives, end in evasions rather than explanations. "I am as Greek as—anything" hints at the essentially hollow nature of her claim, her piecemeal self-construction.

Celia's own formal "system" is epitomized by her rooms. Her "work-room" is littered with the tools of making and creating—easels, books, pens, half-finished drawings, half-modeled clay figures. The in-nermost room, which Celia allows Theron to enter, is one into which not even Celia's servants are allowed. Illuminated only by candles, the room is furnished with vaguely oriental divans and large throw pillows and decorated with reproductions of famous statues. Theron is over-whelmed by the sheer sensuality of it, and Frederic writes that "a less untutored vision than his would have caught more swiftly the scheme of color and line in which these works of art bore their share" (1960:197). It is Celia who explains the decorating scheme to him; it is meant as a formal reflection of her own appearance: "I've made this whole room to match it . . . between us, we make up what Whistler would call a sym-phony" (199). It is not particularly *what* she is making in the rooms that counts, for she is really only reproducing herself over and over as an endless work of art predicated on the pillaging of other historical eras. Susan Stewart remarks about the interior of the bourgeois room that "contained here *is* the self; the material body is simply one more position within the seriality and diversity of objects. Private space is marked by an exterior material boundary and an interior surplus of signification" (Stewart 1984:159).

Although Theron believes that Celia is remarkably rare, she has perversely mystified only the world of commodities that is the basis of her self. Once again, Theron's misrecognition of what is unique for what is only surplus damages his self-perception. When Theron returns to his own house from his first visit to his new friends, he looks around and decides that "the whole effect of the room was . . . bare and squalid to Theron's newly informed eye" (1960:106). Not only does Theron learn to reevaluate himself through the eyes of others, but he also is forced to evaluate what seems to him to be an even larger and more bizarre "new world," opened to him by his new friends.

The emblem of this "new world" is the ethnic other, particularly the Irish. When he first meets the Irish as he tags along after them to the house of a dying worker, they strike him as almost lovely and poetical. Later, however, he is forced to recognize that his previous visions of the Irish have been gleaned from metropolitan sources and that his prejudices are merely received wisdom, a sacred text he has never thought about challenging. When Theron realizes that the Irish live in Octavius and that he has met some of them, he thinks:

What a sinister and repellent name! His views on this general subject were merely those common to his communion. He took it for granted, for example, that in the large cities most of the poverty and all the drunkenness, crime, and political corruption were due to the perverse qualities of this foreign people. (1960:50)

Theron begins to realize that his prejudices have been based on other people's accounts of the crisis of the cities and on the tales of the Molly Maguires that reach even into papers read by young Methodist ministers. But Theron only replaces one type with another. The urban Irish that he first imagines are quickly replaced by the type of the "Celt" that Father Forbes lectures him about. Theron thrills to the priest's sonorous voice offering the last rites to a dying man and learns to value the sonorous tones of Latin over the brogues that he hears muttered around him by more common people. His conversations with the priest and Celia Madden seem to open a tantalizingly new world whose exotic richness threatens to spill into Theron's own household when he shocks his wife with his new and "fine unconcern" about having an Irish washerwoman.

Theron's experience of the coexistence of races summarizes the structure of regional writing in the construction of local identity. His own sect lives almost as a separate community within the town, prompting the remark that "Octavius, so far as the Methodists are concerned, is twenty or thirty years behind the times" (1960:181). His meeting with Father Forbes and Celia Madden at the bedside of a dying Irish worker forces Theron to a "dissenting opinion," and he reflects that the Irish "with all their faults, must have a poetic strain, or they would not have clung so tenaciously to those curious and ancient forms. He recalled having heard somewhere, or read, it might be, that they were a people much given to songs and music" (52).

The discovery that the people about whom he had entertained the wildest fantasies might be exactly the opposite drives him to rethink all the texts he reads. When Theron remembers hearing or reading that the Irish might also be of a poetic temperament, his reading of the story of Abraham suddenly reveals its own opposite. Allowing the ancient Celts to coincide with the contemporary Irish he sees everyday opens a rhetorical space in which they might also coincide with ancient figures in the Bible. He must then confront the fact that the figures in the Bible might be as infinitely interpretable as the Irish. In shock, he realizes that

the people he read about were altered to his vision. Heretofore a poetic light had shone about them, where indeed they had not glowed in a halo of sanctification. Now, by some chance, this light was gone, and he saw them instead as untutored and unwashed barbarians, filled with animal lusts and ferocities, struggling by violence and foul chicanery to secure a foothold in a country which did not belong to them. (1960:62)

This double temporality perfectly matches the information Father Forbes has offered. Theron receives a lecture that destabilizes his own reading of the tenets of his Methodist community and of those of the Irish. Father Forbes explains racial and textual genealogies to him in a speech that he repeats throughout the text:

I spoke of Heber and Heth, in Genesis, as meaning the Hebrews and the Hittites. Now my own people, the Irish, have far more ancient legends and traditions than any other nation west of Athens; and you find in their myth of the Milesian invasion and conquest two principal leaders called Heber and Ith, or Heth. That is supposed to be comparatively modern—about the time of Solomon's Temple. But these independent Irish myths go back to the fall of the Tower of Babel, and they have there an ancestor, grandson of Japhet, named Fenuis Farsa, and they ascribe to him the invention of the alphabet. They took their ancient name of Feine, the modern Fenian, from him. Oddly enough, that is the name which the Romans knew the Phoenicians by, and to them also is ascribed the invention of the alphabet. . . . You see, there is nothing new. Everything is built on the ruins of something else. Just as the material earth is made up of countless billions of dead men's bones, so the mental world is all alive with the ghosts of dead men's thoughts and beliefs, the wraiths of dead races' faiths and imaginings. (1960:74)

When Father Forbes explains the interconnectedness of the Bible and the Irish, he demystifies the stories separating the Methodists and the Catholics. Yet his demystification, which should reveal the hidden social history of the sacred ideas Theron holds, serves only, ironically, to mystify Theron even more. In asserting that the Irish, who seem like interlopers in the United States, are in fact an ancient race and culture, Father Forbes makes relative the existence of all social knowledge. Although Theron is not quite ready to assimilate this information (itself about a more troubling kind of assimilation), it forces him to reevaluate his own status in the world. Rather than hearing an argument for relativism and pluralism, Theron hears instead a new hierarchy of value, and he secretly learns to devalue his former self and his Methodist community.

It is the desire to shock his wife, Alice, that completes Theron's alienation from his former self. His gradual falling away from his own marriage marks a moment in the text at which Theron himself learns to envision Alice and the members of his own congregation as "regional figures." Unlike Celia, Forbes, and Ledsmar, Theron does not find these regional types at all charming; instead, he finds them dull and stupid. He wonders how Alice, "who had once seemed so bright and keen-witted, who had in truth started out immeasurably his superior in swiftness of apprehension and readiness in humourous quips and conceits, should have grown so dull? For she was undoubtedly slow to understand things nowadays" (1960:150). This contrasts with his treasured remembrances of her as a singular country girl, admirably fitted to be his wife—"Alice had been one with him in every thought and emotion" (38). His arrogant confidence to Celia Madden that he cannot take seriously his own congregation or his own wife anymore, that he is just a "showman" (207–208), contrast with his paranoia about his reputation should he be seen lingering in the woods with Celia. For her, then, he has become not inauthentic, for the text has destroyed any single available text for the construction of authenticity, he has merely become entirely reified.

It is through Theron's alienation that we can best read this text as a critique of regionalism. The first half of the novel is punctuated by moments in which Theron seems to snap in and out of a formless terror or in which he suddenly sees himself as leaping ahead in knowledge or, more accurately, experiencing the recognition that he is "the most ignorant man in the world." But toward the end of the novel, his sudden jolts into a state of illumination have stopped, and he is comfortable assuming that he has secretly surpassed his congregation. But secrecy implies interiority, and that is precisely what Theron has sacrificed. His new self is radically exteriorized—his sense of having a secret self derives from his nearly paranoid ability to see himself and his surroundings only through the eyes of his new "friends." As I noted earlier, it is particularly cultural identity that is at stake in the regionalist project, and we can see the illuminati's desire for Theron, fundamentally a regional desire, exposed in Celia's final dismissal of him: "We liked you, as I have said, because you were unsophisticated and delightfully fresh and natural. Somehow we took it for granted you would stay so" (1960:331). But Theron *cannot* stay so. Most of what happens around, and indeed to, Theron is about looking or observing, as one would an object in a curio cabinet. The final mark of his separation from self is his ability (meager as it is) to see himself and his surroundings through the eyes of another. The text's reliance on codes of reading and observation as a dramatization of Theron's increasing "self-consciousness" is the final stage playing out regionalism's logic of strangers and natives.

In fact, we could explore this logic through Theron's steadily increasing ability to watch himself in the classic terms of a reified consciousness. When he first meets his new friends and discovers that his knowledge of the Bible is based on nothing but his religion's standard reading of it, he "found revealed to him an unsuspected and staggering truth. It was that he was an extremely ignorant and rudely untrained young man, whose pretensions to intellectual authority among any educated people would be laughed at with deserved contempt" (1960:61). At the Methodist love feast, Theron thinks "he was conscious of a dawning sense of shame at being even tacitly responsible for such a thing. His fancy conjured up the idea of Dr. Ledsmar coming in and beholding this maudlin and unseemly scene, and he felt his face grow hot at the bare thought" (161). In keeping with his growing self-consciousness, "he had never realized before what a spectacle the Methodist love-feast probably presented to outsiders. What must they think of it!" (154).

As he falls more deeply in love with Celia, he thinks of his own wife Alice:

He questioned whether men, for instance, like Father Forbes and Dr. Ledsmar would care much about her. Visions of the wifeless and academic calm in which these men spent their lives—an existence consecrated to literature and knowledge and familiarity with all the loftiest and noblest thoughts of the past—rose and enveloped him in a cloud of depression. (1960:151)

After Theron has begun to imagine himself distanced from his ministry by having become a performer, the narrator intones: "He viewed with astonished delight the progress he had made in his own estimation. He had taken Sister Soulsby's advice and the results were already wonderful" (239).

The jaundiced vision of his "newly informed eye" (1960:106) reminds us that all the time that we have been reading the novel and thinking that Theron Ware has been corrupted by his new acquaintances, Frederic has in fact constructed a picture of Theron *only* through the eyes of others. "People," he writes, "had prized him for his innocent candor and guileless mind" (1960:19). "It was your face and what it showed of the man underneath it, that helped to settle my mind . . . [your] very face is a pleasure and a help for those in suffering and trouble to look at" (304), Michael Madden says to him. Here the unbearably maudlin scene between a newly confident Theron and the dying Michael, Celia's brother, is predicated on the fact that Michael, a devout Irish Catholic, had previously been watching and approving the young Methodist minister. Michael thus responds to Theron's argument that he is becoming better and more intellectually expansive by telling him bluntly,

You are entirely deceived about yourself. You do not at all realize how you have altered your direction, or where you are going. It was a great misfortune for you, sir, that you did not keep among your own people. . . . Keep among your own people, Mr. Ware! When you go among others—you know what I mean—you have no proper understanding of what their sayings and doings really mean. (305)

Yet, Theron's inability to read what the "sayings and doings" of others mean is primarily a function of his desire to penetrate the true meaning of things, to divine, as his new friends have seemed to do, the meaning of the new world. But Theron's misrecognition stems not only from his belief that a world he previously understood seems to be unfolding itself in new ways at his command. Theron misrecognizes himself because he cannot negotiate his own belated entrance into the new world. His belatedness makes him a subject of and to the world, but it has not, as he believes, given him special access to its social or ethnic hierarchies. Theron believes that he has discovered the real conditions of his relationship to the world, but in believing he is outside ideology, he is only further within it. Paraphrasing Althusser, he has merely reimagined his relationship to the real conditions of his life, not escaped them.

At the end of the novel, Celia Madden, the sophisticated femme fatale with whom Theron has fallen in love, says to him,

You impressed us as an innocent, simple, genuine young character, full of mother's milk. It was like the smell of early spring in the country to come in contact with you. Your honesty of nature, your sincerity in that absurd religion of yours, your general *naïveté* of mental and spiritual get-up, all pleased us a great deal. We thought you were going to be a real acquisition. (1960:331)

The key rhetorical terms in these phrases have an ominous overtone. Theron is simple, innocent, and genuine, but he is a "character." Celia infantilizes him—the mention of "mother's milk" alongside the language of dewy, fresh-eyed country goodness confirms this reading. The word *acquisition* highlights a problem within regionalism as a whole. The lyrical desire for an innocence of character and experience is clear in Celia's initial desire for Theron. In fact, it is not far from Celia's irritated analysis of Theron to the narrator's relationship to William Blackett, Almira Todd's brother in *The Country of the Pointed Firs*. Describing him for us, the narrator writes about William that "it was impossible not to feel as though an untraveled boy had spoken, and yet one loved to have him value his native heath" (Jewett 1981:45). She, too, infantilizes him, as Celia does Theron, and whimsically remarks of William that "once I wondered how he had come to be so curiously wrinkled, forgetting, absent-mindedly, to recognize the effects of time" (143). When Theron realizes that he has become "a bore" to his new friends, he cracks. Having followed Celia Madden and Father Forbes to New York, he is shocked to find out that they have "seen" him all along. He is appalled to know that he is not merely visible to his friends but entirely predictable. He then escapes into the underworld of New York and finally to the West.[16]

Theron's journey through the underworld of New York is a salutary contrast to the popular imagination of who was really flooding the streets of the metropolis. In addition to the "foreigners" Theron fears are the rural men and women drawn to the city because life in the village became tiresome or, more likely, because there was no money to be made anymore by farming in the countryside. Theron, then, becomes part of the larger social phenomenon of regionalism's displaced version of the countryside.

It is interesting to see what happens to him in the city. Like the narrator of *The Country of the Pointed Firs*, Theron ultimately becomes a "poor incoherent being" and ends up tramping the night streets of the Bowery. Getting off the train at Grand Central Station, Theron is already beginning to feel overwhelmed. The station seems immense, and he feels in danger of being swallowed by "incessantly shifting processions of people" (Frederic 1960:316). But because he is in the city following Celia and Father Forbes, Theron cannot let himself lose his purpose; instead, he relies on bravado, on an imaginary idea of himself as a man of the world. But when he is dismissed by his irritated friends, when he is "found out" in his disguise as a man of the world, he descends to the saloons and goes on a two-day drinking spree.[17]

The omniscient narrator does not allow the reader to accompany Theron in his physical descent and degeneration. Instead, Frederic shows Theron only after he has arrived at the house of religious debt-raisers, the Soulsbys. Rather than relating what has happened to Theron, Frederic has Theron describe his debauch to Sister Soulsby. This is an interesting strategy, since Theron is so completely broken for want of sleep and sobriety that his attempts to reconstruct himself in language sound like an apocalyptic vision. "I have come out of hell," Theron cries dramatically, explaining that

I've been drinking for two days and one whole night, on my feet all the while, wandering alone in that big strange New York, going through places where they murdered men for ten cents, mixing myself up with the worst people in low bar-rooms and dance-houses, and they saw I had money in my pocket, too—and yet nobody touched me or offered to lay a finger on me. Do you know why? They understood that I wanted to get drunk, and couldn't. The Indians won't harm an idiot, or lunatic, you know. Well, it was the same with these vilest of the vile. They saw that I was a fool whom God had taken hold of, to break his heart first, and then to craze his brain, and then to fling him on a dunghill to die like a dog. (1960:344)

The language here seems to show that Theron finally recognizes what has happened to him or what he has become. But his inability to talk about what is really troubling him is overlaid with a familiar rhetoric based on his conjectures of what other people were thinking about him. "They saw," repeated twice in the passage, speaks not to Theron's sudden self-knowledge but to his desperate attempt to overcome his alienation in a city whose inhabitants, down to the metaphor of Indians, strike him as severely alien.

It is the enigmatic fraud and professional debt-raiser, Candace Soulsby, to whom Theron flees after his debauch in the city. She takes care of him and sends him out to Seattle. In a novel that so completely exposes the cultural practices underlying the desire for regional folk, Frederic's portrayal of Sister Soulsby stands apart and suggests a new vision of the subject—she is more and less than a regional figure. In some way, she becomes a prototypical cosmopolitan. Theron notices about her practiced manner of public speaking that she has retained the characteristics of the actress she used to be and later realizes that her manner of speaking is accentless, from no place, a universalized urban accent in comparison with everyone else's rustic way of speaking. Sister Soulsby is in control of her own image; she is able to manipulate how other people respond to her. She tells Theron, for example, that she makes her stirring revival music out of the classical music that she personally favors. Even her person becomes an emblem of the simultaneous existence of the ancient and the novel. She wears shockingly low-cut dresses, yet Theron notices that her neck is heavily corded. Her given name, he is surprised to find out, is Candace, which he traces to an ancient Ethiopian name. She claims that she is a good fraud, and it is she who explains to Theron that both the spiritual devotion that she wishes to inspire at the Methodist meeting and the spiritual desire that he wishes to inspire through his sermons must all be stage-managed. "Did you ever see a play?" she asks him.

In a theatre, I mean. . . . But you'll understand when I say that the performance looks one way from where the audience sit, and quite a different way when you are behind the scenes. . . . That doesn't prove that the play out in front, isn't beautiful and affecting, and all that. It only shows that everything in this world is produced by machinery. (1960:177)

Larzer Ziff writes that "the Soulsbys represent the possibility of social control by a meritocracy of common-sensical people who sympathize with the masses and are knowledgeable enough to translate new intellectual developments into a tongue they can understand" (1979:216). This certainly sounds like how they themselves would describe the secret of their success, but in the economy of the novel, the Soulsbys become important because they have ceded any claim to authenticity, or the unity of the subject, and to its authentic relation to the world.

In her ability to become what other people most want her to be, Candace Soulsby finds the means to make quite a comfortable living. But if Theron has misrecognized his "illumination" because he has learned to see only through the eyes of other people, he has entered, unlike Sister Soulsby, a state of profound reification, separated from his own labor power, which (since he is a minister) is equivalent to his self-identity. In his new state of illumination, Theron has learned only that he is not self-identical, but he has failed to make the halfhearted gestures necessary to overcome the sense of reification that Celia, Forbes, and Ledsmar have learned to make. Their master narratives may be incomplete, but in the face of no community at all, each has chosen to join an abstract order of "Greekness," Catholicism, or Science. Sister Soulsby too, enacts this reified consciousness, yet Theron misrecognizes her comfort with it. In fact, when Dr. Ledsmar calls the Soulsbys the "most genuine people" he has ever met, he is probably close to the truth in the world of the novel. It is not that the Soulsbys have managed to escape the problem of reification but that they have managed to accommodate it and profit by it. But even the shrewd Candace Soulsby misrecognizes Theron's ability to adapt to her easy blend of participation and observation. She believes that Theron can get over his infatuation with Celia Madden and should go to the West to renew himself. Looking at him when he first arrives at her house after his debauch, she thinks "under the painful surface-blur of wretchedness and fatigued debauchery, she traced reflectively the lineaments of the younger and cleanlier countenance she had seen a few months before. Nothing essential had been taken away. . . . The face underneath was still all right" (Frederic 1960:341).

But aside from Sister Soulsby's estimate of Theron, the close of the novel offers perhaps even less hope than one would have imagined from Theron's crises of self-understanding in New York, where he confronts Celia and is in turn confronted with the truth about how he appears to other people. As Theron readies himself to leave his ministry forever and begin a new life out West, he imagines himself again before a crowd. This time he dreams he is a politician being swept toward Washington by a tide of adulation inspired by his public speaking. As though he were still a small town minister, he imagines himself exhorting a crowd.

There rose before his fancy, out of the chaos of these shapeless imaginings, some faces of men, then more behind them, then a great concourse of uplifted countenances, crowded close together as far as the eye could reach. They were attentive faces all, rapt, eager, credulous to a degree. Their eyes were admiringly bent upon a common object of excited interest. They were looking at *him* ; they strained their ears to miss no cadence of his voice (1960:354).

This sounds almost exactly like the text's first vision of Theron as "the object of a universal gaze" (1) and then as he preaches to his Octavius flock, in which "the sustaining sparkle of [the congregation's] gaze lifted him to a peroration unrivalled in his own recollection of himself" (157). But after his experiences in Octavius, the parallel is more troubling. As a politician, specifically a senator, Theron would be in exactly the same position in which he found himself with Celia; he would be representing a whole class of people who have no official voice. But in this political fantasy, Theron would finally be controlling the way that other people saw him, by agreeing to become what they wished him to be. Theron would in fact become what Celia and Father Forbes first thought him—a regional representative. Of course, Theron is being sent to the West as a real estate agent, a job that also returns him to the fictions and values of the local.

Garland's and Frederic's texts demonstrate a particularly difficult problem in regional writing. In the first chapter, I discussed how regional writing presents a problem of fidelity in two related but distinct economies. In the first, the regional text that uses rhetorical devices signifying fidelity and authenticity is exposed as being underwritten by the foreign, thereby questioning the region's ability to counteract the endemic fears of the foreign generated by the city. In the second economy, the figure of the participant/observer is brought to a sense of self-identicalness by narrating the fullness of the rural community. But in the two texts in this chapter, the second economy breaks down; the central figure cannot achieve self-identicalness in the face of the region's simultaneous existence with the urban problems from which it is presumptively so far removed. The uneven development of the Midwest and the quasi-urban small town of Octavius seem to have a corresponding effect on the uneven or disjointed development of the regional subject. In the first two chapters of this book, the problem of the regional subject has focused on how a narrator, or outsider, is processed in the logic of regionalism. The problem of how regionalism creates subjects within imaginative regions, specifically around categories of race and ethnicity, is the topic of the next two chapters.

3

The History of a Historyless People

Gertrude Atherton's *The Californians*

There's a good deal of history-making, quiet and noisy, going
on all the time.

Gertrude Atherton, The Californians

Gertrude Atherton's 1898 novel *The Californians* is set near San Francisco in the late nineteenth century. It charts the progress of a serious
young woman in San Francisco's upper class and culminates in her marriage to a world-weary easterner who has come to California for personal
regeneration. Its plot is, as one critic wrote in an otherwise positive review, "not notably novel." After a short summary of the book's various
narrative strands, the reviewer notes that "it is consequently hardly necessary to follow the central thread of the story further in order to appreciate the book, which otherwise bears the stamp of originality" ("Novel
Notes" 1898:254).

While the plot of the novel may not be innovative, its careful negotiation of the terms under which narrative can provide a conventional
destiny for an unconventional character warrants scrutiny. Magdaléna
Yorba, the young woman whose personal development ends in marriage,
is the child of a Spanish grandee and a New England mother. Formally,
the novel proceeds according to a conventional realist plot line. Magdaléna grows, suffers, and marries. But thematically, the novel plots a different story. Magdaléna is excluded from conventional fictional narratives because of her ethnic background. Her ascension to the position of
successful heroine depends on the text's ordering of different kinds of stories according to whether they assign ethnic difference as a personality or
character trait rather than as a social fact which has public consequences
for the classification of persons in the United States.

The Californians foregrounds questions of the importance of texts and textuality by constructing Magdaléna as, first, a reader. Her understanding of herself and the world around her is structured by a series of failed personal comparisons with an archive of Spanish folklore and realist novels. Although her careful reading of this small archive of pivotal texts provides her with models for behavior, each model proves to be insufficient and partial. Magdaléna is neither a conventional realist heroine nor a legendary romantic Spanish beauty. On technical grounds alone, she recognizes that she is an unlikely heroine because she is ugly, unpopular, serious, and shy. Following another characteristic narrative trajectory, Magdaléna aspires to intellectual greatness as a means to compensate for her physical limitations, but she discovers that unlike her more conventionally beautiful friends, she is frustratingly slow to learn and understand things. The novel's self-conscious use of the discourse of literary narratives *about* the nature of fictional heroines, combined with its insistence on excluding Magdaléna from their ranks, presents a crucial problem for the assimilation of ethnic difference in a self-consciously realist model of representation.

Because the text obliquely attributes Magdaléna's inability to be "like" a heroine to her inability to find a fictional model to imitate, it casts the problem of her interior development as a problem concerning the explanatory limits of fictional texts in the public sphere. But what is it that prevents Magdaléna from finding and following an appropriate narrative of interior development? As we will see, the text casts her as a hyperindividuated character paradoxically outside the parameters of a realist model that is the expression of a bourgeois model of individualism.

Magdaléna's reading of narrative is her only private pleasure. She can imagine herself as a heroine when she is alone, but her public position as a wealthy Spanish woman always prevents public acknowledgment of her fantasy of herself as "like" a realist heroine. In the text, Magdaléna's ethnicity is an impediment to her full, conventionally legible subjectivity. That is, it is her *identity* as ethnic—an identity presented as anterior to her own personhood and exterior to her self-understanding—that prevents her from becoming a realist subject. The text's opposition of the ideas of subjectivity and identity are crucial to understanding how it invents a scheme for imagining local difference in a more broadly national literary genre. Magdaléna's ethnic composition is, while unique in the text, assumed to be fixed and eternal, to denote racial characteristics that have been mysteriously and incompletely converted into cultural traits.

It is the novel's objective to find a narrative strategy flexible enough to convert racial difference into personal difference and to transform a crisis in the political representation of the citizens of an imperfectly assimilated territory into a crisis in their literary representation. The novel laments the disappearance of "authentic" Spanish culture in the increasingly Americanized state of California, thereby ignoring the official, legal construction of Spanish ethnicity in the years between the Mexican War, which provides the context for the seizure of California by the United States, and the Spanish-American War, which is the context of the book's composition and reception.

Insofar as it depicts the careful development of characters in an equally carefully presented social world, *The Californians* is a realist novel, and as I discuss later, it is remarkably conscious of and insistent on its participation in the genre of realism. But because the novel uses ethnicity as "the great unknown local fact," as William Boelhower terms it, I read it as a regional novel in order to ask how it represents and values the local (Boelhower 1987:17). Such a reading does not stem simply from the fact that the location of California is ultimately presented as constitutive of the characters' relations to themselves and one another—in other words, it is not simply because the novel takes up a particular region as its ground of action that I want to read the text in the dynamic of regionalism that I have previously identified. Rather, it is because the novel cannot resolve the crisis of Magdaléna's subjectivity unless it converts her Spanish heritage into a more general, although still troubled, regional identity. By casting ethnicity as a problem only of individual identity, the novel moves to privatize and depoliticize Magdaléna's Spanish heritage. Making ethnicity an obstacle to self-realization, *The Californians* portrays Magdaléna as a character caught between modes of representation. On the one hand, she is a realist heroine who struggles toward her future in the placeless, progressing realm of full subjectivity. On the other hand, she is the emblem of a lost romantic culture, struggling to authorize an individual identity in the present by writing herself into and through folktales about her Spanish heritage. Finally, Atherton conflates Magdaléna with California, arguing that Magdaléna's problems as a character are like those of California's relationship to the United States.

As a representative of California, Magdaléna ends up being a regional character, but because her identity is connected to the problem of ethnicity, *The Californians* is a novel that narrates the invention of regional characters and histories as a consequence of rewriting ethnic difference as regional variation. In this chapter, I look at the development and treatment of the space of California. First, I argue that making California into a region entails erasing or smoothing into a single narrative the violence of imperial histories and resistances that marked California's previous relation to the United States. Second, I argue that the novel's depiction of Magdaléna as the embodied trace of these conflicted histories suggests that realism's construction of the subject depends on a certain hollowing out of specific regional identity, thus making it susceptible to narrative and cultural appropriation. In these terms, the text separates Spanish and Mexican identities, demonstrating that the Spanish heritage is national and therefore linked to a legal notion of subjectivity and individuality, whereas Mexican heritage is described as problematically racial.

The Californians' strategy of realizing regional characters is echoed by its characters' curiosity about their place in the national imagination. The text registers a certain anxiety about the relationship between West and East. Besides the casual discussions about California's role in a national economy, the social world within the novel is enlivened by the visits of peripheral characters touring the California countryside and exploring native culture. Jack Trennahan, Magdaléna Yorba's fiancé, remarks, "You do not hear California mentioned in New York once a month. It might be on Mars. The East remembers California's existence about as often as Europe remembers America's" (Atherton 1968:215). This flippant remark speaks not to the peripheral status of California but to its central imaginative function for the United States. In Trennahan's rhetoric, California is a new version of America. It promises rejuvenation of the national economy as well as of the dispirited character that Trennahan represents. In *The Incorporation of America*, Alan Trachtenberg writes in a similar vein about the larger cultural phenomenon of the East's relationship to the West:

The word "West" embraced an astonishing variety of surfaces and practices, of physiognomic differences and sundry exploitations they invited. The Western lands provided resources essential as much to industrial development after the Civil War as to cultural needs of justification, incentive, and disguise. Land and minerals served economic and ideological purposes, the two merging into a single complex image of the West: a temporal site of the route from past to future, and the spatial site for revitalizing national energies. (Trachtenberg 1982:17)

The question about what California means to the nation is certainly not limited to Atherton's novel. Her figuration of the problem draws on a popular tradition that attempts to describe both the meaning and the use of assimilating a "new world." Early travel writing from California describes the spatial and temporal borders that Trachtenberg mentioned. In commissioned letters to the Philadelphia *North American and United States Gazette* (November 1847–January 1848) and the New York *Journal of Commerce* (July 1847–February 1848), William Garner, an Englishman who had moved to California, reported directly to eastern readers about California's great natural wealth. In a letter dated October 1846, he writes that "this country is now opening a field for all sorts of enterprise; not only for male persons, but for females also" (Garner 1970:91). His letters cover a crucial period in California's relationship to the United States: between 1846 and 1848, the Mexican War ended, the Bear Flag Republic emerged, and California was officially annexed to the United States as a territory.

Not only do the letters cover these events, they brim with lists of raw materials, ranging from game animals to the types of trees one might mill into lumber.

Garner's economic incitements are directly related to his analysis of the native Spanish and Indian inhabitants of California and the progress of the United States' annexation of them. Indeed, the three are entangled in such a way that the lists of the various qualities of fruits, animals, and trees parallels the description of the traits of the Spanish—each is reduced to its potential profit. More important, each is offered to the eastern reader as a problem that only U.S. culture and business might resolve or repair. In a letter dated November 1846, Garner writes:

Nature has been bountiful to this country in many wonderful ways, but her goodness has been disregarded by those who have held possession of it for so long a time. The reproductiveness of animals in this country is extraordinary; but indolence, carelessness, and the love of luxury, have within the last twelve years brought it almost into a state of desolation. (116)

Garner's invitation to immigrants is directly linked to a portrayal of California as a land of great plenty and goodness and also a land in need of supervision. The description of its fecundity and the fecundity of its livestock might itself be seen as an unconscious reference to the Spanish inhabitants of California—the fact that both the land and the people show promise and yield riches underwrites the imperious tone of further descriptions of the people. Indeed, in February 1847, Garner reports,

Improvements are daily increasing in this town . . . every step advanced by the Americans for the benefit of the country at large, or any part of it, excites the most pleasant feelings in the breasts of the Californians. . . . [T]he natives already begin to form a distant idea of what California in a very few years must become, by remaining in the possession of a nation that has the will, the power, and the means, to make it what it deserves to be. (179)

This glowing and prophetic statement is confirmed by a letter entitled "A Hint to Speculators" (February 1847), which describes the financial debt that Spanish Californians already owe to Americans and advises emigrants on how to capitalize on that debt.

Yet Garner, like many other tourists, fetishized precisely those attributes he perceived as most inimical to capital—luxury, indolence, glamour, and laborless wealth. For example, he writes in early November 1846 about the California rancher, "If he makes a thousand dollars in one month, or in one day, he will not go to work again until that thousand dollars is spent, and perhaps not until he has run himself one or two thousand dollars in debt" (98). Later in November, he writes with some ire and perplexity,

They have not the least forethought, they will not look one day ahead. The greater part . . . think of nothing in the world but gambling, dress, horse-riding, women, and stealing to maintain these vices. There are many persons who have tremendous large tracts of beautiful and fertile lands, containing from three to eleven square leagues, and the man who cultivates twenty acres of it, without taking the trouble to fence it, is considered among themselves an extraordinary industrious man. (127)

Similarly, just when more and more people are settling in California and "Americanizing" the manners of the "natives," Garner writes in October 1847, "there never lived a more hospitable race of people in the world; but their manners were rude and uncultivated, and their customs such as nature taught them" (206). The childlike innocence regarding global economics and trade that characterizes the Californians might be compared with the ways in which writers such as Sarah Orne Jewett depicted the remaining inhabitants of New England villages. Untouched by the advances of urban technologies, such peoples seem temporally and spatially remote. Particularly interesting are the constant indications by Garner that the Spanish can't look "ahead" or are without "forethought." His description serves as evidence that such people are outside capital, which by its nature, "looks ahead." Casting the people as outside capital and equating them with a more natural identity figures them as one of the many sources of raw material for settlers.

Such alternately romantic and demeaning descriptions of California's Spanish inhabitants are not uncommon in the literature produced about this region. The aggressive imperialism of letters like those of William Garner was gradually transformed as the genre mediating the value of the "news" of the raw material of California itself was transformed from factual articles to local-color stories. This transformation of evidentiary documents like letters into local color was key to the success of Bret Harte's work. His *The Luck of Roaring Camp and Other Stories* (1870) chronicled the massive influx of miners and speculators into the West. Although his stories dealt mainly with the local migrant communities, the material for those stories came from the letters he had earlier written for the *Springfield Republican* and the *Christian Register*. In these factual letters, as in his later fictional stories, Harte provided colorful sketches of the Spanish and Native American mission past, Spanish señoritas, and descriptions of everything from the celebrations of the Chinese New Year to the climate and landscape. For example, in his letter to the *Christian Register* of May 19, 1866, Harte writes about a preserved adobe chapel:

Even the old rural accessories, the market-gardens and nurseries, that once gathered about its walls and resisted civic encroachment, were passing away. A few small *adobe* buildings, with tiled roofs, like longitudinal strips of cinnamon, and walled enclosures sacredly guarding a few strips of hide, still stood there; but I missed their tenants—the half-reclaimed Mexican, whose respectability stopped at his waist, and whose red sash under his vest was the utter undoing of his black broadcloth. I missed also the female of his species—the swarthy-faced, black-haired women, whose dresses always appeared unseasonable in texture and pattern, and whose manner of wearing a shawl was a terrible awakening from the poetic dream of the Spanish mantilla. Traces of another nationality were visible. (1990:3)[1]

The temporal crisis that subtends the figures in the foregoing presents the imaginative transformation of ethnic figures in a genre whose literary genealogy and ideological project are momentarily out of sync. The image of the "half-reclaimed Mexican" is striking, especially since a close reading of this passage shows that such a figure is not actually *in* the landscape that the narrator is observing. Harte simply thinks such a figure would be an appropriate accessory for the local color tableau he has found and framed for his readers. In aesthetic terms, the figures are inflected with the nostalgia of local color. The narrator appears to long for people whose presence would add a colorful touch to the adobe. Although the discourse of aesthetics—underscored by the narrator's lavish descriptions of color and texture—distances the Mexican characters, the political elements of the passage bring the characters into an uncomfortable physical and temporal proximity to the narrator. Specifically, Harte distinguishes between the political problem of the Mexican and the local-color fantasy of the Spaniard. Rather than inventing a Spanish caballero, he invents a "half-reclaimed" Mexican couple. Certainly the use of the word *reclaimed* signifies that native peoples are insufficiently processed raw material. Each character is assigned bestial qualities—the woman is described as the "female of his species," and Harte contemptuously hints that the man has uncontrollable sexual urges. But each portrait is inflected by the romance of the caballero. The woman's clothing, especially, points to the glamorous dress of the Spanish but is undercut by a kind of inappropriateness—it is "unseasonable."

Atherton's presentation of Magdaléna Yorba, the young Spanish American protagonist of *The Californians*, draws on the uneasy temporal coexistence of the culturally declining Spanish and the racially contaminating Mexican, but it does so by trying to close the circuit of the their problematic textual coexistence.[2] Like Harte, Atherton recognized the value of the "nuggets" of ethnic history for her own career as a writer, but because she privileges realism as a genre, she connects her raw material to a more genteel eastern regionalism and not to a more popular form of local color like Harte's.[3] Although Atherton's and Harte's genealogies of regionalism are quite different, they share a relationship to the United States' imperialist concerns in 1898. The larger inability of regional writing to provide a

79

proper racial or literary "paternity" for California's inhabitants results in the obsession that *The Californians* exhibits about the proper use of novels and folklore and the proper way to explain character through a historicized yet depoliticized ethnicity.[4]

Ideologically, *The Californians* might well be considered the story of how the old Spanish empire became a new region in the United States and how Atherton scavenged Spanish American folklore to create a nonthreatening and romantic past for the new state. But by marking out the construction and fictionality of that romantic past, the text also reveals the much more complicated story of how a nationalizing genre—the realism with which the novel itself is a self-conscious participant—imagines a fictional, corrupt "minor" literature—the folklore that defines an anterior and still compelling vision of California. Although the action is set long after the boom years of the Gold Rush, the regional economy by which local-color populations are used as raw material to place California into the national literary market suggests a kind of literary Gold Rush sensibility. As its title suggests, the novel's geographical and rhetorical space is concerned with California, its history, and its inhabitants. As the plural of the title might also suggest, the subjects of California, and the subject of California itself, are multiple.

This is, first, the story of an unrealized character, Magdaléna Yorba, who is almost completely defined by her ethnic identity, which is itself constructed through many conflicted historical narratives. In fact, Magdaléna becomes ethnic only in the *conflict* of various histories. In the novel, the character of Magdaléna is nearly indistinguishable from the mythology of the actual land of California, and the land itself is historically a contested site. The two ruling passions of Magdaléna's life are her brief fantasies of becoming a writer and her ongoing fantasy of becoming a wife. Through writing, Magdaléna hopes to give meaning to her life and to save from oblivion the Spanish romances she treasured in her girlhood. With Jack Trennahan, her fiancé and the "representative of one of the proudest families in a State some three hundred years old" (Atherton 1968:123), Magdaléna hopes to find personal and emotional happiness. Finally, Magdaléna sacrifices the proposed transcription of her beloved Spanish folk stories—as well as her attempt to write a realist novel—for the greater romance of marrying Trennahan, who in turn, finds the romance of her ethnicity too powerful to withstand.

The text is founded on a series of histories of California, three of which I will examine: the Gold Rush, precontact California life, and contact between Californians and Americans. Because the Spanish have a historical national claim to California, Atherton rewrites the romance of ethnicity as a failure of national history and then extrapolates this as a failure of the Spanish nation. The war of territorial and cultural origins that begins and flourishes in Magdaléna is not confined to her body (the product of racial and cultural miscegenation) but is exteriorized on the space of California, also the disputed product of national cultures.

To examine this text's strategy of simultaneously creating Magdaléna and California as historical and literary products, we must turn to the histories and texts that produce the two of them simultaneously. I look at the way the novel describes the American presence in the West and at the kinds of popular literary traces this leaves in the narrative. Then I look at the flip side of this, the description of the Spanish presence in the West and the kinds of narrative traces it leaves in the novel. Finally, I look at how Atherton shows Magdaléna trying to make sense of the histories that have made her.

The historical moment of the Gold Rush is commemorated in the novel as a lovingly preserved legend for the characters, who tell newcomers and tourists about the atmosphere in California in the 1850s. The Gold Rush not only creates a set of folk stories for the Americans, it also finalizes the decline of Spanish culture in California, marking the end of the golden age of the caballero and the grandee. Oddly, the text doesn't linger over the stories of the Gold Rush, nor do the characters express much nostalgia for that time. Even the occasional reflection on it has the ring of a dream or myth. Meditating on California, one character says:

While the Virginia City mines were booming, your backbone felt like a streak of lightning; you hadn't a comma in your very thoughts; you woke up every morning in a cold sweat, and your teeth chattered as you opened your newspaper. You believed every man a liar and dreamt that your veins ran liquid gold. The Stock Exchange was Hell let loose. Men went insane. Men committed suicide. No one stopped to remark. (Atherton 1968:170)

It is the fact that no one stopped to "remark," of course, that is so remarkable. Although there were already many legends of the Gold Rush era circulating in the East that helped authorize Atherton's own book, it is enlightening to ask why she shies away from these literary precedents without "remarking" on them. As Atherton's own historical accounts demonstrate, the Gold Rush brought the first great influx of other nationalities into California. Not just Americans but Europeans, Mexicans, and Chinese flocked to California to get rich fast. As Roberta Greenwood noted, "The Gold Rush . . . was the catalyst for vast and rapid changes in the course of California's history. Among these far-reaching changes . . . were the attainment of self-government and statehood without the intermediate territorial stage" (Greenwood 1992:76). The history of the Gold Rush is silent, hidden, in *The Californians* partially because it, as the catalyst of U.S. interests, allows the absorption of California into the nation without the "comma" of intermediate status as territory. For Atherton, the process of Americanization is less important than its effects; the text is always more interested in cultural economies than the "real" economies of the Gold Rush.

Thus, American involvement in California produces the business and marital partnerships that in turn produce Magdaléna. Magdaléna is the daughter of Don Roberto Yorba and Hannah Polk, the chilly sister of Don Roberto's shrewd Yankee business partner, Hiram Polk (the expansionist imperialist ideology invoked in the name Polk needs little explication). Magdaléna's Spanish father and New England uncle meet on the first day of the official American occupation of California, with Polk, a naval officer, coming ashore as "Commodore Sloat ran up the American flag on the Custom House of Monterey on July seventh, 1846" (1968:10). Literally under the sign of American conquest, the family relation begins. The two men go into business together, and Atherton writes that "the don was fascinated by the quick terse common-sense and the harsh nasal voice of the American" (11), while Polk, for his part, "acquired a taste for Spanish cooking, cigaritos, and life on horseback" (14). In order to complete the circuit between business and family, Polk marries Don Roberto's sister, a beautiful Spanish woman, who "saw how it was with her people, [and] accepted her lot with philosophy" (17). The product of the family business partnerships, Magdaléna Yorba, is "an unhappy and incongruous mixture of Spanish and New England traits" (17). At first glance, she appears to be a highly refined version of the tragic mulatto, but this literary resemblance, although fruitful, must be extended. Magdaléna's racial mixture is an ambivalent sign. On the one hand, her maternal genealogy is impeccably pedigreed as white—her mother is from New England. But her father's pedigree is unstable. In the text, he yearns to become more white, but his class aspiration testifies to his racial illegibility. Upward social mobility was partially enabled by laws allowing "a wealthy person of Indian or black ancestry [to] legally delete his true origins and gain Spanish status. Indeed, scholars of early California history believe that many of the most distinguished early 'Spanish' families could also trace their family roots to Indians and African sources" (Frakes and Solberg 1971:3–4).

When the narrator writes that Magdaléna "had all the Californian's indolence, which was ever at war with the intellect she had inherited from her New England ancestors" (Atherton 1968:20), she invokes racial categories as well as regional and cultural categories. In her description of Magdaléna, the substitution of California as her place of origin rather than Spain, and of New England for the broader America, moves the novel's focus to the history of a place or territory from which the inhabitants can be shown to be imaginatively, even "naturally," constituted.

When she turns to the "natural" constitution of a culture, Atherton runs into a previous narrative of imperialism—an inherited but unsystematically theorized narrative of a mix of Spanish, Indians, and Mexicans. Describing the Spanish Americans, the narrator uses the word *race* over and over, eliminating the differences between any Spanish-speaking characters: Magdaléna, for example, is a "swarthy" skinned woman, a woman as "dark as an Indian." By using metaphors like these, the novel adds to the confusion of race and culture, which threatens the integrity of Magdaléna's identity as a realist character. The product of conquered and conquering, Magdaléna teeters on the edge of temporalities. Her Spanish ways are noted and approved—the Spanish are passing away and becoming invisible. But ironically, her visual appearance is a sign that other Spanish-speaking people are *not* disappearing. In this way, we can see also the intersection of the Spaniard—imagined as a white European—and the Mexican—imagined as a dark native. Buried under the simple opposition of Americans and Spanish is Atherton's urgent and particularly American project of determining culture along a racial axis.

Another way in which we can look at the intersection of Spanish cultures that traverse Magdaléna's body is by examining how Magdaléna's father, a former Spanish grandee, participates in his young territory's initiation into capitalism. Don Roberto still possesses the 300,000 acres granted to him by the Spanish crown, but in order to keep this land, he collaborated with the invading Americans and helped found a bank. The narrator writes that

Don Roberto was a man of wealth and consequence to-day. But through no original virtue of his. He had been as princely in his hospitality, as reckless with his gold, as meagerly equipped to cope with the enterprising United Statesian who first conquered the Californian, then, nefariously, or righteously, appropriated his acres. (1968:10)

From this inauspicious beginning, Don Roberto ends up controlling the cash and interest flow that might very well have squeezed him out of power earlier: "He saw his old friends fall about him: advice did them no good, and any permanent alliance with their interests would have meant his own ruin; so he shrugged his shoulders and forgot them" (15). Don Roberto's attempt to create a new and Americanized identity is undercut in this novel by the narrator's ambivalent descriptions of him. When he speaks in this novel, it is in a grotesquely accented English that reveals the text's anxiety about the coexistence of racial others with the cultural others commemorated in the other history of California.

The novel contains many traces of these oral histories, and their popularity and cultural influence in the time of *The Californians* can hardly be disputed. Ideologically, Atherton presents them as "tribal barbarities [that]

become 'colourful traditions'" (Nairn 1977:168). Through the traces of the Spanish American folktales and stories that inform the development of Magdaléna, Atherton seems to be indicating an anterior, "authentic" culture. Her characters' longing for that time and for those stories forms the outlines of a profound lack of a recoverable history. The suppressed oral histories anchor Magdaléna especially to an irretrievable past.

The text reveals its other history of the Americas in two ways. The first is through a common cultural stereotype to which both the narrator and the characters in the book refer. This stereotype does not apply with any precision to the growing legal category of Spanish Americans; rather, it refers to the Old-World Spanish—the "Californios" who lived in California. The grandees' lifestyle, for example, is described as one of

Arcadian magnificence, troubled by few cares, a life of riding over vast estates clad in silk and lace, botas and sombrero, mounted upon steeds as gorgeously caparisoned as themselves, eating, drinking, serenading at the gratings of beautiful women, gambling, horse-racing, taking part in splendid religious festivals, with only the languid excitement of an occasional war between rival governors to disturb the placid surface. (1968:10)

The language of this passage is heady and sensuous, but its description of Spanish culture is not unique to this text. Already as we have seen, this kind of cultural mythologizing was common in the late nineteenth century, but the difficulty in understanding these grand and romantic descriptions is in seeing the flip side of that kind of language. Reflected in that "placid surface" is another grandee. In American systems of reckoning he is lazy, slovenly, stupid, brutish, and childish. As we will see in the text's representation of Magdaléna, it is only too easy for grandees to become "greasers."

The language of the narrator's rhetorical flights has a larger schematic meaning as the second history of the Old Californians is unfolded in the novel through traces of Spanish cultural production: the songs, ballads, romances, and legends of the great landowning heroes. These are the constructions of history that Magdaléna knows from her childhood. In fact, the heroes of the ballads that ignite Magdaléna's imagination are about some of her own ancestors—she is thus, perversely, descended from these fictions. Interestingly enough, the transmission of these myths and legends to Magdaléna is direct, unlike the other histories informing the novel that are assumed to be "common knowledge." Magdaléna's Spanish aunt sings her the ballads in her gorgeously appointed rooms. Thus, the very orality of the tales marks a point at which Magdaléna inherits history.

Magdaléna . . . loved these gorgeous apartments, and ran through the connecting gardens daily to see her. [Her] delight was to sit at her feet and listen to the tales of California when the grandee owned the land, when the caballero, in gorgeous attire, sang at the gratings of the beauties of Monterey. . . . Doubtless she exaggerated the splendours, the brilliancy, the unleavened pleasure; but it was a time far behind her, and she was happy again in the rememoration. (1968:19)

While the legends of the caballeros, the former owners of the land, are indicated in distinctive, almost disruptive prose, the legends themselves are not translated in the text. Although the stories themselves are not, like the Gold Rush, common knowledge, their general shape is suggested by their reliance on the stereotype of the romantic caballeros. The narrator's descriptions of the grandees' lifestyle is accordingly romantic. Names are brought up occasionally during a conversation between Magdaléna and her fiancé: Ysabel, Alvarado, Castro. Events are mentioned: a mission is robbed of pearls; a don dies of love for the sake of a woman. But nothing more. In the passage I quoted from *The Californians*, we can see that these folktales typically function in the place of Magdaléna's memory of her aunt (the only Spanish blood relative besides her father that she knows). Unlike her brother Don Roberto, Magdaléna's aunt denies the value of American culture, and like the tales she tells, she is not actually present in the text. She herself is only a memory for Magdaléna; she has moved to Santa Barbara to live in a Spanish-speaking enclave of destitute caballeros and señoras. Like the life her aunt "rememorates," she recedes to the South, and the folktales, coming from an absent narrator, are thus doubly removed in time. What defines them is the space in which they are told: the room, scented, private, luxurious, as splendid as the festivals the narrator refers to in the previous passage. A kind of allegory of the book's staging of regionalism itself, her room is kept as though someone still lived there; it is a monument to a woman who will never return.

Atherton can write quite feelingly of the beauty of the Spanish señoras and the dashing caballeros who courted them. But these nostalgic apostrophes are canceled out by disavowals of the distastefulness of an essential Spanish nature. Don Roberto is an excellent example of this balancing act. Even though he used to be a great and wealthy grandee, the moment he becomes an American initiates his fear of regressing to an essential Spanish nature: "Why I no dying with the wife and the little boy? Make myself over, and now the screws go to drop out my character, and I am like before" (1968:258). Such a sentence converts a concern with character into a concern with form—not only does Don Roberto fear reverting to an essential nature, he fears that the labor he has performed in order to construct himself as an American will be lost. He fears that he will "go to die in the streets like the others; with no one cents!" (257). It doesn't matter if the others are Spanish dons or war heroes or even Indians set "free" from the missions. It is the novel's formal mission to make these colonized subjects equivalent to one another.

Not surprisingly, Magdaléna's attempts to write are suggested by conflicts of history. She turns first to Walter Scott and begins to write a historical novel, but the structure and form demanded by his historical narrative seem hollow to her. She finds herself "taking the creator's structures to pieces as best she could and giving all attention to parts and details" (Atherton 1968:76). Magdaléna herself is "not mixed at all . . . just hooked together." This relentlessly structural language, pulling together Magdaléna and her failed novel, suggests to the reader that texts must have an organic relationship to the writer, that Magdaléna must write what she knows, and that she will find her identity in the documents of her own people. But who her own people are is unclear. The parallel between how she writes and what she is (her best friend calls her fabricated, constructed, piecemeal) is the reverse of the previous passages in which she recalls an intensely personal relationship to her stories. In the logic of *The Californians*, Magdaléna's novel about English life is hollow because it does not root Magdaléna to a place, either geographically or imaginatively: "California had whispered to her but she had not understood" (77).

Magdaléna's next attempt to write the history of the legends of the Spanish Californians, her ancestors, takes shape from what Atherton would like us to believe is a more authentic historical pressure. Magdaléna seeks to write the Southland tales as simply and clearly as they were told to her. In doing this, she turns to California and her own position there. The creation of folklore, the work of *preserving* it, implies that it cannot officially reproduce itself, suggesting that official U.S. history is an organic process that "naturally" leaves behind the conquered cultures and nations. Cultural and national differences are artificially located in what becomes, in the act of writing, America's national past. But crucial to my purpose is not only how local color functions in the novel but also who is attempting to preserve it. Because it is Magdaléna, herself the product of two different cultures and traditions, who wishes to preserve her heritage before it passes away, the issue of preserving the past is deeply implicated in the imperialist narrative of both the United States and Spain. Magdaléna imagines presenting the stories of "old California" to a world that has decided to forget them:

It was as much for their sake as for her own that she wanted these little histories to be triumphs of art, that they might arrest the attention of the world. Alvarado and Castro were great heroes to her: it was unjust and cruel that the big world outside of California should know nothing of them; to the present California, for that matter, they were not even names. And forty years before the Californias had bent to their nod! They had lived with the state of princes, and the wisdom with which the one had ruled and the other had managed his armies would have given them lasting fame had not their country then been as remote from Earth's greater civilisations as had it been on Jupiter! (311)

Magdaléna is mistaken when she imagines her work to be about provincial heroes. Alvarado and Castro were government officials of the new Mexican republic. Magdaléna is not writing fiction or commemorating a lost European history, she is fictionalizing a history of national resistance. The purity of the folk history she wants to transcribe is already diluted by a previous, failed struggle against Americanization. The tales, like Magdaléna's own person, are on the borders of two warring states, as well as two warring cultures. She does not complete this folk history but burns it.

Magdaléna's failure begins to answer why the text's competing versions of history must be radically, irreconcilably opposed. Although she gives the tales a more appropriate form—the mimicry of orality—Magdaléna discovers that they cannot be written at all, that her people must remain, as Atherton writes, "unhistoried." Ironically, however, there is an organic connection made in the heart of *The Californians*' presentation of diverse colonial histories. The silence of the Spanish histories and folktales determines the historical connection to the present material conditions of Spanish Americans. At the time of the novel, the grandees who were the subject of the untranslated or transcribed tales were objectionable not because they were Spanish but because they belonged to an old Spanish empire that could not document itself, translate itself, or reproduce its national culture. In the terms of contract and land disputes, it has no "papers," only verbal promises. By conflating with old heroines and grandees the heroes of actual battles of resistance against the U.S. occupation, Atherton demonstrates what happens to a conquered nation—its heroes (no matter which colonial narrative produced them) are flattened out to the same moment of cultural production as the romance.

Thus, Magdaléna's failure can be seen as a testament to the genre of realism, to its triumph as the only "natural" or authentic way to structure experience, even if the experience itself is not authentic. Realism not only verifies the form of the novel and the authenticity of the characters' experiences, it also closes off the possibilities that the text itself has raised. As Magdaléna begins to think about writing a different kind of narrative, she discovers a contemporary novel by Henry James. "It was a week before [Magdaléna] squarely faced the relation of Henry James to her own ambitions. Then she admitted it in so many words: she could not write, she never could write" (1968:322). She cannot realize herself through writing, through observing or creating her own cultural past.

Although the text highlights Magdaléna's attempts to become a full, rich character, it introduces Henry James as though he were a character in the narrative. James's close identification with the mystery of the realist form is hardly accidental. Atherton dedicated *The Bell and the Fog,* a collection of her stories about Spanish California, "To the Master, Henry

James" (Atherton 1905). James's is the master narrative. Becoming real means following a set of formal guidelines through which subjectivity might be performed and appropriately read. The conflation of national form and the pervasive eruption of illegible ethnic traces testify that against the problematic of its own internal literary production, *The Californians* has arrived at what Terry Eagleton terms the "crisis point in the relatively autonomous evolution of realist forms—a point at which the problematic *fictionality* of those stolidly self-confident forms is becoming incorporated as a level of signification within the text itself" (Eagleton 1985:123).

The failure of Magdaléna to become a writer and the structural failure of the stories she is writing suggest an alternative national history whose emergent articulations are formally repressed. Although none of Magdaléna's documents ever appears anywhere in the text, they indicate the shape of that emergent history.

The gold of the grandees, often claimed illegally by Americans, becomes part of the nation's wealth, although the grandees themselves do not. The stories about them also must remain outside the system of production and consumption in which the plunder of this nation now participates. The very orality of these tales keeps them out of textual circulation. Although their history seems "real" to Magdaléna when she hears it in Spanish or when she repeats it in English to her American lover, their transmission is circumvented by the narrator, whose realist voice relentlessly, repetitively, claims that realism is truly valuable and restorative for eastern audiences.

The old tales of the grandees, however, are virtually useless to Magdaléna, as the cultural and national identity they provide her is without depth, power, or subjectivity. Magdaléna's identity is also in the balance, as the novel is about whether she will become a writer or a wife. That choice is really between an internal shift in identity and an external change in identity. In Werner Sollors's terms, will Magdaléna's identity derive from her descent from the Spanish conquerors of California, or will it be predicated on a consensual marriage to an American (Sollors 1986)? The novel locates Magdaléna's divided identity in the conventional language of realism's drama of self-development, but that language breaks down when confronted by racial matters. Magdaléna is, we recall, a "swarthy-skinned" woman, but she has "a sweet inner life, which was an almost constant dwelling upon the poetical past" (1968:21). She is apparently "Mexican" and "internally" Spanish. Only by suppressing the oral histories can Atherton suppress the racial scandal that underwrites the imperialist ventures that produced Spanish California and Magdaléna as the subjects of conventional narrative.

Although the text's controlling silence over its hidden historical texts is embedded in its structure, this silence is once violated. Near the end of the novel, when Magdaléna has given up writing, she meets a vagrant "who looked like a fallen king" and who needs money. Don Yorba turns him away, but Magdaléna asks him who he is. He tells her that he "held the highest offices under the Mexican government," that he is a former grandee, cheated out of his lands by the Americans during the drought of 1864. Sympathetically, Magdaléna asks his name:

It was a name famous in the brief history of old California—a name which had stood for splendid hospitality, for state and magnificence, for power and glory. It was the name of one of her beloved heroes. She had written his youthful romance; she had described the picturesque fervour of his wooing, the pomp of his wedding; of all those heroes he had been the best beloved, the most splendid. And she met him—a broken-down old drunkard. (1968:342–343)

After hearing his story, Magdaléna thinks that she is "glad that she had burned her manuscripts" (345). This is a crucial segment. The Old Californians, who until now have not been invoked in the novel, make an appearance in its plot. This appearance summarizes the novel's desire to convert folklore and ethnic romance into a more conventional realist narrative. Only when Magdaléna relinquishes the romantic stereotype of the Old Californians can the "drunkard" who was once "a king" emerge in the novel as the sign of a crisis in narrative and social assimilation.

Homi Bhabha writes that "the language of culture and community is poised on the fissures of the present becoming the rhetorical figures of the past" (Bhabha 1990:293). But *The Californians* insists that there is an agent behind this transformation. Stories do not simply become figures of the past. In *The Californians*, the stories of the Old Californians cannot be translated in a nationalized system of production and consumption. Conservative though Atherton is, she recognizes the possibility of a minor American literature that would have at its heart the possibility of resistance to the ways in which official American identities are produced.

Atherton manages and contains this minor literature, describing it as a component of California culture by creating another narrative space for it—ethnic history becomes quaint regionalism. This is a conversion Atherton had worked out in other texts. Her other work also is concerned with the stories of old California. In particular, her collection of stories *The Splendid Idle Forties* is composed of the very tales that Magdaléna tried and failed to write. From one vantage point, this collection would actually be the text that Magdaléna was attempting to write. In it are the lovely señoras and dashing caballeros, preserved through the nostalgic lens of regionalism. The circle completes itself in Atherton's historical document *California: An Intimate History*. In this book, Atherton verifies that the folktales Magdaléna listened to as a child and are reworked as fiction in *The Splendid Idle Forties* are indeed based on real history.

a full subject just as the region of California becomes fully subject to the laws and culture of the United States. It is important to recall that Magdaléna is the product of two opposing national mythologies, but that she is also a product of two similar "cast-iron" traditions. Both the New England Yankee and the Spanish grandee may be thought of as remnants of the past. California, though, primeval and new, is a land of promise, a land where anyone can rewrite or refound America. But in placing California outside imperialist relations at the moment it becomes most American through its metaphoric link to Magdaléna, California becomes a utopian site, unable, as Terry Eagleton argued about the utopian impulses of nationalism,

> to trace within the present that secret lack of identity with itself which is the spot where a feasible future might germinate—the place where the future overshadows and hollows out the present's spurious repleteness. To "know the future" can only mean to grasp the present under the sign of its internal contradictions, in the alienations of its desire, in its persistent inability ever quite to coincide with itself. (Eagleton 1990:25–26)

Magdaléna's inability to coincide with herself, her blankness, are emblematic of a text seeking to erase the histories that promise to structure her identity.

By closing with marriage, *The Californians* smoothes into a narrative that expresses unions that are culturally homogeneous. Magdaléna's fiancé is a diplomat and a scientific explorer and is thus able to negotiate the cultures of his new country and his new wife. Such a neat textual containment occurs at the newly invented origin of California as America. Ernest Gellner writes that the nation "claims to defend folk culture even while it invents high culture," and in that sense, this novel reinscribes union history (Gellner 1983:5). It is not a coincidence, I think, that Magdaléna's failed folklore would have been about the Mexican War and that the novel itself was written during the Spanish-American War, during which Cuba was "liberated" from the Spanish.

Controlling folklore allows the nation to make the double movement of silencing the other and forcing it to speak. It also creates a national public by creating a vogue for stories about cultures that only seem to be fading away because the work of retrieval is already under way. But *The Californians* also asserts that retrieval causes the disappearance of an emergent political force, and it therefore concentrates on cultural failure and reappropriation. But for all this, *The Californians* is not ideologically seamless. Although the text ends with the United States absorbing California and Trennahan marrying Magdaléna, much is left unresolved. For instance, the city of San Francisco, in which a great deal of the novel is set, is an uncontrollable threat and, in at least one instance, a threat to the neatness with which the narrator invents and domesticates Magdaléna's ethnic identity.

The seam connecting ethnic and national identity scars the bodies of Magdaléna and California. This seam can be traced, even smoothed over, by seeing how national identity becomes regional identity in certain marked silences in *The Californians*. The narrator's rhetorical tributes to the grandee culture, converted into regional nostalgia, demonstrate the conditions under which Spanish culture can be nationally (politically) threatening and regionally (culturally) exciting. But this resolution is very unsteady. Indeed, as the narrative of Magdaléna's life unfolds, the tension between how she will be perceived ethnically, as the daughter of a grandee or as a "greaser," is already becoming more and more unmanageable.

Although most of the events in the novel take place in the spacious interiors of various mansions or on the elaborately manicured lawns of the summer homes of the first families of San Francisco, there are slight disruptions. As Magdaléna searches for words to write about her dying culture, she is served by the very real but decidedly mute Chinese and Mexican servants who help keep her comfortably enclosed in San Francisco's small but hardy aristocracy. The class components of Magdaléna's heritage cannot be underestimated. Menlo Park, "originally a large Spanish grant, had long since been cut up into country places for what may be termed the 'Old Families of San Francisco.' The eight or ten families who owned this haughty precinct were as exclusive, as conservative, as any group of ancient county families in Europe" (1968:54).

Even though the West has been easternized, and the Spanish sanitized, other, invisible villages keep the small kingdom of Menlo Park working. As wealthy young protagonists wait for a pleasure train to stop, the narrator writes: "On the far side [of the road] was a row of Chinese wash houses, in whose doors stood the Mongolians, no less picturesque than the civilization across the way. Behind them was the tiny village of Menlo Park" (1968:294). But in the city of San Francisco, the neat distribution of wealth and position are disrupted, and the "villages" of Chinatown and Spanish town will seem not picturesque but frightening.

Only the class distinctions in a very tiny segment of San Francisco society keep Magdaléna Yorba from descending into the mass of countless other women of Spanish descent, from becoming "a creature for whom she had no name." Don Roberto, Magdaléna's father, believes that it is in his nature to deteriorate, as the friends of his youth have. "The fear which had haunted him during the last thirty years, [was] that he should suddenly relapse into his native extravagance and squander his patrimony and his accumulated millions" (1968:220). But it is really his unknown millions that keep him from descending to the level of the unknown millions in the city. Indeed, it is not difficult to see that in Atherton's transcription of Don Roberto's speech, the badge of his "manufactured character" (255), he is always teetering between his rightful millions. He does not speak in the "poetic" voice of the caballero or in the standard English of the rest of the characters but in a grotesque pidgin English. In the context of the novel (and of the stories that Magdaléna is trying so hard to write), Don Roberto sounds like a humorous local-color figure.

Don Roberto is hardly the only model of Spanish identity in the novel. On several occasions, Magdaléna wanders into the city of San Francisco. In these sections of the novel, the perfectly created narrative coincidence of both Magdaléna and California as regenerative figures is displaced by the chaos and disorder the city represents. The city is not so easily incorporated into the logic of the novel. It always seems to be on fire, quite literally, always refounding itself, remaking itself. One character, Colonel Jack Belmont mutters that "you never know where you are in this infernal town, anyhow" (1968:53), and that disorientation holds true for more than the characters' geographic positioning. San Francisco is filled with an ominous though resoundingly mute population that is simply *there*, differentiated broadly by class and sometimes by ethnicity. But often, the inhabitants of San Francisco are faceless and nameless. The city's population, primarily a background for a series of plot devices, edges away from the margins of the book when we try to explain how people learn to narrate their individual identities in a national ideology that according to this novel insists on the seemingly irreconcilable projects of national homogeneity and cultural variation.

Even though the text conflates Magdaléna and California as empty spaces available for claiming, San Francisco erupts out of this tenuous configuration. Often Magdaléna is described in natural settings. When she decides to write, for example, her chosen space for composition is the grounds of her family's country manor. But this setting is always overcomposed. It is carefully tended, laid out to include—but also to enclose—the mute graveyard of her Spanish heroes. The traditional, primeval wilds of California are also away from the center of the novel; characters visit places like the redwood forest and the geysers as tourist attractions, but the reader never accompanies anyone on these tours. The really dangerous wild spot in this novel is the city; it eludes the novel's symptomatic taxonomies of character and identity.

San Francisco, the city that industry and capital built, is blind to the distinctions that can be made so quickly in Menlo Park. Eric Hobsbawm writes that by the end of 1849, the population of California was around 14,000 people and that by 1852, San Francisco alone contained 35,000 (Hobsbawn 1979:149).[7] By the 1880s, the city had more than 300,000 inhabitants. San Francisco is the only place Magdaléna can lose herself and erase the distinctions that keep her apart from any experience of her Spanish history or her ethnicity. While Atherton must create Magdaléna as a Spanish American in order to write the story of the loss of her nationality, in San Francisco, Magdaléna is called and seen as a "greaser." Among her wealthy family and friends, Magdaléna thinks to herself,

It was a privilege for these girls to be intimate with her, to call her 'Léna, great as might be their social superiority over the many in San Francisco whose names she had never heard. In her inordinate pride of birth, in her intimate knowledge of the fact that she was the daughter of a Californian grandee who still possessed the three hundred thousand acres granted his fathers by the Spanish crown, she in all honesty believed no one of these friends of her youth to be her equal. (Atherton 1968:124)

But this is already a time of distinctions that would pass away. It is the "many in San Francisco whose names she had never heard" who will be the final arbiters of her identity if she should ever wander outside her house. Indeed, while wandering through San Francisco one night, Magdaléna passes a wreck of a house and sees that "it had been the home of a 'Forty-niner,' and he was dead and forgotten, his dust as easily accounted for as his winged gold." Before that night, San Francisco had been the home of faceless "unknown millions who said 'mommer' and 'popper,' got divorces, and used cosmetics" (1968:95). But once in the city, the tongue-tied Magdaléna forgets her class biases, loses her lonely pride, and bursts out of her constrictive gender and ethnic position. Atherton writes that Magdaléna "cursed aloud. She let fly all the maledictions, English and Spanish, of which she had knowledge" (328). At this moment, Magdaléna becomes, in both languages, her own other and thinks as she walks through the strange streets of the city, "I am nothing" (330). Thus emptied of any meaning, either to herself or to others, she falls into step with a faceless crowd.

The riff-raff of the world was moving there, and when not apathetic they took their pleasures with drawn brows and eyes alert for a fight; but the only types Magdaléna recognised were the drunken sailors and the occasional blank-faced Chinaman who had strayed down from his quarter on the hill. There were dark-faced men who were doubtless French and Italian; what their calling was, no outsider could guess, but that it was evil no man could doubt; and there were many whose nationality had long since become as inarticulate as such soul they may have been born with. . . . The din of voices, the medley of tongues and faces, the crash of music, the poisoned atmosphere, confused Magdaléna. (331)

Magdaléna's loss of her sense of herself is dangerous to the stability of the text and its configuration of California. The city contains multiple nationalities, and the possibility of losing nationality is the result of criminal life rather than of colonial assimilation. The taxonomies by which the people of the city can be meaningfully identified are gone. Even national characteristics seem lost. Regeneration and renewal are not simply for the easterners exhausted from the rigors of high culture.

But Magdaléna does not stop wandering when she feels confused and emptied in the crowd. Counterposed to the "medley of tongues and faces" is the space of the ghetto, which allows Atherton to break down the uncontrollable threat that the multinational crowd seems to pose. Going from dark alley to dark alley, she finally finds her way into a section of the city that seems reasonably safe. Atherton's narrator then draws away from the previous chaotic descriptions of the city and describes the neighborhood:

The women looked stupid, the men weather-beaten, but the prevailing expression was good-natured. In the middle of the street was a tamale stand surrounded by patrons. . . . This, then, was Spanish town. Magdaléna had dreamed of it often, picturing it a blaze of colour, a moving picture-book, crowded with beautiful girls and handsome gaily attired men. There was not a young person to be seen. Nothing could be less picturesque, more sordid. (1968:334)

Finally, the representation of the people about whom Magdaléna has been fantasizing and dreaming is simply that of any slum, in which life is a marginal experience at best. Two things are important to note here. The first is that Magdaléna wants to see Spanish town as a picture book. Its failure to comport with that idea also signifies the disappearance of one version of her own people. But the most important aspect to note in this passage is that while the novel has always placed the existence of the remnants of "true" Spanish culture in Santa Barbara, a city geographically distant but nonetheless in existence at the time of the novel, the "new country" (1968:36) that Magdaléna sees in Spanish town is also an attempt to "revise" her ideas according to the script of the United States. When she thinks that "nothing could be less picturesque," she is only rephrasing the more personal sense of loss that she first articulated in the phrase "there are no more caballeros."

It would be easy to counterargue, following Atherton's narrative strategies, that Spanish town has, like the Spanish, simply degenerated and thus to understand the novel as simply an example of the late nineteenth century's practice of allegorizing and naturalizing racial and cultural imperialism. We could then measure this internal logic against how Trennahan (the East) regenerates in California and Roberto (Spanish) degenerates, but we still would not have an adequate way of making sense of the city in this novel. Indeed, the images here show a distinctly antiutopian side of the nineteenth-century West.

Writing in 1886 about the "perils" of immigration, Josiah Strong pointed out that so large a share of it is pouring into the formative West. Already is the proportion of foreigners in the territories from two to three times greater than in the states east of the Mississippi. In the East, institutions have been long established and are therefore less easily modified by foreign influence, but in the West, where institutions are formative, that influence is far more powerful. We may well ask—and with special reference to the West—whether this in-sweeping immigration is to foreignize us, or we are to Americanize it. (Strong 1963:57)

The miniature ethnic colonies within San Francisco estrange Magdaléna from herself, but they also help her to "foreignize" herself by representing the still-living cultures that the United States failed to take into its union with the same narrative neatness that Atherton displays in her constant patterns of East-West intermarriages.[8] In *Heterologies: Discourse on the Other*, Michel de Certeau explains the ideological impulses behind the many discourses informing the popularity of folklore in the nineteenth century:

The measure of a work is what it keeps silent. And we must say that the scientific studies—and undoubtedly the works they highlight—include vast and strange expanses of silence. These blank spots outline a geography of the *forgotten*. They trace the negative silhouette of the problematics displayed black on white in scholarly books. (de Certeau 1986:131)

The fact that the novel ends with a conventional marriage between two people who were engaged for the greater part of the text replaces a violent imperial history with a family drama, establishing the nation as an act of consent to a proposition of union. Generically, *The Californians* stands at a cusp in the twinned histories of imperialism and regionalism. Although the status of California is no longer at issue as a territory in the continental United States, the people of California are still coming into focus as citizens. *The Californians* constructs Spanish as a legal category linked to autonomous identity and individual rights, and "Mexican" as a racial category linked to insurgent social problems and secret, hereditary alliances with racial otherness. Separating Spanish and Mexican heritage reveals, too, that the arguments over territorial sovereignty and United States politics have once again moved elsewhere—to Spain's overseas possessions. This is why the same journal can announce "Mrs. Atherton's" responses to a literary dinner in a gossip column at the same time that it features an essay highly critical of the intervention of the United States into the affairs of Cuba and the Philippines. The book models an end point to imperialism in Spanish California and thus erases its imperial foundations within a "realist" model of writing. That conversion tells us finally that the people that regionalism might "discover" in Spanish California have, like Spain's political possessions, moved elsewhere.

4

"The Shadow of the Ethiopian"

George Washington Cable's *The Grandissimes*

"OUR CREOLE 'WE' DOES DAMAGE, AND OUR CREOLE 'YOU' DOES MORE"

This rueful confession comes during the tentative beginnings of a friendship between Honoré Grandissime and Joseph Frowenfeld, two of the major characters in George Washington Cable's 1880 novel of 1803 New Orleans (1988:151). While the two men seem to like each other well enough personally, their immediate, if shy, goodwill is complicated by the social and political circumstances between their nations. To Joseph Frowenfeld, Honoré Grandissime represents "the finest flowering" of the New Orleans citizen, but to that New Orleans citizen, Joseph Frowenfeld, the American immigrant in Louisiana, represents U.S. imperialism. Frowenfeld thus appears to the Creoles to threaten all the ways they constitute themselves as a culture—their language, economy, and territorial sovereignty. He especially appears to threaten their racial and ethnic taxonomies. In this chapter, I consider *The Grandissimes*, looking at the contest between the Creole "we" and the American "you" played out against the background of the United States' 1803 purchase of Louisiana. This act doubled the size of the United States but precipitated a crisis over the racial and ethnic constitution and legal status of the new people who suddenly found themselves to be American citizens.

Cable's attempt to isolate the dynamic of how national and local identities are constructed as coextensive rather than antithetical narratives makes it useful for a study of regionalism. It is through the genre and conventions of local-color fiction or regionalism that Cable creates a temporary textual site on which his white characters can maintain both a national and a local identity, even and especially when the two appear to be in immediate conflict. Cable's reliance on regionalism as a narrative strategy allows him to use this genre as what Richard Brodhead calls an access point for the emergence of new voices and subjects into the American literary mainstream. This strategy also allows us to examine, quite literally, the "color" in the genre of local color.[1] Finally, I suggest that the success of *The Grandissimes* in narratively assimilating the Creole to U.S. culture rests on divorcing its black subjects from the domain of the term *Creole* and expelling them from legal personhood in the text.

Expelling and silencing black culture in this novel mark a larger historical project in which regionalism is complicit. The text's rendering of local Creole identity in terms of whiteness helps create the local-color subjects who, like the New Englanders in Sarah Orne Jewett's text, can be assimilated to an endangered notion of the real, or ancestral American. Likewise, it eases the assimilation of Southern territory into a Post-Reconstruction American nation. Subject/citizen and territory/nation are wedded through the novel's varied, disorganized, and variously authorized versions of the origins of its most exclusive Creole family. In turn, this family history allegorizes the various national histories of the text.

The ostensible topic of *The Grandissimes* is the purchase of the Louisiana Territory by the United States. This event is recounted with reference to the pivotal figure of Toussaint L'Ouverture, whose slave revolt in Haiti forced Napoleon Bonaparte to sell Louisiana in a vain attempt to raise enough money to put down the revolt. The context of the novel's publication—the Reconstruction of the South after the Civil War—is similarly acknowledged in the logic of the novel. It, too, is an event underwritten by, but finally inadequate to the reconstruction of, racial matters. In the time of the novel, the major freed black figures become social rather than political problems, without the ability to speak to the racial struggles for which their very existence has provided the terms. As the novel progresses, the identity of the Creole changes. "Creole" comes to mean not just "white," it also comes to signify a cultural identity consonant (as race could not be) with the project of a politically homogeneous nation.

Like *The Californians*, this book is haunted by the many national histories that produced the territory of Louisiana. Taking the fragments of these histories and regional stories as my starting point, I focus my reading on Cable's deliberate use of the conventions of regionalism. I look at the novel's rich use of languages and accents, asking how they help to order the novel's various racial genealogies. I go on to examine how the text's notoriously difficult family genealogies index the United States's difficulty in accounting for the presence of racial others in the national "family."

But although the novel attempts to reconcile the cultural identity of the Creole with national identity as a U.S. citizen, its focus on storytelling reveals that becoming a U.S. citizen means suppressing local historical conflicts. To this end, I trace several instances of Cable's framing of the family stories from which Creoles fashion themselves as a distinct and closed community, examining in particular the authority the stories carry in culture, as well as the ways in which the stories are authorized and authenticated in the text. The divorcing of Creole self-identity from racial creolization makes race a private matter, a matter of "secretless secrets" kept by families and communities. It installs Creole whiteness as a public position that soothes anxieties about legal and social status in U.S. culture. The central secretless secret that I consider is the story of Bras-Coupé. I look at the events of Bras-Coupé's life and the repercussions of his death on the text's negotiation of Creole cultural and political identity. Because Cable's text also functions as an allegorical account of the Reconstruction South's sectional wounds, its figuration of black characters resonates within a Union history. Within that history, *The Grandissimes* invents Louisiana as a traditional pastoral region and the Creoles as quaint locals.

George Washington Cable's 1880 novel *The Grandissimes* is set in 1803, the year of the Louisiana Purchase, and it recounts the process by which New Orleanians learn to accommodate themselves to the new demands of American citizenship, rather than to the imperialist conditions of colonialism under France. Cable chooses to set his novel at the last historical moment of New Orleans's independence from the United States. His characters, poised on this historical threshold, do not need to retrieve a lost national identity; they are instead faced with preserving Creole cultural identity in the face of American expansion. By framing identity as a choice of affiliation, the text appears to offer the figure of the individual Creole as a working model of cultural heterogeniety in a homogenous nation. Against New Orleans and its multiple national histories of origin, Cable marks out in great detail the strategies that his characters use to position themselves as individuals in the communities of place, family, and race. Through his ironic, omniscient narrator, readers are guided through the tangled web of history and genealogy that structure Creole identity, and they witness how Creoles create versions of their past through seemingly incommensurable social and political imperatives. The strategy of underlining the adaptations characters make to changing historical imperatives while trying to remain coherent as "a people"—Creoles, or Louisianans, or even New Orleanians—anticipates Immanuel Wallerstein's observation that "if we . . . cannot come to terms about this name designating a 'people' or indeed about virtually any other name designating some people, maybe this is because peoplehood is not merely a construct, but one which, in each particular instance, has constantly changing boundaries" (Balibar and Wallerstein 1991:77).

Because the character of the Creole is constructed through the changing boundaries of community, through the public and private histories that account for New Orleans as the center of a transatlantic trade, it is important to balance the novel's own scrupulously defined world against that which it sets itself. I lay out both the frame of the history *in* the book by discussing the context of the Louisiana Purchase and then sketch out the frame *of* the text by noting its gestures toward post–Civil War America. The contest of histories produces a doubling of characters through time, through nationality, and finally through race. Which histories is the novel invested in suppressing, which is it interested in mythologizing, and what larger interests dictate those choices?

In 1803, New Orleans was still a part of Europe. It was populated by French, Spanish, Native Americans, and a vast, highly organized community of both free people of color and slaves. First founded in 1718, the city of New Orleans was a town "with loose, flexible race relations and a mobile population" (Hall 1992:64). Although it was surrounded by Choctaw, Natchez, and Chickasaw tribes, far from maintaining hostile relations with them, French settlers often married Native American women and, in times of want, relied on and lived with Indian tribes for prolonged periods of time. The French policy was to try to ally with friendly tribes in order to control the antipathy of unfriendly tribes, but it was defeated by a series of Indian revolts that many slaves joined and aided. France ceded the colony to Spain in 1763. Although official public documents were to be written in Spanish and the state apparatus was distinctly different, the town's French character changed very little. The city became an important port and increased its population through immigration from France and Spain as well as through the influx of free black men and women from Santo Domingo. Because of mobility and the ease of manumission under Spanish rule, the number of free people of color in New Orleans at the end of the Spanish period was nearly 1500 (Johnson 1992: 35–36, 52).

The population of New Orleans must be understood in a variety of contexts. First, as residents of a port city in a colony that figured heavily in international trade and commerce, the population of New Orleans had a distinctly international set of interests. But more important, the loose relations among white, black and Native American populations ensured at some point that the alliances that its citizens made would be neither necessarily nor programmatically based on an essentialized notion of racial purity. Indeed, the history of New Orleans is filled with slave rebellions aided by Native Americans, Native American revolts aided by slaves and free people of color, as well as the more familiar emergence of mixed blood categories to define black citizens. American definitions of race and culture were spectacularly ill equipped to deal with the complex and sometimes multiply determined definitions of national and/or racial identity, which blossomed into refined systems of classification in the colonial context of New Orleans.

It is this inability to reckon with such classificatory issues *The Gran-dissimes* takes up. The novel, set during the purchase from France, which had taken Louisiana back from Spain in 1803, foregrounds the difficulty in classifying peoples in a new national narrative. Such difficulty is under-written by the other great crisis of nationalism and colonialism of 1803—the great slave revolution of Toussaint L'Ouverture in Haiti. The sale of Louisiana, underwritten by racial struggle, comes to represent the crisis of self-government and self-determination that the novel plots. The first crisis of self-government, which can be measured against the narrative of the slave Bras-Coupé, is derived from the fear not only that the United States will set the slaves free but also that the emerging identity of the Cre-ole subject will somehow be incompletely understood as white and Euro-pean. The Creoles' second objection to becoming American, measured against the economics of the sale of territory itself, is that the European land grants in New Orleans will be worthless and speculators will be able to buy historic New Orleans right out from under its first families.

The sale of Louisiana and the militancy with which the Creoles fight against their impending absorption into the Union lead us to the historical moment that allows Cable to produce his fictions. He writes in the context of Reconstruction, the post–Civil War America in which the status of black citizens and that of regions as autonomous elements in a larger nation are still at stake. How Cable chooses to reinvent the "true" history of New Orleans and to mythologize the category of "creole" serve as a kind of lesson for his theories about the resurrection of the South in post–Civil War America. Joseph Tregle writes that the Louisiana Purchase and Reconstruction activated nearly the same anxieties in New Orleans: "The second invasion of 'Yankee buzzards' brought new hordes into the city and state with less than accurate preconceptions as to the community's always complicated racial nuances. Those earlier northern identifications of 'creole' with 'mixed blood' and 'mulatto' now took on infinitely greater significance" (Tregle 1992:171). Against these mirrored historical frames, *The Grandissimes* enacts a remarkable and elaborate series of internal tex-tual mediations and negotiations of local and national history, of language and storytelling, of classifying and ordering peoples. Finally, it smoothes the imaginative and narrative disorder of origins into a clear, nationalized genre.

The Grandissimes is unusually incoherent by late-nineteenth-century standards. It does not move in a predictable chronological fashion, and while the self-referential narrator appears to guide the reader through the abrupt chronological breaks, he withholds a great deal of useful local knowledge from his audience, aligning readers with the character of Joseph Frowenfeld, the Northerner whose arrival in New Orleans acts as a catalyst for the proliferation of local narratives. One critic observed that the novel presents a "story-shaped world, one articulated by the narratives—the lies, the gossipy tales, the myths, the histories—that the inhabitants tell each other" (Swann 1987:257).

Because it gives us so many frames, or contexts, through which to read it, *The Grandissimes* is difficult to classify in terms of genre. It could, for example, be considered a species of family romance, as it is ostensibly about the reconciliation of the Grandissime–de Grapion feud. It could also be considered a powerful reworking of the genre of the "tragic mulatto," as the events of the text are determined by racial conflict, many of which can be traced to the hand of the free slave Palmyre Philosophe, who "had stood all her life with dagger drawn" (Cable 1988:135). *The Grandissimes'* meticulous and celebrated deployment of dialect and Cable's preservation of the customs of community and place situate it in the genre of local color.

The events are described in a series of sketches. While the novel does not have a chronological structure, it progresses by connecting events to the characters' memories of them, seeming to use a strategy of subjective association rather than objective knowledge. Barbara Ladd contends that the reason for the structural disjunctures of the novel stems from Cable's persistent arguments with his editors: "The obscurity and the confusions of Cable's texts stem directly from the strategic displacements by which he not only tried to avoid treating too directly but also tried to avoid sidestepping too shamelessly the implications of the colonial history of Louisiana, slavery, and miscegenation for the present" (Ladd 1996:46).[2] At the very least, a symptomatic inaccessibility structures local knowledge in this text. The question of why the text seems to struggle between an explicit treatment of the problems of race and a treatment of family romance is less interesting to me than the question of how the fragmentation of the text allows a reading of the late nineteenth century's ability to articulate race in terms of nationality, family, and ethnicity.

Contemporary critics of *The Grandissimes* also noticed its structural difficulties. The most enthusiastic reviews mention its demands on reading. Writing about the public's newly awakened desire to see New Orleans for itself after reading this text, Edward Hale stated, "They all want to know how much is historically true, and how much is imaginary in this; . . . they want to see exactly the frame in which such charming pictures are to be hung" (Hale 1980:90). This emphasis on framing is perhaps the most penetrating observation Hale could have made. The text is inside out because it privileges the frame—the context—over the "charming picture."

Another reviewer noted that the novel offers up a "gallery of impressions," "a gallery of portraits in which individuality is confused" (Clay 1980:36). In this gallery of impressions, there is no natural, organic relationship among the portraits, no historical progression, no privileging of linear time. No single portrait has any intrinsic meaning. The ordering principle in any gallery, Cable's included, is the relation between frame and portrait, text and context. Each frame offers a way to understand each portrait, but each portrait becomes a frame for the others arranged next to it. There is only discrete impression next to discrete impression. These frames of history provoke a very particular reading of the novel's representations of identity. The deliberate exteriority of *The Grandissimes'* construction allows Cable to create the characters of the Creoles who are also necessarily without interiority—the traditional aspect of identity that the genre of realism constructs—and who must then be read *only* against the histories that they tell themselves about their community and its multiple origins. The characters, then, are created not as psychologically rich individuals in the fullness of unfolding linear time but as creolized individuals through the multiple unfolding of the text's histories. The lack of interiority, the construction of deliberately one-dimensional, even sketchy characters in whom "individuality is confused," is a crucial aspect of the negotiations among time, history, and language that structure the text as a whole. It is precisely this exteriority that produces the empty figure of the Creole, without racial components or conflicting political affiliations, as the novel's central subject.

The Grandissimes' exterior structure extends to its elaborate geography of the city of New Orleans. Almost all the text's action is situated in the city's streets, which are named and marked for the reader. But something in the excess of orientation, in the elaborate placement of the buildings, streets, and alleys conceals their implication in social locations. For example, the narrator presents us with the spectacle of Aurora going to visit her landlord: "On the banquette of the rue Toulouse, directly in front of an old Spanish archway and opposite a jeweller's store and a large, balconied and dormer-windowed wine-warehouse—Aurore Nancanou, closely veiled, had halted" (1988:120). This language frames her exactly— "on," "in front of," "opposite."

This authenticity, this excessive contextualization, this insistence on detail, is an immediate reminder that it is only by such contextualization that any character—veiled or not—may be apprehended. For example, the veiled Aurora is in the right place, but she has gone to the wrong Honoré Grandissime. There are two Honorés, one a white man and one a free man of color (fmc), but for Aurora, it is impossible that she has gone to the wrong one, since the black Honoré cannot even exist for her. When the narrator calls it "a perfectly natural mistake," he elides the fact of miscegenation into Aurora's unintended acknowledgment of it. Cable structures her misrecognition of racial mixing by explaining it as the logic of eternal misrecognition in the streets of New Orleans. Reviewers' remarks that people wished to go to New Orleans to see how much of Cable's writing was real and how much was imaginary confirm that the perceived authenticity, or the effect of reality in this text, is not dependent on the coherence of the characters but on the context that produces the exotic, blended character of the Creole. Lafcadio Hearn, among others, vouched for Cable's careful scholarship and his acute and accurate memory of place in order to verify the novelist's account of the Creole as a type (Hearn 1924). The narrator, courtly and ironic, must often break away to explain that the particular site about which he is writing has changed or disappeared. Interjections like "Do not look for it now; it is quite gone" (Cable 1988: 156) are sprinkled throughout his descriptions of New Orleans. The narrator moves between the time of the text and the time of his construction of the text, asking for a simultaneity of vision, an ability to read both linearly and vertically.

The workings of interiority and exteriority, public and private, resonate through the remarkable architecture of the buildings themselves. Nineteenth-century New Orleans writers lingered over the architecture of the city. For example, Grace King's collection *Balcony Stories* uses the balcony as a space on which one can sit and be both at home and on the street and be both in public and with one's family. In his collections of regional stories and sketches about New Orleans, *Old Creole Days*, Cable also focuses on the construction of the buildings, describing the courtyards of tiny hidden gardens enclosed by the rows of houses in the French Quarter. In his collection of Creole sketches, Lafcadio Hearn describes the inside of a Creole courtyard:

Without, cotton-floats might rumble, and street-cars vulgarly jingle their bells; but these were mere echoes of the harsh outer world which disturbed not the delicious quiet within—where sat, in old-fashioned chairs, good old-fashioned people who spoke the tongue of other times, and observed many quaint and knightly courtesies forgotten in this material era . . . without, it was the year 1879; within it was the epoch of the Spanish Domination. (Hearn 1923:148)

Such metaphors of interiority might be correlated to the ways in which Cable's presentation of Creoles tends to blur traditional realist models for understanding the architecture of Creole subjectivity. They testify to his novel's fantasy of an internally empty but externally coherent ethnic subject.

In *The Grandissimes*, the traditional opposition between the physical spaces of inside and outside establishes spaces and persons that can function perfectly well in the public and private sphere. The narrative rarely takes place in the interior of the Creole home. Joseph Frowenfeld's shop for example is also his home. It is on a street corner, which comes quite naturally to be known as "Frowenfeld's corner"; all characters eventually pass through it. Masses of people congregate outside it and through it comes the gossip of the street and in it are exhibited the relics of Creole life:

Frowenfeld's window was fast growing to be a place of art exposition. A pair of statuettes, a golden tobacco-box, a costly jewel-casket, or a pair of richly gemmed horse pistols. . . . It was natural that these things should come to "Frowenfeld's corner," for there, oftener than elsewhere, the critics were gathered together" (1988:113–114)

The window becomes a space of exhibition, with a variety of objects displaced from an ordering chain of economic value. They are fetish objects—together they form no coherent narrative, but their fetish status points to the concealed social relations that allegorize a larger narrative of dispossession. Similarly, the Grandissime mansion has a front porch allowing twenty women to walk abreast, just as they would promenade in the place d'Armes. Aurora and Clotilde's little house, with its scrupulously hidden poverty, at first seems a space in which only the things that are "private" or domestic can happen, but even this is strategically counterbalanced by the simple fact that they don't own the house—they rent it and can barely afford to pay their rent at that. It is a contested site—the very fact of having a rented home drives them into the public sphere of rentiers and counting houses. The little house is the sad double of the plantation lost to the Grandissime family in the feud that has stripped them of their property. Because they live in this little hovel, the outside—or as Hearn put it, this "material era"—has a claim on the Nancanou women.

There is a similarity in the ways in which the Northern character, Joseph Frowenfeld, becomes disoriented in the streets of the vieux carré and in which he becomes lost in the genealogies of the text's characters. These maps too, have odd turns, hidden courtyards. The blurrings, the contradictions of interior/exterior, the confusion of creolized identity are as prominent in the history of family as in New Orleans architecture. Family history is itself carefully framed by the ritual act of storytelling, which is itself delivered in the accent and voice of the Creole.

The stories through which the Creoles narrate themselves are in dialect. The most immediate and striking aspect of the novel is its cacophony of languages. Cable meticulously transcribes each character's utterance, noting the dropped consonants and elongated vowels. He tries to preserve the sound of the Creole accent in translation. That means not just that readers can imaginatively reconstruct an entire pattern of speaking but also that they seem to have access to history from what seems to be the unmediated other. But as Gavin Jones pointed out, Cable's use of a historically researched dialect reinforces the racial *mixing* of the white and black populations of New Orleans rather than giving each population a distinct linguistic identity. While the use of dialect links Cable's writing to local-color fiction, his deployment of it demonstrates the political stakes in appropriating dialect to serve the literary purpose of describing distinct and "untouched" cultures.

In the chapter entitled "Aurora as Historian," the narrator rhapsodizes, "Alas! the phonograph was invented three-quarters of a century too late. If type could entrap one-half the pretty oddities of Aurora's speech—the arch, the pathetic, the grave, the earnest, the matter-of-fact, the ecstatic tones of her voice" (Cable 1988:145). The text offers wild variations of French and English, some of which remain untranslated, untranslatable, while others are rendered in historically precise detail. There is, for example, Parisian French, slave dialects, gumbo French, gutter French, creole French, and delta French. The precision with which the narrator notes each of these adjectives is crucial, as is the transcription of each accent with exquisite care. The closely limned portraits of speakers struggling for the correct phrase in the proper language, the careful transcriptions, and the thoughtful translations exist because language is in transition itself. It is the contested site of citizens trying to construct themselves in different (and often opposing) national discourses.3 Creole identity is a private, local identity in this text, and the process of becoming a citizen, of entering the United States as reconstructed persons, is part of an ongoing process to invent and occupy an official public sphere. The thicket of languages, accents, and family histories accord with the text's working out of ideas of public and private spaces and the constitution of subjects who are legally able to appear in each of these spaces.

"I HAVE THESE FACTS . . . BY FAMILY TRADITION;
BUT YOU KNOW SIR, TRADITION IS MUCH MORE
AUTHENTIC THAN HISTORY"

The problems in reading *The Grandissimes* are announced by the beginning of the text. The first chapter advertises the play of histories and the doubling of characters. The first scene of the Grandissime clan shows them at a masked ball where each is dressed as his or her own ancestor. The characters cannot, of course, be read against a corresponding ancestor and thus placed into an easy genealogy. Dancing together are a monk and a dragoon, an Indian princess and a *fille à la cassette*. Shoulder to shoulder stand all phases of New Orleans history in no particular order.

The costumes, coded through the relations of family history, are not disguises because the book insists that a historical intermingling inflects the characters in the time of the text.

The same kind of narrative logic is at work when the Northern "immigrant" Joseph Frowenfeld, the ostensible moral center of the book, finds himself talking to the Nancanou women in their home. Aurora Nancanou slyly shows him a portrait of her grandmother, and Frowenfeld remarks that it is very like Clotilde, Aurora's daughter. " 'Dass one *fille à la cassette*," Aurora replies, "My gran'-muzzah; *mais*, ad de sem tam id is Clotilde . . . Clotilde is my gran'-mamma" (1988: 148). The crucial phrase here is "at de sem tam."

The simultaneity of identity, the disregard for logical historical relationships, becomes the organizing principle of the creolized identity in this novel. Aurora is not reading Clotilde in linear time but through the doubled time of Creole identity. This counters Frowenfeld's understanding of national history as a logical, linear progression; Clotilde can be daughter or grandmother but not both. To make sense of the relationship, the reader must, like Frowenfeld, separate the double from its other. The attempt to separate text and context becomes apparent when Frowenfeld sorts through the mysteries of the Creole identity to understand the web of histories that allows the subject to live at the same time as its uncanny double. He resolves to

begin at once the perusal of this newly found book, the Community of New Orleans. True, he knew he should find it a difficult task—not only that much of it was in a strange tongue, but that it was a volume whose displaced leaves would have to be lifted tenderly, blown free of much dust, re-arranged, some torn fragments laid together again with much painstaking, and even the purport of some pages guessed out. (Cable 1988:103)

The "rearrangement" of New Orleans history at the hand of the American "immigrant" begins the task of national reconstruction. Because each person seems to have a double, each appears to Frowenfeld as uncanny, as always in possession of a secret history. This is why hiring the Creole assistant, Raoul Innerarity, proves such a boon for Frowenfeld's scholarly if somewhat blundering textual reconstructions. Raoul was "a key, a lamp, a lexicon, a microscope, a tabulated statement, a book of heraldry, a city directory, a glass of wine, a Book of Days, a pair of wings, a comic almanac, a diving bell, a Creole *veritas*" (118). This description is itself a kind of mirror of the creole *veritas*, with text heaped on text. Like the masked ball, like the objects in Frowenfeld's window, like the frames of history through which the Creole negotiates identity through time and language, the objects describing Raoul are jammed together in no particular order. They are methods of reading, means of classifying and restoring secret histories.

Raoul's disclosures to Frowenfeld are points of origin, the places from which we can get into the textual cacaphony that for Cable represent the Creoles' self-fashioning. We can, for example, find the doubled characters strewn through the novel: Aurora is twinned against Palmyre; Clotilde is placed against the *fille à la cassette*; Honoré is twinned with a sister and doubled with a half-brother; and even Frowenfeld is paired with another Northerner, the cynical doctor Charlie Keene. Indeed, part of the process of reading the text is the slow attempt to place everything in the proper order, to restore relations and to reread information in a proper, chronological sequence. The abruptly told fragments of family histories are revelations that appear as "little explosive ruptures" (1988:102), as they do for Frowenfeld. They rupture the sequence of events in the text and thus appear to stop the history of the Cession that this book chronicles.

The family histories against which the larger history of colonization in Louisiana can be read position every Creole character as a historian or storyteller. But when the narrative pauses in order to let each character tell a particular version of history, it begins to stagger under the weight of stories of origins. In rejecting a teleological narrative of Louisiana's colonization, the text seems constituted in the first half by a series of beginnings, all of which seem to tease the reader with the possibility of finding a logical, or a real origin. Indeed, what Frowenfeld wants is time organized and made logical. His own private book of tables, which record the changes in temperature and barometric readings in a daily progression, searches for a narrative or pattern by which the international and often competing histories of the territory might be made logical. This is also why Raoul is so important to him. The way he "dovetailed story into story and drew forward in panoramic procession Lufki-Humma and Epaminondas Fusilier, Zephyr Grandissime . . . would have shamed the skilled volubility of Sheherazade" (1988:188). But none of the origins in this book—from the Indian queen to the origins of the Grandissime–de Grapion feud—really explains anything or anyone.

Although the text appears to be celebrating Creole self-fashioning in multiple languages, times, and histories, none of the histories or original stories is rendered in the voice of the Creole, which is otherwise so carefully preserved. The text abruptly introduces its key historical facts and normatively supplies them from the perspective of the omniscient narrator. For example, when Charlie Keene explains to Frowenfeld the history of Palmyre la Philosophe, he asks,

> "Don't you know who that woman is?"
> "No."
> "Well, I'll tell you."
> He told him. (1988:59)

The narrator interrupts and closes the conversation, beginning again in his own voice. The jump between " 'I'll tell you' " and "He told him" is unremarked. When Aurora explains her relationship to Palmyre, she begins " 'Sieur Frowenfel, 'w'en I was a lill' girl—" (144), but her narrative disappears after that short introduction. The narrator fills in the content of Aurora's history; her voice frames but does not complete it. Similarly, the narrator appropriates the moment in which the most tragically speechless character, Honoré Grandissime, fmc, attempts to explain to Frowenfeld why he needs a spell to make Palmyre love him. Cable writes, "He handed the apothecary—but a few words in time, lest we misjudge" (108).

Although these multiple beginnings seem to fracture the text, they allow us to see the hidden histories that made Louisiana into a Creole territory resisting the encroachment of the Americans. When the narrator writes "a few words in time, lest we misjudge," he is signaling an urgency in the text's inability to account for all the historical beginnings of the text, but he is also accounting for a certain anxiety over this complicated story of origin. The "we" that the narrator constructs is clearly an American reader who is aware of the "secret" origins of miscegenation, which accounts for the two Honoré Grandissimes. This reader is finally constructed as likely to misjudge or misunderstand it. The story that follows this phrase appears to give voice to the voiceless Honoré, but the narrator has control over his history. The voice of the last colonizer has begun to sew the story of miscegenation into a larger script of racial reconstruction.

In the time of the novel, the story of Numa Grandissime's firstborn son, the black Honoré, must be told in order to legitimate and place him. There are, after all, two Honoré Grandissimes. The marked absence of Honoré fmc's history is echoed in the tale of the two Honorés that follows, which is itself separated from the text by the space between the word *misjudge* and the words that open the following paragraph: "The father of the two Honorés was that Numa Grandissime." There are two fields of history here, the one unintelligible without the other, and it is impossible to say which is the "word in time." Such care from the narrator to give us the phrase "in time" to unravel Creole identity at the crucial intersection of temporal disjunctions, which might be read against the uneven histories of colonization, is emblematic of the way the novel organizes tangled histories from an imperial perspective.

In "Sly Civility," Homi Bhabha describes the colonizer's compulsive demand for narrative. "The colonialist present requires a strategy of calculation in relation to its native subjects. This need is addressed in a vigorous demand for narrative, embodied in the utilitarian or evolutionary ideologies of reason and progress" (Bhabha 1994:98). Joseph Frowenfeld, who is calculating a history in his book of factual tables about geographic and climactic events in New Orleans, is the recipient of most of the stories of shrouded national origins (most of which are also stories of racial inter-mixing). Although he is set on smoothing these texts into a teleological nar-rative, he, as colonizer or representative of U.S. imperialism, does not require the Creoles to narrate themselves. That is, although Frowenfeld asks, or accedes, to hear the stories that the characters tell him, he does not compel them to do so. Such compulsion would more neatly fit with the text's internal schematization of the United States as an imperial force bent on taking over Louisiana and more neatly fit in with the white Honoré's suggestion to the new Yankee governor that he "would *compel* . . . this people to govern themselves" (Cable 1988:95). This ambivalence about self-government and narration converge when the Creoles tell stories to Joseph that are about their identity as a people or a community. In doing so, they return over and over again to the story of Bras-Coupé, the escaped slave who most challenges their identities as governed and self-governing and as masters and narrators.

Rather, the compulsive narration of the Creoles, the compulsion to confess, to account for themselves to a representative of the United States underlines their ambiguous status in colonial terms. They are both the agents of colonial exploitation in Louisiana and the victims of U.S. colo-nialism. Their stories thus produce them as agents and victims, exotics and masters. Their narratives, built on maintaining racial difference, are also preceded and shaped by an occluded history of violence. They artic-ulate, as Homi Bhabha labels all colonial discourse, "an 'otherness' which is at once an object of desire and derision, an articulation of difference contained within the fantasy of origin and identity" (Bhabha 1990:67). But their fantasies of origin and identity are located on the body of a slave. All the Creoles' stories about their families, their land, their feuds, and how they got to New Orleans in the first place are articulated to, and irrevocably implicated in, the single, monolithic story of an escaped slave. This story stands at the nexus of the plot of Louisiana's purchase by New Orleans as a result of the monumental uprising of Toussaint L'Ouverture, an event that leads the white Creoles to believe they will become colonial subjects. But it also stands at the heart of their identity as colonizers in the territory of New Orleans, at the center of a transatlantic trade and empire whose most valuable commodities were not just produced by slaves but were slaves themselves.

All personal histories include the public trauma of Bras-Coupé's rebellion only to excise it or turn away from it. In their compulsion to narrate them-selves to Joseph Frowenfeld, the Creoles produce a double bind; they are both colonial and imperial subjects.[4] The slave rebellion of Bras-Coupé is a much-anticipated narrative. The novel is littered with references to it, suggesting that it is a much-told story, even in the face of the fact that it is almost never told completely.

For example, the entire Frowenfeld family, immigrating to New Orleans at the beginning of the book, wonders aloud at the vastness of the swamps. The captain of the ship tells them "in a *patois* difficult, but not impossible, to understand, the story of a man who chose rather to be hunted like a wild beast among those awful labyrinths, than to be yoked and beaten like a tame one" (1988:10). Upon his first meeting with the secondborn white Honoré, Frowenfeld is again teased with the story of Bras-Coupé. Honoré says to him only, "Ah! Mr. Frowenfeld, *there* was a bold man's chance to denounce wrong and oppression! Why, that negro's death changed the whole channel of my convictions" (38). Raoul, story-teller and painter of the famous picture "Louisiana rif-using to hanter de h-Union," asks Frowenfeld if it would be a "disgrace to paint de pigshoe of a niggah" and exclaims later, "Ah, my soul! What a pigshoe I could paint of Bras-Coupé!" (117). Aurora, telling her own story to Frowenfeld, says, "Ah! 'Sieur Frowenfel', iv I tra to tell de sto'y of Bras-Coupé, I goin' to cry lag a lill bebby" (145).

If *The Grandissimes* might be loosely described as the story of how a colonial emissary, Joseph Frowenfeld, American immigrant, pieces together the stories of the Creole culture he has entered, the story of Bras-Coupé might be described as the story that underwrites the precarious sense of the pre-American creole identity. Its public secrecy acknowledges the vast archive of racial secrets that underwrite the mixed racial history of the Grandissime family itself. This archive is everywhere announced in the book and includes everything from the practice of voodoo by other-wise "untainted" Creole aristocrats to the laughing acknowledgment of why a favorite Grandissime cousin is unlikely to ever take a legal wife. The stately, magisterial violence of Bras-Coupé centers the novel. Here is how the story is introduced to the readers: " 'A very little more than eight years ago,' began Honoré—but not only Honoré, but Raoul also; and not only they, but another earlier on the same day,—Honoré, the fmc. But we shall not exactly follow the words of any one of these" (1988:169).

The narrator's reconstruction is a composite of the voices of the Creole. But he does not simply give us the single, composite story; he gives us the story in the classical terms of democracy—from many, one. And in his use of the word *we*, the reader is again interpellated as an American citizen. The story of Bras-Coupé is thereby shorn of its local inflection and smoothed into an official account. Such an official account might be under-scored by the seemingly conscious self-referential historical or objective quality of the narrative. "Bras-Coupé, they said, had been in Africa, a prince among his people," going on to say "of the voyage little is recorded" (196).

Thus Cable constructs a larger frame to read the significance of

Bras-Coupé. Like the events that structure *The Grandissimes*, the legend of Bras-Coupé is about resistance to assimilation into a new culture. Bras-Coupé is an African prince brought as a slave to Louisiana. He is quickly given to understand that he will have to work on a plantation. When he rebels and refuses, he is made a gamekeeper and accompanies his master all over the plantation. To keep him docile, he is promised a wife—the favored slave Palmyre la Philosophe—but on his wedding night, he becomes drunk and strikes his master. To escape the mandatory punishment of death, Bras-Coupé flees the plantation and hides in "the dismal swamps," a description linking his personal rebellion to the slave revolt of Nat Turner (1988:177). But before Bras-Coupé escapes, he curses the people and crops on the plantation. He cannot be caught by any means, and his curse comes true; the crops of the plantation fail, and the health of all those on the establishment fails. Bras-Coupé is eventually caught and hamstrung, but he will not lift the curse until he is confronted on his deathbed by his owner's wife and her child. As he dies, Cable writes, "the voice failed a moment, the departing hero essayed again; again it failed, he tried once more, lifted his hand, and with an ecstatic, upward smile, whispered, 'To—Africa'—and was gone" (193).

The story of Bras-Coupé is a cultural icon for the Creoles; his effects after he has died are nearly as powerful as his curse was when he was alive. The Grandissimes love to listen to this story; they tell it at the great family gathering, after they have finished the *chanson de negres* and seen the calinda dances. As Charles Swann points out, the Creoles know "that somehow the tale contained the secrets of the culture" (Swann 1987:267). But the story of Bras-Coupé signifies differently for the back and white populations. Its "secret" is that in order to figure themselves as a culture, the Creoles must rewrite the story of race. That the family tells it at the birthday of their most distinguished member reveals that they use the story as a commemorative narrative, which draws them together and gives them an identity as a people.

It is not difficult to see, as I explain later, that the story of Bras-Coupé is a perverse template for white Creoles to express their own discontent with becoming subject to alien American imperial power. Agricola, for example, announces grandly concerning the incipient government of the United States and its perceived plans for total colonization,

English is not a language, sir; it is a jargon! And when this young simpleton Claiborne attempts to force it down the public windpipe in the courts, as I understand he intends, he will fail! Hah! Sir, I know men in this city who would rather eat a dog that speak English! I speak it, but I also speak Choctaw. (1988:48)

Choosing to highlight Choctaw as one of his ancestral languages, Agricola believes that he is guarding the door of racial purity and establishing his family as a unit that moves through history with both integrity and distinction. The fact that the Grandissime clan, indeed all Creoles in this text, already understand themselves as doubled through history should not blind us to the invocation of Lufki-Humma as an originary source. The Grandissimes and their stories are driven by a preoccupation with race. Lufki-Humma is their celebrated foremother and was introduced at the opening ball. But even though Lufki-Humma is an Indian princess, her origination of the Grandissime clan is also an ending for her own clan. This certainly contrasts with the line of descendants that leads to Honoré, fmc. His race does not perish but lives alongside the Grandissimes as an uncanny shadow version of themselves.[5] The Grandissimes can thus claim an originary tie to a North America that is not yet part of the United States, but even in invoking the purity of their descent from the Indian princess, Agricola points to the secret history of racial assimilation that underwrote the French experience of colonization in North America.[6]

Even though the story of Bras-Coupé argues against the possibility of assimilation, it indicates rebellion and acts as a metaphor for the final textual excision of all other characters of color. For example, the chapter immediately following the narrator's retelling of the story of Bras-Coupé is entitled "Paralysis" and is about the fate of the firstborn Honoré. Honoré, fmc, makes a parallel between himself and Toussaint L'Ouverture through the figure of Bras-Coupé when he says, "Ah cannod be one Toussaint l'Ouverture. Ah cannod trah to be. Hiv I trah, I h-only soogceed to be one Bras-Coupé" (1988:196). He speaks of his own powerlessness to change the facts of his existence in New Orleans and focuses on the failure of Bras-Coupé to achieve his freedom.

The parallel between Bras-Coupé and Toussaint L'Ouverture is still instructive if it is turned. While the revolt of this African prince frightened his historical contemporaries, the subsequent story of Bras-Coupé's rebellion thrills his contemporary auditors. The violence of Bras-Coupé's predecessor, Toussaint L'Ouverture, also terrifies the citizens of New Orleans, and it is his rebellion that forced Napoleon, the "dread Corsican," to set Louisiana adrift. For the white creole citizens of 1803 New Orleans, Bras-Coupé represents a pure relationship to self, a pure relationship to social structures, and a pure contempt for the country of the conqueror. For example, when Bras-Coupé is asked for his name upon first arriving at the plantation, he seizes the opportunity to name himself as an unwilling captive, making "himself a type of all Slavery, turning into flesh and blood the truth that all Slavery is maiming" (1988:171). His eventual escape from captivity seems noble, his death patriotic. He becomes the symbol of national and cultural independence for white Creole culture, a status reinforced by his dying words. But even as Toussaint L'Ouverture underwrites Bras-Coupé's rebellion, so Bras-Coupé underwrites the dying words of the

Grandissime patriarch, Agricola Fusilier. Lying on his deathbed, he exhorts his kin to live by the phrase "Louisiana Forever."

The legend of Bras-Coupé and its ramifications for Creole cultural nationalism in the face of American expansion signify quite differently for those characters of color who try to use it to express their dissatisfaction with the conditions of their lives. The characters of Honoré, fmc, and Palmyre la Philosophe, Bras-Coupé's wife, embody the most poignant and violent legacy of Bras-Coupé's life. One character says, for example, that it seems as though the "spirit of Bras-Coupé has gone into Palmyre. She would rather add to his curse than take from it" (1988:188). She recognizes in Bras-Coupé "the gigantic embodiment of her own dark, fierce will, the expanded realization of her own lifetime longing for terrible strength." But she and Honoré, fmc are, unlike Bras-Coupé, nearly voiceless.

Although the genre of local color relies on dialect, the use of various dialects and accents in this novel often conceals the question of who has access to speech. The characters' ability to communicate in a variety of languages is not merely instructive for understanding their twinned colonial and imperial identities; it represents a necessary ability to speak in public, official discourses (and therefore to speak as a citizen) as well as an ability to speak from within their own culture. Part of the symbolic power of Bras-Coupé is his ability to realize himself in language. When he is first asked his name, he replies that it is:

Mioko-Koanga, in French, Bras-Coupé, the Arm Cut Off. Truly it would have been easy to admit, had this been his meaning, that his tribe in losing him, had lost its strong right arm close off at the shoulder; not so easy for his purchaser to allow, if this other was his intent; that the arm which might no longer shake the spear or swing the wooden sword was no better than a useless stump never to be lifted for aught else. But whether easy to allow or not, that was his meaning. He made himself a type of all Slavery, turning into flesh and blood the truth that all Slavery is maiming. (1988:171)

When Bras-Coupé curses the Grandissime family at his wedding, he stands in the hall, "making strange signs and passes and rolling out in wrathful words of his mother tongue what it needed no interpreter to tell his swarming enemies was a voodoo malediction" (1988:181). Bras-Coupé seems to have the power of making his words into deeds, but he also reveals the power imbalances structuring access to language in the novel.

It is therefore instructive to attend to the way black characters appropriate and redeploy the legend of Bras-Coupé. The firstborn Honoré, a wealthy quadroon, feels estranged from the power of Bras-Coupé, but

Palmyre glories in him. Palmyre uses the "arm" of Bras-Coupé to reembody him for her own private and individual revolt. Her appropriation of Bras-Coupé's power is the fulfillment of her initial desire to "show his mighty arm how and when to strike" (1988:178). She chooses to strike at Agricola, patriarch of the Grandissime family, by sending him "the image, in myrtle-wax, moulded and painted with some rude skill, of a negro's bloody arm cut off near the shoulder—a *bras-coupé*—with a dirk grasped in its hand" (314). The figure comports with the text's description of Palmyre, who has metaphorically stood all her life with "dagger drawn." Palmyre's attempt to reembody Bras-Coupé by seizing the sign of his disempowerment in slavery is doomed to failure. As the Grandissime family makes a fetish of the story of Bras-Coupé, Palmyre makes a literal fetish of him, but her creation of this fetish serves only to allow the Grandissimes to finally dispense with him by killing the slave woman who carries the fetish on Palmyre's behalf.

The owner of that slave woman is Honoré, fmc. Honoré, educated in France and an inhabitant of New Orleans for at least as long as his legitimate white half brother, is similarly unable to counter the prevailing racial ideology in white Creole culture. In a passage that deliberately refers to and inverts Bras-Coupé, the free man of color begins, "with many pauses and gropings after word and idiom, to tell with a plaintiveness that seemed to Frowenfeld almost unmanly, the reasons why the people a little of whose blood had been enough to blast his life would never be free by the force of *their own arm*" (1988:195; italics mine). But just as Honoré, fmc, is always described as the specter of his white half brother Honoré, he and Palmyre are also specters of Bras-Coupé. Their separate attempts to fulfill his curse by murdering the patriarch of the Grandissime family bring the story of Bras-Coupé to its final closure and ironically smooth the way for the union of the Creoles and the United States.

The text's narrative of origins highlights the potential danger of slave dialect. While Palmyre and Honoré, fmc, are free quadroons, the character who is ordered to carry the fetish of Bras-Coupé to its destination is not. Clemence, the slave of the free man of color, is caught carrying the fetish by a mob of white Grandissime men. Sure that she can talk her way out of the punishment of lynching, Clemence reminds the men that they all know her well. An itinerant vendor of pastries and cakes, she has entertained the townspeople for years by singing little songs she spontaneously improvises specially for each customer. Clemence's dialect songs contain ironic commentaries about the power imbalances in New Orleans society, but she believes that the colloquial language of her improvisations conceals their import. But as the narrator explains, she presumes too much on her insignificance.

Although the Grandissimes sacrifice Clemence in order to banish the ghost of Bras-Coupé, Clemence's murder does not resonate with the anxieties about assimilation as did the death of the African prince. In formal terms, the narrative doesn't author or authorize Clemence's death. Bras-Coupé becomes an uncanny version of Creole identity; the narrative of his life is revelatory. Everyone in the white creole community who hears or tells it also authors it. The novel demonstrates that the invocation of this story by persons of color signifies to the white creole community not their likeness to white culture or their loyalty to French identity but their secret predisposition for revolt. No one tells Clemence's story except the narrator, and there is no one to punish for her death: "A pistol-shot rang out . . . ; it was never told who fired it" (1988:323).

Clemence's lynching is one of the few events of the novel not framed by multiple tellings or interpretations. Because Clemence is a slave, she is the arm of her master Honoré, fmc. Because Honoré, fmc, is the shadow or specter of the racial divisions that trouble the Grandissime family, he cannot afford to carry Bras-Coupé's legacy. Clemence carries the fetish of Bras-Coupé's to bewitch Agricola. but she has no motivation for so doing and no character except what slavery gives to her. "To Clemence the order of society was nothing. No upheaval could reach to the depth to which she was sunk. It is true, she was one of the population. She had certain affections toward people and places; but they were not of a consuming sort" (1988:251). As Bras-Coupé "made himself a type of all slavery," Clemence, too, makes herself, but not representatively, only performatively. Clemence is a gossip, a window—like Frowenfeld's store—through which all the news of the street comes. She has no interior that can be measured. She makes herself over for everyone that she meets:

She sold some of her goods to Casa Calvo's Spanish guard and sang them a Spanish song; some to Claiborne's soldiers and sang them Yankee Doodle with unclean words of her own inspiration, which evoked true soldiers' laughter; some to a priest at his window, exchanging with him a pious comment or two. (252)

I have argued that the white Creole characters in the text lack interiority because they all have racial and historical doubles that embody the hidden genealogy of Creole culture, but Clemence's lack of interiority also might be measured against a common stereotype of slaves. Writer Lafcadio Hearn, Cable's friend and sometime collaborator, expresses the commonly held idea that black creole servant girls

are consummate actresses, and can deceive even the elect. They can ape humility, simulate affection, pretend ignorance, and feign sorrow so that the imitation is really better than the reality would be, and serves the same purpose. They can tell a lie with the prettiest grace imaginable, or tell a truth in such a manner that it appears to be a lie. (Hearn 1923:188)

Such observations allow us to see that while white characters are doubled externally, Cable's attempts to deal with black characters forces him to construct them not as doubled but as duplicitous. They possess a deep and unreachable interior life shaped by the external and immovable fact of slavery. Clemence is thus a "study" to the narrator. It is one of his insistences on authenticity that he pretends not to know anything about her. Distancing himself from her, he writes that "We know she was a constant singer and laugher" (Cable 1988:251). Clemence's language has no power. While Bras-Coupé terrifies the Creole by bringing down a voodoo curse, Clemence uses the worst curse possible and the most ineffective. As she sees that she is near to being lynched, she cries out, "You ain' got no mo' biznis to do me so 'an if I was a white 'oman! You dassent tek a white 'oman out'n de Pa'sh Pris'n an' do 'er so!" (322). Doubling herself with a white woman makes explicit the racial categories that must remain separate if the Creole is to survive as a subject of the U.S. government. The narrator's decision to back away from Clemence as if she were no more than a tragic anomaly in the events of the novel is part of his general strategy of distancing himself from the narrative in its entirety. While this text has trouble beginning, it has no trouble ending. By its conclusion, its multiple beginnings have been neatly stitched together into a coherent whole.

George Marcus writes that the doubled self is a construction that challenges the unity of the main ideological premise of Western bourgeois culture—that the self is irreducible and an autonomous actor in everyday life. The double self questions the coherence of personal identity "which economic, political, and legal institutions assume, and on which cultural understandings of mental health, character, and personal virtue are established in everyday life" (Marcus 1990:191). The tropes of exteriority in *The Grandissimes* and the narrative's doubling of every white character with a black character presents the Grandissimes' obsession with Bras-Coupé as an obsession about the purity of their family. The ending of the book smoothes over the many Creole voices into a composite linear voice and expels the racialized doubles from the community of New Orleans. The novel ends with a series of marriages that open the family to a new culture and also attempt to purge it of racial mixing.

The Grandissimes is difficult to classify formally, but it is, at the very least, a historical novel, as it delineates and artificially resolves an historical crisis. The novel ends with the main characters marrying each other and with New Orleans joining the United States. Bluff, pompous Agricola Fusilier, the standard bearer of the sentiments of the French Revolution, dies with the words "Louisiana Forever" on his lips. But the sentiment dies with him. Although his kin order that this phrase be carved on his tombstone, they also agree, when visiting this grave, that "forever seemed a long time."

The process of Americanization is not easy. U.S. citizenship is finally the way to make whole the doubled self; it offers a standard, linear time, a single national identity to organize all facts. There is now "one logical language" located in a single, logical, continuous space (Gellner 1983: 20). The effect of Americanization in the text can be measured by U.S. immigrant Joseph Frowenfeld's increasing skill at understanding the appropriate family relations of his new Creole friends. This should not be surprising. As Etienne Balibar writes, "The history of nations, beginning with our own, is always already presented to us in the form of a narrative which attributes to these entities the continuity of a subject" (Balibar and Wallerstein 1991:68).

The newly Americanized text offers a new kind of subjectivity to its characters and in a uniquely suited ideological language: economics and capital. The plantation of the Nancanou women is restored, and the two Honorés are made one through a business partnership. On the sign of the family business is now simply written "Grandissime Frères." These business settlements are cemented by the marriage of Honoré and Aurora, an act that ends the time-honored family feud, thus making whole again the ancestral unity of the two houses of the Grandissimes. Interestingly, this marriage is sealed by another, historical prophecy. Old Agricola, the last standard bearer of Louisiana's independence, is forced to admit that he promised the union of these two long ago, so in marrying they consent a history written without their knowledge. Reconstruction and restitution provoked by imminent Americanization are the fulfillment of history, its logical terminus. The final marriage is that between Frowenfeld and Clotilde. This is even more matter of fact; while they certainly seem to love each other, their relationship is figured as strictly contractual. The rhetoric of their union is that of the business partnership. The narrator informs us that the two signed "regular articles of co-partnership, blushing frightfully" (Cable 1988:286). In addition to the copartnership, which Clotilde begins by investing her plantation economy inheritance in the American pharmacy, the marriage joins the American citizen and the Creole.

Of course, all cannot end happily. There are still two people who cannot be incorporated into the new family and economic partnerships. Smoothing over the differences of the white characters demonstrates that seemingly national divisions, such as French or American, can be translated into ethnic terminology. Clotilde's Frenchness will be roughly equivalent to Frowenfeld's Germanness in this partnership. This newly minted ethnicity does not extend to race, however. Although Honoré Grandissime, fmc's money literally underwrites the continuing status of the Grandissimes in America, it also brings him into the very national economy that will strip him of his place as a citizen of New Orleans. Palmyre and Honoré, fmc, remain outsiders until the end and ultimately are shipped away conveniently to France. The marriage of these two characters seems likely, since Honoré, fmc, tried to convince Palmyre to marry him throughout the text. Their marriage is thematically prevented by the shadow of both Bras-Coupé and the white Creole Honoré. Whatever restitution there is for Palmyre and Honoré, fmc, can only be financial. They are completely excluded from the novel's construction of American citizens. Especially interesting is their relation to the novel's rendering of Creole tales. At the end of the novel, the two have sailed away to France, and when they are recalled, it is within the confines of a romantic story of thwarted love. Describing their fates, the narrator quickly introduces a boat captain who saw the two in Paris. The text deploys the familiar rhetoric of the romance: "Did the brig-master never see the woman again? He always waited for this question to be asked him, in order to state the more impressively that he did" (Cable 1988:331).

When it enters the United States, Louisiana displaces its two silent citizens. As Joseph Frowenfeld bitterly notes, the community of New Orleans supported three distinct but related ways of constructing its people: nation, race, and caste. It is into this murky last territory that Palmyre and Honoré, fmc, were categorized under French law. As free people of color, they occupied an established position in Creole society. But once Louisiana was sold, their status changed, and they became second-class citizens in a strict American hierarchy rather than marginal figures in the more fluid European racial schematization. Because the United States has no such category to describe its people, Honoré and Palmyre must be reinscribed into their new nation as black and thus deprived of even the marginal self-representation that they had in New Orleans. They become commodities and not subjects. And so in the shipbuilder's narrative, Palmyre Philosophe becomes the romantic "Madame Inconnue" of France (331).

All the characters are thus accounted for in a brisk and straightforward way. The jagged layers of history, the doubled identities, and the hidden history of racial rebellion have been smoothed into one logical narrative space, submerged into the narrator's national voice. Yet the Creole characters, although purified racially in the terms of the text, are still without conventional literary aspects of interiority. At the beginning of the text, the Creole was without interiority because he or she was constructed through histories, not within a single tradition. Here, the Creole has no interiority because he or she has been reconstructed as a type. The intrusion of the narrator in the final chapters seems to offer us an epilogue, neatly laid out and altogether distanced. Catherine Belsey writes that the epilogue of nineteenth-century novels describes

the new order, now understood to be static. . . . Harmony has been re-established through the redistribution of the signifiers into a new system of differences which

Social Equality! What a godsend it would be if the advocates of the old Southern regime could only see that the color line points straight in the direction of social equality by tending toward the equalization of all whites on one side of the line and of all blacks on the other. We may reach the moon some day, not social equality. (Cable, "The Freedman's Case in Equity," 1885:34)

Cable later discusses the differences between these two forms of recognition in "The Silent South":

All the relations of life that go by *impersonal right* are Civil relations. All that go by *personal choice* are Social relations. The one is all of right, it makes no difference who we are; the other is all of choice, and it makes all the difference who we are; and it is no little fault against ourselves as well as others, to make confusion between the two relations. For the one we make laws; for the other every one consults his own pleasure. (Cable, "The Silent South," 1885:53)

But even in distinguishing between civil relations and social relations, Cable reaffirms the system that allows the partnership of the white and black Honoré—Grandissime frères—at the end of the novel to paradoxically *remove* the black Honoré from the Grandissime family. The impersonal triumph is recoded as the lack of personhood and demonstrates again that the foundation of the Creole local-color figure is predicated on the excision of those black characters that underwrite the sense of the Creole as a person with " 'character, intelligence, and property' " that is, the kind of character fit to rule or represent himself (Cable, "The Silent South," 1885:78).

5

Disorienting Regionalism

Jacob Riis, the City, and the Chinese Question

In the first two sections of this book, I argued against the critical consensus that pastoral regionalism turns away from the social problems attending capital and imperial expansion. My readings assert that the genre of regional writing helped make sense of these problems by narrating figures of cultural difference as potential participants in national culture. In this reading, genteel regional fiction negotiates literary representations of persons who are illegible in the logic of realist literature, describing them as familiar subjects in familiar literary terms. Pastoral regionalism is thus the signal genre for the accommodation of ethnicity in American fiction and culture. In this final section, I turn to urban local-color fiction. I look at Jacob Riis's 1890 *How the Other Half Lives* (*HtOHL*), and in the following chapter I look at novels about Tammany Hall.

By turning to urban fiction, I close the circle of this project. As we have seen in writers like Jewett, Garland, and Frederic, the roots of general problems in industrial capitalism (such as immigration and bourgeois self-estrangement) are attributed to eastern cities. The crises in identity and community that these urban problems evoke become the backdrop for pastoral regionalism's master plot. While I have been asking how urban material is processed in outlying locations, here I ask whether regionalism's project had affinities with urban texts that also interrogate the same nexus of location, identity, and community. I contend that pastoral and urban fictions share narrative strategies, relying on similar ideas about the local's relation to the national. Urban and pastoral local color—particularly slumming literature—share strategies by which the observer/narrator arrives at a sense of individual wholeness by contrasting his or her sense of self with that of strangers or foreigners.

Urban local color's narrative practice of slumming and pastoral regionalism's practice of tourism each rely on a narrator's ability to occupy the twinned position of participant and observer. The two genres share similar techniques that draw on tourism and observation: a reliance on descriptions of folkways, the use of dialect, the imaginative exchange of natives and strangers. By privileging the tension between estranged narrators and strange subjects, pastoral and urban regionalism rely on similar appeals to the audiences' desire for travel and for authentic experience.

Urban local color is not exactly parallel to pastoral regionalism. Rather, urban local color replaces past/temporality with space/proximity, engaging the very historical facts that pastoral local color suppresses. Peopling the narratives of urban local color are "real" strangers: immigrants, tramps, workers, partially assimilated ethnic populations. In depicting cultural and ethnic differences that exist simultaneously with a standard, if equally fictional, American middle-class experience, urban local color makes the stranger and the native not merely *likenesses* of each other but *like* each other. Pastoral regionalism suggests that cultural difference might be compatible with American political citizenship, but urban local color phrases that possibility negatively. Cultural difference might produce political difference and so must be disarticulated from ideas of American citizenship.

I believe that any analysis of Riis will bear out a convergence of narrative techniques between urban and pastoral regionalism, but it is equally important to note the similarities in their readership. The difference is that in pastoral regionalism, the reader—middle class, white, and urban—is asked to *recollect* the past, with all the market implications that entails. In urban local color, though, the same normative audience is asked to *reform*—to take an active role in the production of ethnicity, community, and space. The motivation behind urban local color was not, then, to assuage the reader but to scandalize and recruit. The same audiences likely to read pastoral regional fiction were, if not identical to the bourgeois readers of reform journalism like that of Jacob Riis interpolated as nearly identical through pastoral and urban regionalism's shared narrative strategies. The object of urban local color was not to preserve or to chart the survival of distinct local traits but to reform cultural differences into political homogeneity.

Cultural and political differences, uneasily balanced around figures of ethnicity, are always in conflict, always poised *temporally* to undermine each other. In *HtOHL*, Riis's emphasis on ethnic differences seems discordant next to his overall project of political reform—reforming the body politic as well as reforming immigrant communities to participate in that body. Before I analyze *HtOHL*, I consider the dynamics of slumming, the strategies that urban local color and pastoral local color share, and then ask what these strategies tell us about the project of accounting for cultural diversity in a public sphere of shared readers. In particular, I want to see how Jacob Riis recruits discourses of public and private to describe "inner" qualities of ethnicity. What relation does "inner" life have to a project of reform or to an idea of assimilation?

I begin with a parallel between urban local color's slumming and pastoral regionalism's tourism. Urban local color's genealogy has roots in reform efforts and sensational journalism, as well as infamous literary antecedents such as U.S. serializations of urban life that borrow from Eugene Sue's *Mysteries* and precursors like Charles Loring Brace's *Dangerous Classes and Fifty Years Work among Them*.[1] Like its gentle country cousin, urban local color shares an interest in legislating the value of citizens, property, and local culture. Alan Trachtenberg's description of literary slumming, for example, points out the role of literary slumming in publicizing the city and the reporter:

Exploration of forbidden and menacing spaces emerged in the 1890's as a leading mode of the dailies, making spectacles of "the nether side of New York" or "the other half." The reporter appeared now often as a performer, one who ventured into alien streets and habitations, perhaps in disguise, and returned with a tale, a personal story of the dark underside of the city. (Trachtenberg 1982b:126)

Like pastoral regionalism, the sketches of slumming reporters prompted audiences to go to see for themselves the picturesque poverty of street life in New York. The connection between the tales of the exotic and the tourism those tales inspired formed the matrix of the market economy and the narrative economy of regional fiction. The reasons driving participation in slumming expeditions (whether professional or amateur) matter less to this argument than the effect that this tourism had on the potential "reality" of the subjects being observed. Accordingly, the most fully realized figure in Trachtenberg's description is the reporter, and his reality is paradoxically underscored by his ability to assume the habits and local knowledge of the "unreal" subjects under observation.

The reporter's personal story of the awful city, offered to readers like a rare and redemptive object, is affiliated with the circulation of authenticity and private experience that I traced in pastoral regionalism. As I indicated, although the two are derived from different literary genealogies, the development of a literary venue for urban local color and the literary arena for pastoral regionalism point to the concomitant development of a niche marketing of the local. In his study of the changes in newspaper and magazine production and consumption in the late nineteenth century, Christopher Wilson notes that one of the results of news standardization for the metropolitan reporter was the "growing value of *local* urban news, a demand which was itself a by-product of the new prominence of collective national news gathering" (Wilson 1985:33).[2] The stress on local news required a particular kind of occulted knowledge.

Tourism is only the first, most obvious structural parallel between pastoral regionalists and urban local-color writers. Richard Brodhead pointed out the ways in which regional writing provided a point of literary access to those populations most often excluded from the profession. Wilson makes a similar argument about the new celebrity reporters:

> The modern professionalized notion of authorship especially answered longings which derived from two sources: the widespread "crisis of authority" in the late nineteenth century and the desire of "outsiders" to enter the American mainstream through emerging entertainment industries . . . literary professionalism was hardly imposed by a conspiracy of publishers and editors upon an unwilling or passive populace of writers; on the contrary, many sought modern authorship as a way "up" or "out." (Wilson 1985:14)

Wilson's observations are particularly relevant to those writers who made their fame and fortune chronicling the other half.

While writers like Sarah Orne Jewett and Gertrude Atherton might have been able to cash in on local knowledge in order to gain access to a literary establishment that might have otherwise considered them of minor interest at best, urban local color reveals the mechanism by which an author gains access to—and authority over—public culture more broadly. As other critics have observed, the minor status of regional writing and the generally minor status of women writers in the late nineteenth century converge in productive ways through the circuit of pastoral local color.[3] The emergence of the celebrity reporter and the "crisis" of immigration and the other half point to a similar convergence: marginalized communities struggling for political recognition and writers eager to distinguish themselves by recruiting discourses of community, culture, and public anxiety in order to enter public life as professional writers. But the knowledge that writers needed to write urban local color is significantly different from the knowledge that one needs to write pastoral regionalism.

Stephen Crane is a logical beginning for examining the regional writing of the city. Although many writers of the late nineteenth century devoted some time to documenting the ethnic chaos of the city—I am thinking here of the Marches' search for an apartment in William Dean Howells's *A Hazard of New Fortunes* or Henry James's depiction of a polyglot New York in *The American Scene*—Stephen Crane is nearly a perfect model of Wilson's entrepreneurial reporter. Out to make himself a celebrity through a new profession reliant on observation, he is at once reformer, *flâneur*, and reporter. He is therefore at the center of a series of useful models to interrogate the conjunction between the literary and the material. While Crane wrote slumming fiction and sold it to a hungry audience, it is not clear that he finds the curiosity of the middle- and upper-class readers of his sketches to be worthy. In fact, at moments it seems clear that he parodies and inverts his audience's desire to see the objects in the literary curio cabinet of the slums. Crane's texts foreground the labor of representing an other whose identity is especially dangerous because of its spatial proximity to the middle classes. In his fiction, Crane makes the double gesture of satisfying his audience's desires while demonstrating that its true object of desire is unobtainable precisely because it violates a fictional economy by being *too real*.4

Parodies of the literary impulse to stare at the poor are apparent in the local-color sketches that Crane wrote for the *New York Press*. The two sketches that I am particularly interested in are "An Experiment in Misery" and "An Experiment in Luxury."5 Written in 1894, the sketches are fictionalized accounts of how an anonymous young man gathers material in the city in order to write his own private local-color sketches. In "An Experiment in Misery," Crane places his anonymous but sincere young man next to a tramp sleeping in the street. The young man wonders aloud what this tramp must be feeling, and his older companion retorts that he "can tell nothing of it" unless he is in the same condition, remarking dismissively, "It is idle to speculate about it from this distance" (Crane 1986:34:).6 The word *distance* is compelling here. Clearly, the two are physically very close to the tramp in the street. But the distance from which they speculate (and I stress again the doubled economies of speculation, as I did in the second chapter of this book) is immense. Looking at and speculating about the condition of the tramp cannot return to the young man what he really wants—understanding of the plight of the urban poor. Ultimately, he decides that he must, like pastoral regional narrators, come as close as possible to the region's real natives in order to more fully "see this and make part of it." The young man tells his friend, "I think I'll try it. Rags and tatters, you know, a couple of dimes, and hungry, too, if possible. Perhaps I could discover his point of view or something near it" (34). Then, repeating the tone of both distance and "authenticity," the omniscient narrator of the sketch tells us, "From those words begins this veracious narrative of an experiment in misery" (34). The narrative voice subsides, and the drama of the young man is highlighted. After being outfitted as a tramp by an artist, the youth "went forth to try to eat as the tramp may eat, and sleep as the wanderers sleep" (34). Crane focuses on the collector of regional stories; his emphasis that it is an artist who outfits the young man acknowledges that the young man perceives the poor as picturesque objects of pity, and the young man's use of the word *discover* situates him in a discourse of anthropology.

In "An Experiment in Luxury," the companion piece to "An Experiment in Misery," the same young man in a different disguise penetrates the inner sanctum of the home of a wealthy man. He feels more acutely the sensation of not belonging, a sense of falseness in the manner in which he gains entrance to the home of the wealthy people. Having been admitted by a supercilious butler, the young man thinks, "He was an invader with a shamed face, a man who had come to steal certain colors, forms, impressions that were not his. He had a dim thought that some one might come to tell him to begone" (Crane 1986:45).

These sketches are not about the people the young man *befriends* but about the people the young man *becomes*. Nonetheless, "An Experiment in Luxury" limits the possible subject positions he can occupy or imagine. As I have noted and as the language clearly reveals, the stories are about the process of collecting folklore. The literary slummer, a middle-class man, inadvertently demonstrates that identity in urban locations is relational and locational. Depending on what one wears and where one stands, one is perceived to be either a tramp or a millionaire. Yet the narrator does not feel comfortable passing as a wealthy man. In fact, cowering before the butler, the anonymous social experimenter feels like a tramp in the house of the wealthy. His inability to maintain his reportorial distance in this final sketch shows us that there has been a breakdown in the project of surveillance and that the task of becoming *like* someone becomes uncomfortably like becoming that person. The task of local color is the province of the middle classes only. It is telling that the young man feels that he is "invading" the inner sanctum of wealth. He does not feel as though he is stealing from the poor, because for literary slummers, the poor are in fact the true invaders of the city, and *they* are stealing, sometimes quite literally, as he discovers, from people like him.

Similarly, the kind of enrichment available to the young man in the house of the wealthy, characterized by "colors, forms, impressions," points to a relationship mediated by culture, not economics. This field of culture throws into relief the kind of culturalized interest in the poor that helped bolster the economic and political reforms that were contemporary with literary slumming. But Crane's reliance on style as the point of authentic access to culture indicates the contradiction in the idea of authenticity for which his characters and his larger audiences might be searching. Referring to Crane's style of parody, Michael Davitt Bell says that "the universal condition of the world of Crane's fiction . . . is that all of its styles are imitations, tawdry recyclings of outworn and ill-understood originals. Nothing, here, can be experienced in itself" (Bell 1993:139).

There is a similarly ironized strategy of pastoral regionalism in Crane's sketch "Stephen Crane in Minetta Lane, One of Gotham's Most Notorious Thoroughfares" (Crane 1986).[7] This time, in the persona of a tired news reporter, Crane tries to gather material on the titillating crime of Minetta Lane, rumored to be a particularly dangerous and exotic area of the city. Crane writes, "Indeed, it is difficult to find people now who remember the old gorgeous days, although it is but two years since the Lane shone with sin like a new headlight. But after a search the reporter found three" (180). About Mammy Ross, one of the three specimens Crane finds and "one of the last relics of the days of slaughter," Crane writes: "Her reminiscences, at once maimed and reconstructed, have been treasured by old Mammy as carefully, as tenderly, as if they were the various little tokens of an early love" (182).

This image of the old reprobate—a "relic"—remembering her days of crime by her kitchen stove so clearly parallels pastoral regionalism's evocation of an old matriarch sitting and rocking by the fire that the rest of the language seems only to seal the comparison. The reminiscences, here of neighborhood crime rather than village celebrations, are reconstructed in the same dim half-light of the most sentimental of regions. The residents of Minetta Lane recall its glory days of crime and drunkenness, and remember how Minetta Lane used to be a region unto itself, entirely black and feared by the police and citizens of other neighborhoods. They miss the old days and realize that things "just aren't like they used to be." Part of their feeling of loss is derived from the fact that they are being squeezed out of the region. The complaints about the new people moving into the neighborhood resonate with the complaints of crotchety old villagers muttering about invading city folk. But the complaints, however satirically presented, demonstrate that nostalgia was already a tired convention.

Stephen Crane's journalistic reconstruction of Mammy Ross's memories seems intended to force his audience to read the sketch "regionally"—that is, to recognize the possibility of nostalgia for a community that has its own internal logic but whose identity is now fading away under the city's pressures. Here Crane equates his public's desire for the spectacular sinfulness of the urban experience with their desire for the innocence of the pastoral experience. By locating such "innocence" in the perilous city that is its opposite, Crane offers an oblique commentary on middle-class taste for regional fictions. In such an ironic schematization of pastoral or local innocence, the figure of "puzzling blankness"—a term I used in the third chapter to talk about the enigmatic lack of interiority in figures of difference—is the middle class as a whole, seeking to counteract what Jackson Lears calls a pervasive sense of weightlessness by consuming the experience of more "real" or more primitive peoples. In staging such a parodic inversion, Crane argues that the value of the region and a generalized nostalgia for it cannot be understood as generated by any individual region. Rather, value is arbitrated by the narration of regional experience. The meaning of the region is relational, and as we shall see for Jacob Riis, the meaning of ethnicity is relational as well. As Michael Bell writes: "what is still very much at issue is the relationship between established styles and authentic experience—or the scarcity and fragility of authentic experience in a world dominated *by* established styles" (Bell 1993:145).

Bell's argument about the recognizable style of slumming illuminates reviews of Crane's sketches. Many of them note a quality of pictorial representation underpinning Crane's presentation of the poor. The *San Francisco Argonaut* noted on July 15, 1896, about Crane's *Maggie* that the "scenes" are not "the kind of beautiful pictures to hang on memory's wall" (Stallman 1972:106), and the *Book Buyer* wrote in the same month that *Maggie* is a sequence of "extraordinary tableaux" in which the "selection of forcible and picturesque words, the same blinding glare of primary colors flashing out into a panorama of illumination" mirrors his previous work (107). The reviewer also asserted that "there is nothing amazing in a writer's knowledge of slum life of New York" (108). Another contemporary reviewer says authoritatively (also in the same month and year) in New York's *Commercial Advertiser* that "Mr. Crane has discovered those localities and revealed them to the astonished gaze of the world for the first time" (109).

Taking a different tack from these reviews—which note a kind of artistic and stylized version of the other half, such as the *Indianapolis News* (August 14, 1896) reviewer's dry advice that Crane "might at least learn to blend his colors a little" (Stallman 1972:116)—are those praising Crane's veracity. The *Boston Courier*'s June 1896 review of *Maggie* states that

the coloring of the whole story is deeply defined and real. We meet with people in books that we would shun upon the streets, and it is well if we do not draw our literary skirts aside from them, for it is absolutely necessary to us that we know something of "how the other half lives," even if we must learn the same from books . . . [Crane] realized this, for he lifts his pen suddenly as if in anticipation of the pure reality, the missionary angel of real life, that his abrupt endings would suggest. (110)

In a review of "George's Mother" in the June 1896 number of *Critic*, the reviewer hits the same notes of "realism," saying that Crane "simply turns on the light, and we perceive at once what the actual conditions of life are to the other nine-tenths in New York" (Stallman 1972:111). A similar review from the *San Francisco Wave* (July 4, 1896) argues that *Maggie* is not "a single carefully composed painting, serious, finished, scrupulously studied, but rather scores and scores of tiny flashlight photographs, instantaneous, caught, as it were, on the run" (119).

When Crane's reviewers of his tales of New York's Bowery insist on a certain level of verisimilitude or detect a kind of authorial self-reflexivity, they draw on the already well-known conventions surrounding the presentation of the other half. Some of these conventions, as I have argued, are drawn from the world of the reporter, but many of those scandalized responses link the reporter's exposé to the general aims of Progressive reforms. Indeed, accounts of slumming obtained some of their power from the standard reform efforts that cast the ethnic populations and the working class as dangerous to public health, public morals, and public democratic life. Slumming texts worked by highlighting the least assimilable aspects of ethnic populations, aspects that seemed to make the working poor "naturally" different from the middle-class Americans, who in turn felt both threatened and titillated by such differences. But the "natural" differences of the urban poor seemed most ready for reform. In this paradox is the crux of the reformers' difficulty in differentiating between the traits of ethnic groups and the inner life of the individual ethnic subject.

In his 1890 reform text *HtOHL*, Jacob Riis's narrative voice assumes authority over the city as a whole, drawing boundaries and maps. But Riis's authority is problematized at the level of the local when he describes the various populations of each neighborhood. In order to create local descriptions and snapshots and to maintain local authority, Riis's text follows the conventions of the urban exposé that informed Stephen Crane's fiction, conventions that were themselves par of a larger representational economy of regional fiction. Unlike pastoral regional writers, Riis relies on the narrative techniques of spatialization over temporalization. Doing so allows him to attach his vignettes about the customs and lives of immigrants to larger and placeless institutions and ideas like the law, government, morals, and citizenship. His local regional tactics allow him to construct a general idea of reform, an idea that follows a kind of superlogic in being rooted in local terms and on local ground.

Jacob Riis, sometime police reporter and celebrity reformer, was one of the late nineteenth century's most tireless speakers on the problems of urban poverty. In *HtOHL*, his arranging and collecting authorial hand marks all the information he gathers, and his narrative first-person voice is everywhere in the prose. His intrusive and guiding first-person narrative "I" (and photographic "eye") grounds and supports his readers as he takes them through the "other half." Although its ostensible subject is tenement reform, the text itself seems to be a primer for the authority to move between and within sections of the city. Beginning with the initial map-making metaphors that Riis employs, to the actual maps and blueprints he provides, the text is like a tour through mysterious foreign lands.

Riis's narrative strategy bears the marks of pastoral regionalism's cultural/political interchange, but his observation of local customs or house-hold economies is remarkably uninterested in preserving the cultures of his ethnic subjects. The ethnic subject, however, is still inflected by elements drawn from regional fiction and a regional sensibility, and the power imbalances between the stranger and the native are even greater than in the pastoral region. This is especially evident when we discover that the specific knowledge of communities in the metropolis is unidirectional; that is, there is no exchange between the observer and the subject. The subject of urban local color, unlike that of pastoral regionalism, has no knowledge that he or she wishes or needs to impart to the observer. No folkways or lessons internal to the urban communities that Riis describes are offered to readers as intrinsically valuable.

The most famous aspect of the text is the photographs Riis uses to support and to verify his narrative. The photographs mimic the narrative, and taken together, they suggest that the text's organizational and narrative strategy is driven by surveillance. Images of individuals and photographs of interiors or street culture allow the photographs to help make the interior of various ethnic groups visible and legible according to a script of how character itself could be understood. Drawing on the popular archive of photography as a "universal language" that can make the invisible visible and a sitter or place comprehensible, the photographs illuminate not just the ideological points Riis wishes to make about the constitution and disposition of the "other half." They also naturalize the archive of representation being used to constitute the other half in ethnic groups.[8]

The combination of photographs and vignettes and maps and statistics make *HtOHL* about the practice of looking itself, rather than about explaining or parroting the objects being observed. The text of Riis's *HtOHL* is about the idea that cultural identity is itself like an individual subject and that it can be reformed and understood exactly as character would be to the realist writer. But the subtext of Jacob Riis's work—even given that he indulges in every kind of essentializing racial stereotyping in order to *place* his subjects—is that identity itself is locational. It is a matter of perspective, a matter of where one stands, bearing out William Boelhower's contention that "neither the concept of 'American' nor that of 'ethnic' is separately definable, for neither is an immediately given or individual entity in itself" (Boelhower 1987:20). The text asserts that perception and perceptual evidence are the keys to the upper half's knowing or understanding the "other" half, and to this end, surveillance is the strongest narrative strategy. But ocular evidence is often unstable in this text, and as I shall demonstrate, Riis draws on it selectively.

As a writer and photographer, Riis wants to show not just environmental conditions; he is also interested in perspective as an organizational strategy. In describing urban problems, Riis more than once falls back on a variation of this phrase: "It depends on the angle from which one sees it" (1971:56). Riis divides his study between descriptions and pictures made at street level and generalizations made from a "bird's eye view." Riis moves easily from being an impassioned reporter, searching out and presenting facts that only he can know, to being an all-seeing eye, disseminating information that is both particular—it takes an overview to see—and general—it is constitutive of the very metropolis itself. For example, describing for us the territory of the Bend, he writes:

The whole district is a maze of narrow often unsuspected passage-ways—necessarily, for there is scarce a lot that has not two, three, or four tenements upon it, swarming with unwholesome crowds. What a bird's-eye view of "The Bend" would be like is a matter of bewildering conjecture. Its everyday appearance, as seen from the corner of Bayard Street on a sunny day, is one of the sights of New York. (1971:49)

To make sense of the area, Riis must figuratively try to survey it from above—a "bird's-eye view"—and to observe it from street level. In this passage, Riis shows a city within a city, full of tenements and neighborhoods that cannot be detected simply by looking. Riis's text breaks down the city, making it plain and visible. He stakes out the "secret city," preventing the use of city space in "unofficial" or subversive ways. For example, he happily reports the closing of an unofficial roadway on Cherry Street, noting about its previous function: "It is on record that the sewers were chosen as a short cut habitually by residents of the court whose business lay on the line of them, near a manhole, perhaps" (1971:32). The secret roadway that cannot be seen from either street level or from the bird's eye view also determines Riis's imagination of the population of the metropolis. Riis illuminates this hidden city because it can be read as a space that can be, when made visible and put "on record," reabsorbed into the official city. Likewise, he notes the "secret byways" in the back alleys (34) and the "winding ways and passages" of young thieves, which makes the police's pursuit impossible (176).

Even by looking at the table of contents, we can see that Riis's organizing strategy is to make sense of the "hidden city." He moves from a bird's-eye view of the history of the tenement in the first two chapters, to "The Mixed Herd" in the third, slowly differentiating and distinguishing. In quick succession after this come the chapters on individual ethnic groups and ghettos, which might be seen as chapters privileging the view from street level. He begins with the totalizing view of seeing the city as a whole as "this queer conglomerate mass of heterogeneous elements" to a place in which "one may find for the asking an Italian, a German, a French, African, Spanish, Bohemian, Russian, Scandinavian, Jewish, and Chinese colony" (1971:19). In the third chapter, he glosses his distinction between

the city as a whole and the character of individual neighborhoods by supplying an image of a color-coded map, writing that "a map of the city, colored to designate nationalities, would show more stripes than on the skin
of a zebra, and more colors than any rainbow" (20), and he underscores
this metaphor by correlating the map with a summary of the racial characteristics of all the ethnic groups living in the city.

As places are mapped and given a distinct character, people are placed
in categories as well. Riis breaks up "The Mixed Herd" into distinct ethnicities—the chapters take up, among others, Jews, Italians, Bohemians,
and Chinese. It is when he begins to delineate the different ethnic groups
into neighborhoods or colonies that he makes gestures toward a generalized imperial ideology. In "The Mixed Crowd," Riis writes,

As emigration from east to west follows the latitude, so does the foreign influx in
New York distribute itself along certain well-defined lines that waver and break
only under the stronger pressure of a more gregarious race or the encroachments
of inexorable business. A feeling of dependence upon mutual effort, natural to
strangers in a strange land unacquainted with its language and customs, suffi-
ciently accounts for this. (1971:20)

His attempt to "account" for the patterns of immigrant demographics
and population distribution in general throughout the city of New York
is animated by his narrative attempt to "account" for the character of the
inhabitants of each ethnic group. The seeming incoherence between his
professionalized persona as a statistician and his persona as a storytelling
narrator can be reconciled when looking at the shared political agenda
behind these different accounts.

Riis's ambivalent narrative persona stages knowledge of the poor and
of the city in a variety of ways and thus stages knowledge about the "reality" of life in the city as a product of various kinds of expertise. Riis's ideas
about the necessity of making maps and showing the geography of the city
are an important element of his creation of specific regions of the city.
Here his expertise is that of the professional Progressive reformer, relying
on objective data, external evidence. Pastoral regionalism has no boundaries, and one needs no map to return; the old homestead, perfectly preserved in memory, has no beginning and no end. But urban regions are
clearly marked and physically delimited. Riis draws on such language to
map out the different sections of New York. "We have crossed the boundary into the Seventh Ward" (1971:36), he informs his readers, and later
he crosses more boundaries, enters colonies, turns corners, strolls through
ghettos, over lines, even into regions. The text itself is structured as coher-
ently as Riis claims the city should be.

Riis's introduction to the inhabitants of the various neighborhoods,
though, relies on the personal expertise of a narrator of pastoral region-

alism. Riis positions himself as a reader's guide, although he is himself a stranger visiting and investigating the strange and foreign territories of the slums' different sections. He balances his position as both outsider and insider by making his *readers* the true strangers—the more recent intruders, ranked according to how recently they arrived, just as immigrants themselves were categorized. In many of his illustrative vignettes, he invites the reader into the streets and homes of exotic foreigners with elaborate verbal instructions that literally guide them through geography of the book and the city. Maren Stange noted the conjunction between his proprietary imperialism and his technique of surveillance:

> Riis's representation of the touristic point of view offered a "respectable" perspective on the photographs he showed; in addition, it helped him further flatter his audience, implicitly assuring them that they were the "half" designated by history and progress to colonize and dominate . . . by conflating the language and perspective of geographical inventory and settlement with that of social surveillance and control, Riis was able to imply as well that his audience's mobile and "colonial" position in relation to the slums it "visited" was a natural one. (Stange 1989:17–18)

Such a narrative position looks, in its ambivalent identification with the subjects of observation and the anticipated audience of the text, like the narrative position of a regionalist narrator.

For example, in the section "The Down Town Back Alleys," Riis writes about a tenement called "The Ship" that it has been "famous for fifty years as a ramshackle tenement filled with the oddest crowd. No one knows why it is called 'The Ship,' though there is a tradition that once the river came clear up here" (1971:38). After that little bit of local historiography, Riis writes that readers should put a face on the rumors, test the street gossip about the tenants, and *see for themselves*. And just as we are prepared for a kind of bland description or a barrage of statistics, not uncommon occurrences in the text, Riis writes about the tenement house, "Suppose we look into one?" (38). As he prepares to describe the tenants in question, he advises: "Be a little careful, please! The hall is dark and you might stumble," thereby extending the visual metaphor.

Once inside, Riis as the narrator makes himself transparent, and a woman briefly narrates in the first person what life is like in her tenement. Although her story is touching and puts a local face on the unlocalizable information of gossip, the whole section has been so artfully framed that we wonder whether the woman is fictional and the story itself simply a generalizable caption for a material face in any one of a dozen photographs in the book. Which piece of information is more "real"? At this point, the text begins to groan under an excess of signification of the real. But if his referents are unavailable to be read as real because they are so intensely mediated by the guidebook language and by the photographs he relies on, Riis's audience is in the process of becoming real, not simply as the privileged mobile half Stange describes in her critique, but distinctly as a coherent middle class invited into the slums to help remake them in their own image. When the parents of a baby in the tenement "the Ship" talk about the death of their child, Riis quotes the father: "If we cannot keep the baby, need we complain—such as we?" and then breaks into a passionate peroration to the very audience he is already leading through the building. "Such as we! What if the words ring in your ears as we grope our way up the stairs and down from floor to floor . . . they are true" (1971:38). In this quick interchange between second-person pronouns, Riis manages to redirect the "we" of the tenement parents to become the "we" of the collectively better off, moving in and out of alliance with his subjects and his audience.

Sometimes Riis ensures that the sights he shows are obviously coded as "real." In such instances, he frames the conditions of his own knowledge of or participation in the scene that he will later describe, for example, by mentioning that he himself had a guide and translator. In a footnote, Riis reveals that he was able to make some of his textual and photographic observations *only* because he had a guide. In the chapter "The Sweaters of Jewtown," Riis writes: "I was always accompanied on these tours of inquiry by one of their own people who knew of and sympathized with my mission. Without that precaution my errand would have been fruitless; even with him it was often nearly so" (1971:100).

His efforts to chronicle some of the stories of the poor often put him in a strange position. No matter how much he tries to negotiate the idea of being both an insider and an outsider—he states at one point that "in this metropolis, let it be understood, there is no public street where the stranger may not go safely by day and by night, provided he knows how to mind his own business and is sober" (1971:26)—Riis is nonetheless aligned as a spectator not with a sympathetic guide from the community he wishes to enter but with one of his many friends in the police department. At one point, determined to experience a police raid on a bar, Riis writes that he accompanied the police as "a kind of war correspondent" (61). Indeed, the sense that Riis was involved with policing infuses the images in his work and informs the structure of surveillance and control he attempts to establish throughout the text.[9]

Such attempts at control and surveillance are not entirely successful. By now it has become commonplace to point out that totalizing theories of surveillance neglect the possibilities of resistance. This text, though, complicates this sense of utopia as well, since resistance is always rendered in the terms of the book's adjudication of personhood and cultural identity. Maren Stange comments,

Riis's actual physical presence as mediator between the audience and the photographs virtually embodied the overseeing "master" narrator familiar to readers of realist literature. Not only were the pleasures of reading recalled, but also the ostensibly incontrovertible authority of such a "point of view" was evoked on Riis's behalf, dismissing any possibility that the photograph itself might offer an alternative, or even oppositional reading to his. (1989:13–14)

Although the text does seem to dismiss the possibility of an oppositional reading, its different orders of knowledge and evidence lead to the idea of knowledge itself as contingent and disciplinary. Riis's master narrative thus suffers much the same fate of many other narratives of the master in a strange land—it cannot align the interior and exterior lives of objects of his study or make them equivalent to the assimilated citizens he appears to wish to produce. Here especially, it seems that although the text is structured to order and categorize the city, some elements of the project always escape Riis and his camera.

Riis's reliance on boundary metaphors to describe and divide New York spatially is enhanced by his description of the character of each ethnic group he documents. Through anthropological descriptions, Riis creates seemingly natural markers, or boundaries, by which an observer can understand the foreign population of New York. One of the categories by which Riis describes foreign populations is that of what is most visible in each local culture. Thus he mainly focuses on overt markers of difference—clothing, physical characteristics, manners of arguing or transacting public business, and styles of housekeeping. But after a lecture at a church, when a minister asks Riis if he doesn't focus too much on "the material condition of these people" at the expense of "the inner man," Riis responds, "You cannot expect to find an inner man to appeal to in the worst tenement house surroundings. You must first put the man where he can respect himself. To reverse the argument of the apple: you cannot expect to find a sound core in a rotten fruit" (1971:209).

Although Riis's narrative does indeed focus on the outer man in relationship to his surroundings, he is also, contrary to his response to the minister, interested in finding the inner life of communities, if not subjects, and so places his outer man in inner surroundings. His focus is on different communities' use of the streets and neighborhoods but also on various meanings of "home" and the nature of family organization. Part of his strategy in describing and humanizing the other half is to demonstrate how "like" the middle classes they are in their attempts to raise both their families and themselves in the world.

The likeness to the middle-class family can be explored only through the similarity of their homes. The home, then, becomes the site where Riis feels that he gets closest to the "common humanity" of the immigrant, but it is also the site that capital is most successful in destroying. Riis's access to the homes of his subjects is key to finding the conditions that prevent the "inner man" from adjusting to external circumstances and from assimilating. The relation between the inner man and his outer environment is built on a continuum leading from the individual to the family to the nation. The visibility and coherence of all parts of this continuum are complicit with one another. In creating this continuum, Riis understands the immigrants in question as empty units that can be made into citizens, or subjects of various social and legal laws that will more closely align them with the middle class. His invocation of ethnic stereotypes is always joined to his evaluation of their ability to regulate their homes and to subject themselves to external regulation.

The communities whose home and street life Riis measures are those of the Italians, the Jews, and the Bohemians. In each section, Riis finds much to celebrate, and he devotes much time to transcribing the bustling and colorful street life of various neighborhoods. Here, like the regionalist narrator, he wishes to become transparent, to open himself like a photographic eye and record the strange ways of the charming folk.

On the street, he attempts a kind of invisibility. Seldom does he tell us how he has chosen a specific site or if there were any confrontations or miscommunications between himself and his subjects. "No need of asking where we are, the jargon of the streets, the signs of the sidewalk, the manner and dress of the people, their unmistakable physiognomy betray their race at every step" (1971:85). These are comments about the Jewish quarter, which Riis describes with great verve. But his initial level of comfort is tied to the fact that he doesn't need to ask for his location. His use of the word *betray* when he describes the "race" of Jewishness strikes the reader as less interpretation than an invocation of an unmistakable external sign that registers the "truth" of the inner life and character of the Jews. It is important to Riis to record the self-identicalness of the Jews, the commensurability between what they act like and what they are. His discussion of Italians in New York is similar: "Their vivid and picturesque costumes lend a thing of color to the other wise dull monotony of the slums they inhabit" (47). Here the narrative slows to scenically appreciate Italians, even though its aim is to eradicate local differences in the service of assimilation and economic reform.

In these two instances, the Italians and the Jews are each sewn into civic structures of the United States. The Italian, lured to the United States by promises of a wealthy padrone, is "persuaded . . . by false promises to mortgage his home, his few belongings, and his wages for months to come for a ticket to the land where plenty of work is to be had at princely wages" (1971:43). Such not being the case, the Italian works himself out of his quasi slavery. Writing about the Italian control over the dumps of New

York, Riis notes that "it augurs unsuspected adaptability in the Italian to our system of self-government that [the rivalries to control franchising] have more than once been suspected of being behind the sharpening of city ordinances" and goes on to say the Italian is ordinarily "easily enough governed by authority" (44).

Similarly, although Riis excoriates the Jewish immigrant for his apparent thralldom to money, he cannot help but recognize the necessity of his labor. Like the Italian, the Jew is also adaptable to the legal as well as the economic systems that seem to control his fate.

Oppression, persecution, have not shorn the Jew of his native combativeness one whit. He is as ready to fight for his rights, or what he considers his rights, in a business transaction . . . as if he had not been robbed of them for eighteen hundred years. One strong impression survives with him from his bondage: the power of the law. On the slightest provocation, he rushes off to invoke it for his protection. (1971:90)

Although Riis stresses here the Jewish immigrant's desire to protect his financial rights, it is not difficult to see that the discourse he invokes is about the protection of the law. In arguing that the Jewish immigrant wishes to accept outside arbitration for "slights" or "provocations," Riis also comments on the Jewish community's willingness to accede to or be governed by laws outside those of its own ethnic community. Seeking outside authority in both personal and public disputes means that the community, however apparently self-enclosed and rigidly internally structured, has also conceived of a place within a larger national structure, thus entering into a nationalized economy of both material production and the production and maintenance of individual rights.

The relation between home and ethnicity most fully elaborates this book's assimilationist impulse. Riis begins his discussion of the Jewish quarter by focusing on the crowded nature of the streets. "It is said that nowhere in the world are so many people crowded together on a square mile as here" (1971:86). Similarly, when he writes, "Thrift is the watchword of Jewtown, as of its people the world over" (86), he is indulging in the most common stereotype about Jewish culture in the nineteenth century.

Riis does not use the stereotype of greed without reason, nor does he use it in order to resecure or certify it. Rather, Riis's goals seem twofold in his description of the Jewish colony. The first goal is to lament a certain economic condition that makes the tenement house and the factory one and the same and that leads to both the deterioration of the home and the exploitation of labor in the Jewish ghetto. In this way, he wishes his readers to see the people as victims rather than masters of money. But the second goal is to introduce his readers to the Jewish quarter by showing verbally and visually the Jewish involvement in trade, thus confirming, with modification, the same stereotype. He writes that Friday morning is bargain day and that "is the time to study the ways of this peculiar people to the best advantage. . . . Friday brings out all the latent color and picturesqueness of the Italians, as of these Semites. The crowds and the common poverty are the bonds of sympathy between them" (1971:91). Riis describes people selling their various wares and, in the etchings based on his original photographs, depicts complementary scenes of street life. The perspective in each is from a street corner somewhere on the edge of the action, and in the etchings, the perspective is elongated by placing the point of view slightly higher. Because the readers are slightly above the market, the effect is a position of the scene, but not uncomfortably in the scene. Riis writes about the market day: "Pushing, struggling, babbling, and shouting in foreign tongues, a veritable Babel of confusion. An English word falls upon the ear almost with a sense of shock, as something unexpected and strange" (95).

Although the sound of an English word may be strange, the market's festival atmosphere strongly contrasts with the dead silence with which the stranger is greeted in Chinatown, and even the "strange" sound of an English word does not have the same impact as does the transcription of Chinese accents in his chapter on Chinatown. The babel of language in Jewtown invites contact; the ability of the Chinese man to speak English indicates, paradoxically, the desire to keep out the inquiring reporter.

The street scenes in the Jewish quarter appeal to Riis's aesthetic sense more than do the frightening, empty avenues in the Chinese section, but he partially uses this backdrop of external life and liveliness to set up the real problem that he finds in the Jewish quarter: the use of the tenement—the home—as a factory. In his chapter "The Sweaters of Jewtown," Riis creates the lack of established middle-class social spaces as a mark of potential social deformation. He writes: "It is idle to speak of privacy in these 'homes.' The term carries no more meaning with it than would a lecture on social ethics to an audience of Hottentots. The picture is not overdrawn" (1971:106). Indeed, it is in this hidden part of the Jewish district that Riis finds that he needs a guide. The language of barbarism implicit in the term *Hottentot* defamiliarizes even these model immigrants.

This sense of the collision of the domestic and the social is clear in the photograph of a young woman working in a sweatshop (figure 1). The title of the photograph is " 'Knee-pants' at forty-five cents a dozen—a Ludlow Street sweater's shop." The central figures are three young women and three men at work making trousers. The interior of the house is crowded with the materials for sewing; cloth spills over onto the floor and the extra chairs. But even though the home has clearly become a workplace, the almost invisible traces of domesticity still function as the centering motif.

Figure 1: "'Knee-pants' at forty-five cents a dozen—a Ludlow Street sweater's shop" (Jacob Riis, *How the Other Half Lives* [1971], 96; photograph from the Jacob A. Riis Collection, #149, © Museum of the City of New York, reproduced with permission)

Hanging between the two windows is a framed photograph of a baby, a typically bourgeois decoration, and here the symbol of exactly what is missing from this domestic space: where in this apartment occupied by three "couples" are the babies, and where are the young children? In the text, Jacob Riis asserts that while the parents make over the home as factory, the children are forced into the street in order to play. But the photograph of the baby not only focuses attention on the problem of the children who cannot play and learn in the home, it also marks the presence of the children who remained in the home, transformed along with the domestic space from children into laborers themselves. And finally, in the time of the photograph, the photograph of the baby symbolically commemorates the *absence* of the typical middle-class family, acting as the center of an invisible line that appears to be keeping the three men and the three women apart.

The photograph shows a man who is in the process of crossing that boundary toward two of the women. His back is to the camera, which highlights the face of the young woman holding the scissors. The rest of the people in the photograph are turning or have turned away from the eye of the camera, making the direct gaze of the young woman with scissors more central than any other aspect of the photograph. Indeed, she seems isolated; the others are concentrating on their work, and they are mainly anonymous. The young woman is an image of the transformation of domesticity into labor. She is covered with unfinished garments, and the scissors she is holding up to her mouth are quite violent; they seem to be literally cutting off her speech, interrupting her flirtatious smile. Amy Kaplan writes that Riis's "mission of reform suggests that proper housing could transform the world of the alien immigrant into a vision of middle-class domesticity. The home, he implies, can make the boundary line disappear by turning it into a mirror" (Kaplan 1988:16).

In this photograph at least, Riis seems interested in showing the ways in which domestic harmony has been disrupted by the sweatshop. The places he visits are defined by their inhabitants, so rather than simply going to the Jewish quarter, Riis narratively escorts us to "Jewtown." The photographs of the text parallel this conflation of location with otherness. The most visually exciting photographs in the text are those of the outside, of the life of the streets in various quarters. It is here that urban local color becomes visible and where whole communities can be defined from street level. But it is also these general street shots that make the photographs of the interior of the tenements so shocking and that lend to these interior shots the ideological components of not just squalor but danger to the middle-class family. Once Riis has escorted his readers to a specific ghetto, he often chooses to move inside a tenement in order to demonstrate exactly how the environment of poverty has inflected the "natural" traits of various cultures, creating out of them a strange and "unnatural" world of factory/home, and family/boarder. Genetic and capital reproduction are too proximate in the Jewish community; the space of the home and the metonymic space of the nation are thus thrown into chaos.

Riis's critique of the Jewish household is that it escapes a generalized sense of homelikeness and so disturbs the likeness between the ordered home and the ordered nation. But in his observation of the Chinese, he finds exactly the opposite problem. The homes are ordered and private, but the very kind of privacy they have established is dangerous to the project of assimilating citizens. The Chinese and Chinatown elude Riis's desire to control and describe New York's ethnic communities. His inability to account for the Chinese and his startling inability to offer reform suggestions for the community stem from their unwillingness to be observed and their unwillingness to be governed or described by either Riis's hegemonic gaze or the institutions he represents.[10]

For Riis, the Chinese are visible, but they are not legible through any of the strategies he has used to describe other ethnic groups. The Chinese thwart his Progressivist program of controlling and "re-forming" ethnicity in relation to the middle class. In fact, it is the very "nature" of the Chinese to maintain a dual identity. "I am convinced the [Chinese] adopts Christianity, when he adopts it at all, as he puts on American clothes, with what the politicians would call an ulterior motive" (1971:77). This ulterior motive makes Chinese men visible in the ethnic landscape, but because they appear to be controlling their relationship to larger structures of authority and identity, it separates them from the Italians and the Jewish immigrants, whose doubled "internal" and "external" natures are clearly developed through Riis's reading. The Chinese, like the "secret centers of corruption," trouble Riis because they have become a mysterious site of agency outside the city's controlling gaze. These foreign subjects cannot be placed into any system by which ethnicity and United States citizenship can be adjudicated.

Riis begins his tour with "Chinatown as a spectacle is disappointing. Next door neighbor to the Bend, it has little of its outdoor stir and life, none of its gaily-colored rags or picturesque filth and poverty. Mott Street is clean to distraction" (1971:77). The fact that Riis draws on language referring to pictorial regionalism to frame his opening image of Chinatown is less interesting here than the fact the Chinatown cannot be scripted in this language. The discourse of regionalism is simply inadequate here; the life of the street is unavailable. No one seems to be around, so Riis cannot account for Chinatown, he literally cannot "count" the Chinese. It is not simply that there is nothing to look at that bothers Riis. It is that he appears to be watched as he moves through Chinatown. The red and yellow banners of Chinatown seem to have a "blank, unmeaning stare, suggesting nothing, asking no questions, and answering none." As quiet are the dwellings of Chinatown, which "are fenced off by queer, forbidding partitions suggestive of a continual state of siege" (78). After Riis sets this scene, he intrudes into the narrative as "the stranger" rather than "a curious wanderer" or "a visitor," writing that such an interloper is "received with sudden silence, a sullen stare, and an angry 'vat you vant.'" The "state of siege" refers to the relative autonomy of Chinatown as well as to its active resistance to intruders. "The one thing they desire above all is to be let alone" (83), Riis writes, but the text wishes above all to uncover the Chinese, to show them for "what they are."

Just as the economy of public and private life are disrupted in other sections of the city, so too they are disturbed in Chinatown. But unlike the case of the Bohemian cigar makers, for example, who work in their apartments all day, the Chinese, according to Riis, are directly responsible for controlling their own environment. The partitions—the odd forbidding entrances—are erected by the Chinese. Additionally, they have deliber-

Figure 2: "The official organ of Chinatown" (Jacob Riis, *How the Other Half Lives* [1971], 79; photograph from the Jacob A. Riis Collection, #260, © Museum of the City of New York, reproduced with permission)

ately inverted and appropriated the very elements of civic life that are meant to act for the good of the public. Riis writes that "Chinatown has enlisted the telegraph for the dissemination of public intelligence, but it has got the contrivance by the wrong end," continuing his description by saying that "every day yellow and red notices are posted upon it by unseen hands" (1971:82).

It is this notion of unseen hands that troubles Riis. He cannot detect the source of these secret communities or "read" the messages they post. The photograph of Chinatown crystallizes his anxiety. Standing near a telephone pole is a Chinese man walking toward the camera (figure 2). Hands in his pockets, hidden from view, the man stares expressionlessly at Riis, "asking no question, receiving none." The photograph suggests that the very hidden hands that are so dangerous might belong to this anonymous man. The photograph also returns to one of Riis's first obser-vations about Chinatown—its emptiness. In this outside shot, unlike that of the Jewish quarter or the Bend, there are no other people on the street and no accompanying photograph of the interior of a house or flat. Indeed, the solitude of this anonymous man underscores his observation that the Chinese "rise up as one man" and "act . . . 'alike,' in a body, to defeat discovery" (1971:83). Similarly confounding to Riis is the fact that while the telegraph is supposed to disseminate information for the public good, the Chinese have appropriated it for their own "unseen" ends. The gambling notices represent an appropriation of the "proper" use of city property, a kind of theft allowing for a measure of self-governance that escapes the best intentions of the police. Immediately after he has finished describing the inversion of the telegraph, Riis tells us an anecdote about Chinatown. A crime that Riis has "a very vivid recollection of" remains unsolved because the Chinese suspects "appear to rise up as one man to shield the criminal" (8).

The section on the nature of the Chinese is subtended by descriptions of law and authority. The Chinese wish to protect the interior of their ten-ements, and so they force Riis to pay for the privilege of taking a photo-graph. When he has to pay, he playfully writes that he had to send two pigs to "his offended majesty of Mott Street" (1971:82). The appropri-ation of public space, especially instruments of communications to main-tain a group existence outside "discovery," comports with Riis's sense that Chinatown is a colony governed and legislated by a private, even secret government:

Even discarding as idle the stories of a secret cabal with power over life and death, and authority to enforce its decrees, there is evidence enough that the Chinese con-sider themselves subject to the laws of the land only when submission is unavoid-able, and that they are governed by a code of their own, the very essence of which is rejection of all other authority except under compulsion. (1971:82)[11]

Their rejection of authority and the installation of private self-govern-ment strike Riis as the primary factor militating against their inclusion in the United States. Riis holds out no hope that the Chinese can be assimi-lated, yet he argues at the close of this section that Chinese women should be encouraged to emigrate so that the Chinese man "might not be what he now is and remains, a homeless stranger among us" (1971:83). When Riis argues that privacy is meaningless in "Jewtown" because the home has been turned into a factory and thus the economy of family reproduction is converted into the economy of factory production, he makes an analogy between the interior life of the immigrant, his community, and his house-hold. In Chinatown, he argues, "whatever is on foot goes on behind closed doors" (78), implying that the Chinese have managed to maintain a sense

of privacy necessary to withstand assimilation. This is a seemingly paradoxical position for Riis, for it is his contention that the establishment of
the private home is the most important aspect of assimilation.

In *The Peril and the Preservation of the Home*, a series of lectures delivered in Philadelphia and printed in 1903, Riis argues that "upon the preservation of the home depends the vitality of our Republic; that if the home
were gone, we should be fighting against overwhelming odds in the battle
to maintain it and would as surely lose" (Riis 1903:13).[12] This crystalliza-
tion of *HtOHL* seems at odds with his description of the Chinese—after
all, they have created homelike spaces in which to live, and nowhere in the
section on the Chinese does he maintain, as he does about the Jewish tenements, that the home spaces have been violated by sweatshop labor. His
failure to articulate the "nature" of the Chinese community to the logic of
the supreme value of the home is not simply an inconsistency within the
book; rather, Riis's bafflement in the face of his exploration of the Chinese is informed by other contemporary discourses about the peril the
Chinese posed to definitions of democracy and identity.

Riis's fears about the Chinese and their homelessness are echoed in
other documents about Chinese presence in the United States. The "homeless stranger among us" was bought, as Riis notes, to labor. Thus the position of Chinese immigrants in the United States was immediately bound up
with discourses about slavery and citizenship. Debates, especially in California, although ostensibly on labor issues, were advanced in the rhetoric
of slavery—even those arguments that opposed the Chinese on the grounds
that they took gainful employment away from native workers used the discourse of slavery to ground their antipathies. Such debates are echoed in
Riis's discussion of the traffic in white slavery, which, he hints, is not
unknown in the hidden homes of Chinatown.

In fact, in this chapter, it is interesting how often the terminology of
slavery and bondage appears. The "authority" that the Chinese seem both
to abrogate—ceding personal authority to a group that "acts as one
man"—and to claim—refusing to "show" themselves as willing citizens—
also seems to play out in relation to other institutions and citizens in the
United States. The Chinese came to the United States during the Gold
Rush. John Higham writes that from 1860 to 1880, the Chinese com-
prised about 9 percent of the population of California, and Ronald
Takaki records that they constituted "a mere .002 percent of the U.S. population" in 1880.[13] From nearly the time of their arrival in California, the
Chinese were the targets of racial violence and hatred. Used by various
employers to work in mines, on the railroad, and on ranches doing heavy
labor, they constituted a small, but mobile and cohesive workforce. During the boom years, when there seemed to be more than enough work for

everyone who wanted it, they were not the target of a sustained organized popular enmity. Although they were often locally driven out of richer mines, they were able to pick up work in other places.

When the railroad was complete and Chinese laborers began competing more directly with "native" workers, they became the target of workers' organizations' political platforms, culminating in a series of federal laws capped by the 1882 statute suspending the entry of Chinese labor for ten years. According to Higham, in 1892, "the Geary law not only continued suspension for ten years more, but also required every Chinese in the United States to prove through white men's testimony his legal right to be here. At the turn of the century, suspension became permanent exclusion" (1984:36). Seemingly in opposition to this policy of exclusion, Riis writes: "Rather than banish the Chinaman, I would have the door opened wider—for his wife; make it a condition of his coming or staying that he bring his wife with him. Then, at least, he might not be what he now is and remains, a homeless stranger among us" (1903:83). Other influential texts of the period also described the Chinese as homeless. Otis Gibson, a minister sympathetic to the Chinese in California, writes that when the Chinese cut off their queues (an act legislated by the California legislature), "he denationalizes himself, he becomes a waif in the world, without a people and without a country" (1978:120).

The importation of Chinese resembled slave labor—a notion reinforced by a California statute of 1849 barring black men and Native Americans from testifying in a court of law against a white man. This statute was ruled to cover Chinese five years later in the 1854 case *People v. Hall*, thus equating black and Chinese men under the law. Ronald Takaki cites an 1853 issue of the *San Francisco Alta*: "Every reason that exists against the toleration of free blacks in Illinois may be argued against that of the Chinese here." In addition, magazine cartoons "depicted the Chinese as a bloodsucking vampire with slanted eyes, a pigtail, dark skin, and thick lips. Like freedmen, the Chinese were described as heathen, morally inferior, savage, childlike, and lustful. . . . Chinese men were seen as sensuous creatures, especially interested in white women" (Takaki 1989:101). The fear that the Chinese were interested in white women also resonates with the pervasive fears of racial mixing and miscegenation at the heart of antiblack prejudice in the late nineteenth century.

Like the free blacks with whom they were racially equated, the Chinese stood at an intersection of the formation of class identity. Again, their imaginative alignment with freedmen has origins in their perceived status as

slave labor, a charge emphatically denied by the president of the Six Companies, the Tongs or Consortiums importing the Chinese, who writes in a letter that "*in no single instance is a Chinaman in the United States a slave.* That if *these Chinese laboring men* are called *slaves*, then *all men laboring for wages may be called slaves.*" (Gibson 1978:334)

Alexander Saxton and Ronald Takaki contend that part of the reason that the Chinese Exclusion Acts garnered so much public support was because they came at a time of massive unemployment and class conflict. But as Alexander Saxton pointed out, "Neither trade unionists nor anyone else in nineteenth-century America arrived at conclusions involving matters of race simply through processes of economic reasoning," and so we need to look at the ways in which class hostility, racial fears, and anti-Chinese sentiments inform one another in Riis's reading (Saxton 1996:301). I believe that *HtOHL*'s critique of the Chinese as a racialized other and a secret society must be read against Jacob Riis's partial attempt to understand the "nature" of the Chinese only when he could not understand their culture.

On the one hand, the historical and legal circumstances of Chinese presence in the United States militated against becoming "at home," a term that in Riis's book might be read as the attempt to establish domestic space and pursue a social mobility that might eventually erase racial or ethnic distinctions. On the other hand, the very homelessness of the Chinese might be read against the anomalous cohesion of Chinatown in New York, which, in Riis's book, speaks to their desire neither to be assimilated nor to adopt highly individual identities that might be balanced against their assigned racial or ethnic identity.

Once again we return to Riis's ambivalent argument about the Chinese: Whereas the public life of the immigrant in "Jewtown" signifies his domestic life, which itself acts as a kind of metonym for the assimilable "interior" life of the immigrant, the Chinese do not provide Riis with such a spectacle of assimilation. In fact, their secrecy and privacy are extended to the "unnatural" home life of the Chinese, who are seen as seducing young white women with the opium pipe in order to make them "slaves." Riis argues that these young women are seduced to live with the homeless strangers from "homes that have no claim upon the name" (1903:80). Evaluating the status of the women, he finds that they have been manipulated by the tyrant Chinese masters into believing that they are their own "bosses" but are really caught in a web of coercion and violence from which they can escape only through death.

Riis's final indictment of the Chinese is that they not only maintain a stringent secrecy about their homes and thus their interior lives, but they also seduce young women away from their own homes. This invocation of this opiumlike addictiveness of the Chinese home adds another layer to the arguments about slavery, the free man, and the home. The Chinese are here imputed with a kind of "white slaver" function parallel to their own status as quasi slaves. Riis's desire to open immigration to Chinese women is a last-ditch attempt to keep white women away from Chinese men, thereby safeguarding the middle-class home, and creating the possibility of a "real" home in Chinatown.

The implied reversal of the proper boundaries between themselves and white women also informs Riis's description of the Chinese man's radical reversal of his observational strategy. A Chinese man who "eyes" Riis up and down concludes that if he doesn't "lickee" Mrs. Riis, then she must beat him. The imposition of his own standards onto Riis and his subsequent evaluation of his manliness leave our reporter speechless. Yet even in the Chinese man's appropriation and inversion of Riis's own tactics of evaluation, he cannot escape the general judgment passed on his race. Riis makes remarkable parallels between the Chinese and the Jews and Italians (sometimes even down to the animal metaphor), remarking that both the Jews and Chinese worship money, noting that gambling is the ruling passion of the Italians and the Chinese and asserting that the Chinese and the Italians prefer to solve their own crimes by finding and stabbing the criminal. Yet despite all the similarities he describes, Riis cannot equate them. In *HtOHL*, nearly every immigrant group is in some way equivalent to the others, and in making pictures, through both photography and a remarkably coherent set of visual metaphors, Riis reduces each ethnic group to a likeness of the others, holding them up to the middle-class public as a dark likeness or equivalence to themselves. But in transgressing both the status of the observer and the centrality of the home, the Chinese come to seem finally ungovernable and, as such, unprepared for assimilation.

Not all texts attempting to "expose" the plight of the other half approved of the methods that Riis later made famous. Otis Gibson wrote passionately against invading the homes of the Chinese in San Francisco:

Our "special policemen," for a consideration are always ready to take visitors through these dens, to show them "The Chinese as they are." These good visitors go away and write up the Chinese in America, giving as historical facts the impressions received from such a night adventure, together with the statements of unprincipled, corrupt men. I protest against this method of studying the Chinese question. Suppose the table turned, and curious Chinamen escorted by some "kind and intelligent policeman" should make a raid upon American bedrooms, about twelve or one o'clock at night, solely for the delectation of the Chinaman. (Gibson 1978:93)

As the example of Chinatown demonstrates, although Jacob Riis often asked for certain poses and used them to confirm already prevailing public images about the "other half," the limits of the technology could not account for every move or every kind of artifice. For example, it was possible for subjects to turn away from the camera, and many did (Stange

1989:11–12). Some also demanded money or goods in exchange for a photograph sitting.[14] And by accepting some of the responsibility for their own images, some of the subjects of the photographs help reveal Riis's methods.

In one instance, his own hidden hand becomes visible when we read his descriptions of photographs of street gangs.

While I was getting the camera ready, I threw out a vague suggestion of cigarette-pictures, and it took root at once. Nothing would do then but that I must take the boldest spirits of the company "in character." One of them tumbled over against a shed, as if asleep, while two of the others bent over him, searching his pockets. (1903:174)

This photograph shows two little boys holding a third down, all three of them apparently laughing and having a wonderful time. Although Riis is very clear that he did not pose the photograph, he is equally clear that he was annoyed that his subjects posed themselves. It was possible not just for those little boys to see themselves through the eyes of another but also to try to see themselves as they believed others would like them to be. Thus, the little boys already seem to know that they can pose "in character" and that they will appear in an intelligible and public system of representation. Their refusal of Riis's gaze helps to rescue them from that totalizing gaze of power that Reginald Twigg notes Riis's book seems to inspire in readers (Twigg 1992:309).

Riis's writing and his photography were tied to a kind of turn-of-the-century tourism as well as to a Progressivist desire to eliminate the conditions that created the vice and disease of the slums. Riis's reliance on these twinned discourses recognizes the potential for urban slum dwellers to reimagine themselves outside legible scripts for identity and therefore to break the homology between home and nation. For example, in a footnote Riis tells his audience that a whole group of immigrants managed to leave their tenement and remain together, and in an aside:

The Sheriff Street Colony of rag-pickers, long since gone, is an instance in point. The thrifty Germans saved up money during years of hard work in squalor and apparently wretched poverty to buy a township in a Western State, and the whole colony moved out there in a body. There need be no doubt about their thriving there. (1903:20)

Riis uses the word *body* deliberately here; all the language is about the idea of incorporation. The colony is defined by ethnicity—"thrifty Germans"—but also by place—they are the "Settlement Street Colony." They act in a body, as Germans, but also as a corporation, as people who live on Sheriff Street and agree to endure hunger and poverty in exchange for a better living in the future. From the region in which they live, they purchase a town, thus enacting the reverse of the historical trend toward the city. They also tap into a particularly American frontier mythology by creating a town in the West where there was none before. They remain salutary figures in the text. The Germans, "long since gone," show the reader that Riis recognizes (perhaps only in its safe and soothing absence) the potential for cultural and ethnic cohesion that does not prevent what seems to him the natural and desirable ability to become an American success.

Riis's praise of the success of the Sheriff Street Colony of ragpickers should be measured next to his predictions of what might happen if the coherence of ethnicity were disturbed. Riis presents some of his most provocative instances of crime and corruption through stories of individuals without a strong ethnic or family identification. They have become socialized by associating with other like-minded people, and such associations are criminalized. The mass, or the "common herd," "the unmixed crowd," came to seem dangerous to Riis. While he occasionally complains about the venality of ward politicians, who buy the votes of the poor with alcohol, he astonishingly does not include any sections or any photographs of the ward heeler. He writes that "the colonization of voters is an evil of the first magnitude" (1903:75) but says no more about this particular "colony," this alternative way of breaking up and organizing sections of the city. This is a serious omission, for Riis criminalizes the culture of saloons, in which the ward boss did his work, and the growler gangs of young men, who were often controlled by the ward bosses.

In a chapter entitled "The Man With the Knife," Riis tells the story of a "poor and hungry and ragged" man who, looking at the carriages of the wealthy, remembers his own starving children and springs into the crowd with a knife, "blindly seeking to kill, to revenge" (1903:207). Riis casually vouches for the truth of the story, and while he appears to have sympathy for the man with the knife, this man is also the body that Riis uses to call up the specter of more violent mass bodies. Riis photographed the other half to make visible the problems of poverty, casting himself as a visionary when he tried to discuss the consequences of this poverty. He writes about the anonymous, nameless "man with a knife" that he and his knife "had a mission. They spoke in their ignorant, impatient way the warning one of the most conservative, dispassionate of public bodies had sounded only a little while before: 'Our only fear is that reform may come in a burst of public indignation destructive to property and to good morals'" (1903:207). In other words, the man with the knife warns that if the upper and middle classes did not fix the wretched conditions under which the "other half" lived, mass action and violence would ensue.

In the final section of his text, Riis envisions an ideal situation. Including a blueprint of a model tenement, Riis tells us that it has been built and has

dupes or essentialized ethnic voters but as apparently, if not actually, emergent and potentially disturbing voices in the field of representation itself.
This model of emergent literary representation comports with historian
Zane L. Miller's description of the political and geographical "zone of
emergence" in the turn-of-the-century city. This "zone," defined by the
emerging middle class, represented not the poorest of the poor or the
wealthiest of the wealthy but those citizens interested in jobs, electoral politics, and social issues. It thus was a volatile and socially heterogeneous
group from which politicians wished to recruit votes and to which they
wished to give a unified voice. Tammany novels might therefore be considered a "zone of emergence" from which a heterogeneous population of
working-class and immigrant people can be interpellated and unified by
the bosses of Tammany Hall.

To explore the possibility of the "undifferentiated" people becoming
citizens, I focus on Tammany's ascribed power to refigure seemingly "natural" communities of people, such as Irish tenement dwellers, into "unnatural" alliances like voting blocs. I concentrate on how the figure of the
Boss is constructed, how he produces himself and his constituents through
the imaginary trope of the machine, and, finally, how "the people" circu-
late endlessly in that machine as political subjects.

It is this last point that brings us to Tammany Hall as the end of a
book on regionalism. Tammany gives us a way to read the regionalist
project as a circuit attempting to connect the struggle over the political
representation of ethnic subjects with a literary form that serves as a partial access point for figures of cultural difference. Just as regionalism
opened the public sphere to voices challenging the homogeneity of U.S.
culture, Tammany Hall offers itself as a point of access to the public
sphere for previously un- or underrepresented peoples. Tammany is the
nexus of a crisis in the constitution of the public and its interests. Michael
Warner points out that our own era has produced a rhetorical crisis in
the ways in which individual subjects enter public discourse because "so
much political conflict revolves around identity and status categories"
(Warner 1994:377–378).

Studying political novels in order to study regionalism allows us to see
the social components that underwrite the literary production of "identity
and status categories." Tammany novels reconstitute the public sphere by
inverting regionalism's interchange between the public experience of
tourism and the private experience of memory. As I demonstrated in earlier chapters, the past that is recalled in regional works of fiction is domestic. Much regional writing revolves around the domestic sphere of women
and labor, the village, or the preindustrial community as a kind of residual
domestic space itself—a rural haven in a heartless urban world. In casting
the region as doubly domestic, the genre reconstructs an imagined unity

out of cultural/regional diversity. That enterprise is corrupt, since the national unity of regionalism's reading public depends on an endless supply of local-color artifacts whose difference from one another decreases with each passing year. In the most extreme version of this argument, Tennessee and Maine, as produced for Howells's reading public, are mass-produced versions of the same location. All regional figures are the same mass-produced figure, infinitely exchangeable, empty of but irreducibly marked by cultural difference.

Similarly, nineteenth-century regionalism is constituted by an anxiety over the reading public and a related anxiety over who belongs to the national community. Coded as racial or ethnic others, disenfranchised laborers, or lost initiates or exiles, the figures of cultural difference in regional texts demonstrate the problem of determining who counts as a citizen, and under what conditions different kinds of communities appear. These individual figures, rendered as national subjects through cultural difference, gain political value by becoming metonymically representative of the regions they inhabit. The Tammany novel restages regionalism's precarious resolution of these conflicts.

It dramatizes the problematic constitution of the public sphere. It does so by grappling with the debates about this sphere through the historical figure of Tammany and by incorporating those debates into its figuration of Tammany as a site of representation. Tammany constitutes, if not a counterpublic sphere, then a public sphere that seems to run alongside the "official" public sphere of late-nineteenth-century civil society, endlessly producing citizens whose loyalties are both oriented toward recognition by the public and inimical to its interests. The production of citizens out of persons with vested and interested local identities destroys the fantasy of regional difference and national coherence. Michael Warner argues, following Habermas, that "the bourgeois public sphere is a frame of reference in which it is supposed that all particularities have the same status as mere particularity. But the ability to establish that frame of reference is a feature of some particularities." Warner goes on to explain that "the bourgeois public sphere has been structured from the outset by a logic of abstraction that provides a privilege for unmarked identities: the male, the white, the middle class, the normal" (1994:383). Warner notes that for Habermas, the body of the ruler is necessary only in the public sphere revolving around nobility. In the public sphere of late capitalism, with its theatrical presentation of the rulers' public personae, he links the unmarked bodies of normative participants in the classic bourgeois public sphere to their reembodiment as vested subjects.

The perpetual depiction of the body of the Boss in Thomas Nast's satirical illustrations therefore serves an important political function. First, the body of the Boss invokes the uneven development of the public sphere, which exposes the limited character of access to it. While the public sphere may well be fragmented, the case of Tammany demonstrates that it was, in fact, always internally problematic, that there were numerous publics in the late nineteenth century, and that they struggled over the relative definitions of private and public, of interest and disinterest in terms of specific identities. Those identities were partly embodied and imagined as grossly physical. The body of the Boss, especially as popularized by Thomas Nast, was always huge and bloated, perched atop piles of money or on heaps of screaming citizens. Its enormity indicated a certain excess and intractability, a huge physical presence akin to the physical presence of the immigrants it seemed to call into being as citizens.

Pictorial depictions of the corpulent boss suggest a feudal image of Tammany, whose power always had to be secured by the display of his representative body to his people. This feudal aspect of power underlies popular visions of the Tammany Boss, but here the feudal or noble public sphere that it conjures up as coexistent with a civic public sphere of progressive reform and the common good indicates an unevenly developed but mutually constitutive sense of the public and of citizenship. While popular accounts linked Tammany to Irishness, novelistic accounts and historians have differed in this assessment. Looking at Tammany as the province of one ethnicity or as a machine that ensured the perpetuation of a solid ethnic identity like Irishness mistakes its crucial function as a marker of how fungible an ethnic identity could be for a subject interested in becoming a public actor.

I address these issues by examining *The Boss*, by Alfred Henry Lewis. His pastoral local-color and political novels link the ideological work of regionalism with the management of social difference. This introduction to *The Boss* gives a brief history of the connection between a genteel late-nineteenth-century regionalism and the earlier antebellum tall tale. That connection, like all literary histories, is accurate but not as neat as we might wish.

Critics have traced late-nineteenth-century regionalism of the kind praised and promoted by William Dean Howells in his capacity as editor of *Harper's Monthly* to cruder tall tales of early- and mid-nineteenth-century settlers' experiences. But it has not been commonly acknowledged that later-nineteenth-century regionalism did not merely subsume and replace "oral" tall tales. Stories written in dialect or in the broad vernacular of the comic ethnic character continued to be produced and marketed in nearly the same venues as the more genteel stories by Mary Wilkins Freeman or Sarah Orne Jewett. In the same year that William Dean Howells called for a literature that would introduce citizens to one another and show that men were more like than unlike one another, the *Century* magazine was busy printing a series of Irish stories that used heavy local-color touches. They resembled not only the literature Howells approved of but also the popular stories of Sut Lovingood by George Washington Harris, which appeared newspapers from the 1840s to the 1850s. The genealogy of regionalism usually advanced does not account for the continued popularity in quarters other than the upper middle class for texts that presented the immigrant, particularly the Irishman Mr. Dooley, "as he was" and whose "realism" is a reminder of the content of the earlier tall tales of Davy Crockett, Mike Fink, and Sut Lovingood. The survival of texts that read like antebellum tall tales reminds us that although genteel regional writing may have been the signal genre for the introduction of social and ethnic difference, it never managed it successfully. The representation of ethnic difference found an outlet in many literary forms.

Alfred Henry Lewis brings into focus the coexistence of different kinds of regional writing. He began his career as a writer of sketches and tall tales set in a fictional western town called Wolfville. These stories, collected into several volumes, rely on the textual features commonly associated with regional texts. They are written in elaborate dialect and feature the exotic mores and habits of Americans who seem foreign, even though they are unquestionably U.S. citizens. The Wolfville stories also resemble tall tales of the antebellum era and accordingly privilege plots underscoring the construction of a social arena that has begun to mimic the urban centers of the East. In all the stories, Wolfville is in the process of civilizing itself, of bringing itself into closer identity with the social mores of the East. This means that the town of Wolfville is perpetually in crisis. It was settled by people who want to escape the old strictures of the East, but it is also trying to establish laws for its citizens that will help give it a recognizable shape. Neither the content nor the existence of the *Wolfville Tales* is surprising, for stories about the West sold well throughout the nineteenth century. What is surprising is that Lewis turned his attention away from Wolfville in order to address the problem of urban politics. In both his novel *The Boss* and his biography of Richard Croker, he, like Jacob Riis, brings to bear on his subjects an authorial strategy that I have been calling regional. But his approach to regionalism in his earlier work demonstrates that his approach to the urban problems of ethnicity and politics more resembles the techniques he used to deal with the problems of self-governance on the frontier than with the Progressivism advanced by Jacob Riis.

The stories set in Wolfville, like the problem of the ward constituent in *The Boss*, show us that problems of identity always underwrite problems of community. The Wolfville tales are not invested in realist models of writing in which subjects are produced through the construction of rich psychological interiors and in which they learn to moderate their public appearance in finely graded social situations. Rather, the problems of identity in the local-color tales of Wolfville are public problems—that is, nothing falls outside the bounds of the public interest. The private does not exist in these stories, an observation we might use to argue that the characters in Wolfville are not particularly rich or deep because they do not need the kind of interiority privileged by genteel regionalism or realism. What is at stake is not their status as private subjects but their ability to work toward the public construction of an efficient community. To this end, even such nominally private affairs as marriage engagements and "falling in love" are matters for the entire town to witness and adjudicate, since it is the town that will be affected by the development of any private and interested relationships.

Similarly, the problems of identity and ethnicity that Lewis portrays in his Tammany novel also are public. The citizenship of ward constituents is not fashioned at the level of the individual subject nor is it a product of individual desire. Rather, the process by which the ethnic constituents of the Tammany machine are introduced to the public world of citizenship and representation is by group or community. The ideal of the private citizen is not even at issue for Tammany. This problematic constitution of the citizen on a grid of public and private disrupts Jacob Riis's attempt to find the "inner" man in order to give depth or reality to the urban slum dweller. Only by finding that inner man can Riis identify previously unassimilable aliens and prepare them for self-representation and thus to join the public sphere rather than remain in the "private" sphere of the ethnic. Riis's insistence on using the private to underwrite a public conception of identity underlies regional writing more generally. In each case, the two forms of appearance in the social field require that each text rewrite certain markers of shared national identity as a feature of individual character, thus allowing the trace of the foreign to underwrite conceptions of empty, homogeneous citizenship. But the critiques of Lewis's novel and the general Progressivist critiques of Tammany locate the danger of machine politics in its derangement of public and private spaces and identities.

Writing about the construction of a Tammany-style apparatus in San Francisco, Alexander Saxton describes what I have been calling Tammany's strategic transposition of public and private investments as a challenge to traditional concepts of loyalty. A Tammany-style manipulation of "political power to personal advantage" implied a "concept of political power not as accrued from the trust of certain groups of constituents, but as a kind of natural resource subject to private expropriation like a gravel quarry or gold mine" (1996:211). The confusion of public and private that distorts the representation of Tammany novels' characters also informs the vast Progressivist critique of Tammany-style government. The indifference of Tammany to making "appropriate" distinctions between public and private—in fact, Tammany's perceived disposition to appropriate the public in the service of private interests—reinforces larger cultural anxieties about kinds of representation that Tammany afforded ethnic or working-class constituents in the city. Tammany was not interested in individuals except as they could be converted into votes, but in order to get the vote to as many people as possible, Tammany acted as an interchange between private individuals (or raw material, like gravel quarries or gold mines) and public citizens.

Because this chapter deals with two entangled modes of representation—political and literary—a short history of Tammany might be helpful, although it is difficult to assign some versions of Tammany to the domain of history and others to legend or fiction. Tammany began as a political club in New York and took its name from a Native American figure, Tammemund. Constituted as a "wigwam," Tammany's earliest incarnation was nativist and federalist, and it excluded foreigners. After the Civil War, its constitution changed, however, and it gradually came to welcome foreigners in its ranks. By the time of Boss Tweed, whose image and name became interchangeable with Tammany itself, it was infamous for its role in citywide graft and boodle. Tammany was castigated for its role in economic scandals, and it was also infamous for its role in Irish immigrant life. In many contemporary accounts, Tammany and Irishness signal and indicate each other. Although many of Tammany Hall's bosses were Irish (John Kelley, Richard Croker, and Charles Francis Murphy), not all of Tammany's constituents were Irish. Histories of Tammany highlight its role in producing Irish citizens, since it was popularly described by contemporaries as an Irish institution, but it must not be understood as a *specifically* Irish institution. "Facts" about Tammany, like the "graft" Lincoln Steffens chastised the bosses for raking in, circulated in highly partisan ways. Indeed, two historians note that "the source cited most often on the issue of machine politics is Edwin O'Connor's *The Last Hurrah*" and "that it is an open and disturbing question whether O'Connor adopted his account from the scholar or vice versa" (Boulay and DiGaetano 1985:33).

Much of the debate about Tammany during the nineteenth century centered on its strong mythic character, and to counter its inflated status, Tammany exposés tried to put a face on the Tammany machine, to impute to it the kind of agency missing from public accounts. An example is Rufus E. Shapley's anti-Tammany novel *Solid for Mulhooly: A Political Satire*, first published in 1881 and later reprinted in 1889. Shapley appended a preface to the 1889 edition that responded to "constant demands . . . for copies [of the book] which cannot be supplied—notwithstanding the fact that it has been widely circulated by republication in the columns of newspapers" (1970:8). The notation that *Solid for Mulhooly* was available in newspaper serialization must have struck readers as odd, since much of the text of *Solid for Mulhooly* is interwoven with unattributed quotations that in the novel purport to be editorials from a variety of daily newspapers. The new preface to *Solid for Mulhooly* states that not only was the text reprinted in the newspapers but that its narrative was occasionally propelled by the strategic reprinting of fictional newspaper editorials.

It is not especially important for us to decide which parts of the novel were from the newspaper, and thus "real," and which were invented by Shapley, and thus "fictional." Rather, the text's use of both fact and fiction place *Solid for Mulhooly* at an intersection between the market for "news" and the market for "fiction," predicating as a condition for reading the Tammany novel an interest in public, civic issues. The conflation of the public of the novel reader and the outraged public who would be drawn into a discussion about Tammany's systematic ravages of the body politic are inscribed in the novel's occasional use of the second person.

Why continue to talk of the free-school on the hillside as the hope of the Republic, when everyday under your very eyes, you see the indubitable proof that the despised grog-shop is the true birthplace of statesmanship, and the maligned gin-mill the very cradle in which shall be rocked into manhood the coming American politician? (Shapley 1970:21)

The invocation of the reader's public and private duties as a novel reader are juxtaposed with the text's description of Mulhooly, the Irish-American boss, who "soon came to look upon his ward as a property which he owned, or as an empire which he had the right to rule as with a rod of iron . . . he lived but for the public" and who, even more dangerously, "came, in time to see of himself and his political associates as 'we, the people' " (1970:46, 48).

This caustic passage refers to the narrator's indignation about the ethnic and moral constitution of the city's political leaders, but it also hectors the middle-class reader, drawing on a particular link between "private" pleasures of novel reading and the public duties of debating the decay of urban politics. Making this textual gesture interpellates the reader and articulates him or her to an unmarked class position that counters a specific, local, and marked position of class and ethnic threat. Similarly, Shapley strengthens the link between the private pleasures of novel reading and the public duties of critiquing urban politics. He adds urgency to his references to "real" political situations by appending a contemporary anti-Tammany newspaper clipping—this time from an actual newspaper—to the end of his novel, lest the reader be fooled by the fictions of the novel into thinking that "Mulhoolyism," as he calls boss rule, has disappeared.

Finally, Shapley's text is amply illustrated by perhaps the most cele-brated anti-Tammany polemicist, Thomas Nast, whose drawings of Boss Tweed and the Tammany Tiger in *Harper's Weekly* were well known. The ease of circulation of news about Tammany installs all information about Tammany in the public record as "fact" even if the news is simply specu-lation. In an ironic illustration of the interdependence of representations of Tammany with Tammany itself, Morton Keller writes that Boss Tweed, who escaped from jail in 1875 and fled to Spain, was apprehended in Spain and returned to the United States by "authorities who identified him with the aid of a Nast cartoon" (1968:182).

Alfred Henry Lewis's 1903 novel *The Boss*, the focus of this chapter, exemplifies Tammany's intertextuality. In addition to writing *The Boss*, Lewis wrote a biography of Richard Croker, who was the boss of Tam-many from 1886 to 1902. Written in 1901, the biography of Richard Cro-ker is remarkable in its nearly total lack of traditional information about him. Instead, the text is the accumulation of an enormous amount of research in the daily life of the other half. Going around to the saloons and ward meetings, Lewis asked the people whom Croker represented to talk about him, so that his biography is self-consciously modeled on the opin-ions of the people whose lives Croker helped shape. This allowed Lewis to construct a vision of Croker from the point of view of his constituents and to fill in a standard history of Tammany with local histories.

While the political and social opinions of various ward constituents are documented and supplemented by long tirades about politics more generally, there is no real data about or interpretation of Croker himself. Instead, Croker is merely a lens through which Lewis assesses the social conditions that give rise to the relation between Tammany and its "peo-ple." By avoiding a hagiographic or hostile presentation of Richard Cro-ker, Lewis wrote a kind of antibiography, a document whose displacement of the conventions of biography itself installs Tammany and its boss as an empty location in which unforeseen social arrangements come into exis-tence. Parts of the novel *The Boss* are modeled on the information Lewis uncovered when he wrote the biography of Richard Croker. The issues and concerns that helped shape the novelistic accounts of Tammany Hall were already at work in the public record of the operations of Tammany. I am not suggesting though that there is no difference between the novels written about Tammany and Tammany itself. Rather, the novels and the various historical and public documents anxiously converge when we look at how they construct "the people." Historical and fictional work each worry the question of how the Boss might be mobilizing and config-uring the "other half" beyond ethnic categories into solidarities based on other kinds of alliances.

The temptation of reading Tammany novels is to see them as *romans à clef,* which will yield more pleasure and profit if we know their historical context. Although Alfred Henry Lewis's eponymous Boss was modeled after Richard Croker, the character of the Boss cannot be located in the novel *The Boss,* and he is similarly depersonalized in contemporary anti-Tammany discourses. Josiah Strong, for example, argues, "As a demagogue, he shifts his position as the political wind shifts. The boss does not create the situation; the situation creates the boss" (Strong 1907: 157–158). Thus, it does not matter who the Boss "really" is—only that he occupies the position of being boss. The first-person narrator of Lewis's novel, who ultimately becomes the Boss to which the title refers, does not even reveal his name, and no one ever refers to him by it. Rather, the chapter titles are organized as follows: "How the Boss Came to New York" or "The Boss Sees the Power of Tammany." Such titles reveal the emptiness of the Boss's character and shift traditional conceptions of the subject of the novel into the domain of what Mark Seltzer has called "the case" model of nineteenth-century knowledge of subjects. The novel's characters must be understood only in relation to the public institutions and discourses that shape them. In such narratives, people are given character only by these conditional social positions, and so the novel—and the figure of the Boss—thwarts the expectations of the middle-class reader, trained by the genre of realism to expect certain kinds of psychological fullness and subjectivity from its literary characters.

As Seltzer argues of realism:

[Realism] is formed from the outside in—filled, as it were, with the social—and the project of accounting for persons in the realist text becomes then an account of persons as "socially constructed." The radical pressure that the later nineteenth-century realist and naturalist text places on the category of persons—in positing that the individual is something that can be made—is bound up with an imperative that this making refers back to the constitutive agency of the social. (1992:94)

Lewis creates the eponymous character of the Boss as a first-person narrator who has no name and very little of what might be described as individuality. He narrates his story in the vernacular to an unnamed reporter, supplying to his interlocutor only the facts of his tenure as a political animal and the strategies that compel his actions in the political sphere.

The Boss arrives in America from Ireland as a boy, runs afoul of a ward heeler on his first day and, in court, makes the acquaintance of the Boss, Big John Kennedy. Boss Kennedy takes a shine to the young immigrant, tutors him, and allows him to rise in the Tammany organization. First the boy runs errands, founds a boy's club devoted mainly to fighting, becomes a confidant of the Boss, and, after Big John Kennedy dies, gradually takes over the Tammany organization. While the nameless hero is rising in the ranks, Big John Kennedy is giving him the political lessons that he will be able to use during his own tenure as boss.

The text traces out a fairly likely route by which a young immigrant might become a ranking member of the Tammany machine, but it does not attribute any kind of personal identity or motivation to any of its characters. The character of the Boss is, paraphrasing Seltzer, constructed as radically social; his identity is made known to readers through politics, through his public life. The lack of any description of the Boss's thoughts, feelings, sympathies, or sense of interiority counters a reading practice based in realist novels, in which depth is privileged. It returns us to a completely different idea of character—less like that of genteel regional fiction and more like that of antebellum tall tales or the hero of a picaresque novel. But the lack of interiority, of a kind of "inner self," also makes the figure of the Boss the embodied will of the people and the transparent window through which the public might glimpse their aggregated features. At one point the Boss says:

I went behind the bars by the word of Big John Kennedy; and it was by his word that I emerged and took my liberty again. And yet who was Big John Kennedy? He was the machine; the fragment of its power which molded history in the little region where I lived. As mere John Kennedy he would be nothing. (Lewis 1967:37)

A Boss is a "fragment" of power; as a mere man he would be nothing. But if the Boss, often conceived and vilified as the head of an organization, is merely a fragment, what is the larger whole to which he belongs? As I have argued, if the Boss is the emblem through which the public might perceive the people, the slippage between the description of the Boss as the whole and the fragment of the machine speaks to the way in which his position might be seen as a mirror of the larger official institutions of the city itself. It is this aspect that is important, because the Boss is the obverse image of those institutions and therefore dematerializes them, but his actual physical presence is familiar to his ward constituents. He cannot be fixed in either a social space or a physical place by the *other* "other half," the bourgeoisie who excoriate Tammany's political machinations. To them, the Boss is illegible. "As most men know, there is no such post as that of Chief of Tammany Hall. The office is by coinage, and the title by conference, of the public. There exists a finance committee of, commonly, a dozen names" (Lewis 1967:223).

The Boss is even absent from the production of his own "memoir." Having never learned to write, he is only dictating his story, leaving no trace of his own hand. In fact, his power is contingent on the systems of official power on which democracy, "the conference of the people," is founded. His "word" by which some go free and others are detained resonates with two seemingly incommensurable forms of power; the first local and intimate, as in speech but not writing, and the second magisterial and proclamatory, as in the decree of the king. The Boss's power is dependent on the successful mixing of the two. Indeed, one of the contemporary quotations from the *Oxford English Dictionary* under the word *Tammany* is from Oliver Wendell Holmes, who wrote in 1885 that "the Tammany Ring is to take the place of the feudal lord."

Through the Boss, the power and authority of the bourgeois "other half" of the city can be located for the faceless, nameless ward inhabitants, and in turn, through the figure of the Boss, the fearsome mob becomes embodied. It is not simply that the people "coin" the Boss but that the Boss coins the people. He mediates and brings into political equivalence two chaotic cities: one, the mysterious tenement wards, and the other, the well-ordered middle-class districts.

The most famous compiler of facts about the "other half," Jacob Riis, explains the doubled city by describing the physical and ethnic geography of various neighborhoods and by referring to an uncanny subterranean city, pointing out New York's sinister and secret infrastructures, the hidden physical connections between the city's poorest neighborhoods. For Riis, this moment signals a break in his depiction of well-defined ethnic neighborhoods housing subjects with equally well-defined identities. The hidden connections might be extended through the figure of the Boss, who is, after all, a kind of government official, a figure who creates access points to hidden or forbidden spaces.

I emphasize the rhetoric of the Boss's role as ruler of the city to underscore the nineteenth century's anxiety over the governance and regulation of its citizens. One way the ward boss was theorized was as *regius*—the head of the region. But in order to be head of a larger region, itself the product of many neighborhoods, the Boss needs to traverse seemingly impermeable categories and boundaries—social, ethnic, class, even sexual boundaries. The Boss says about himself, "I laid out my life as architects lay out a building. A dictator is so much unlike a poet in that he is made, not born" (Lewis 1967:81). Countering "born" with "made" creates the Boss as a figure who works for his ascension rather than simply inheriting it, and the juxtaposition of "dictator" and "poet" firmly places him in the twinned fields of political and literary representation.

Big John Kennedy says, "My pull's my pull; it's my property as much as a bank's money is the bank's, or a lawyer's brains is the lawyer's . . . my pull is my capital" (Lewis 1967:182). If the Boss's language or persuasive capacity is a kind of capital, he is right to equate it with power. His pull might be seen as emanating from his invisible hand, redistributing wealth among his constituents at the same time he exposes the actual workings of capital's uneven distribution according to the "unregulated" invisible hand. We can contrast the Boss's reliance on the arts of persuasion to his masculinity as it is described in the novel: the Boss fights, hangs around in saloons, pals around with violent buddies.

The entanglement of cultural and natural identity makes the Boss's relationship to family and gender especially interesting. The Boss can, after all, reproduce. In his manipulation of voting, the Boss literally makes bodies appear where there were none before. He explains that

a man votes with a full beard; then he votes with his chin shaved; then he shaves the sides of his face and votes with a mustache; lastly he votes with a smooth face and retires to re-grow a beard against the next campaign. Ten thousand men should tally forty thousand votes. (Lewis 1967:215)

This wily tactic not only demonstrates the Boss's political technique, but it also presents the apparition of seemingly stable individuals changing (even if momentarily) their identities by manipulating stable, physical signs of those identities. It is impossible to tell who is who when people manipulate their identities, and impossible to predict what they will do based on their "natural" identities. The Boss creates a constituency that can propel him to victory—that mysterious combination known as "the people" to whom the Boss attributes the source of his power.4

The production of people where there were none before is both a natural and a cultural act metaphorically tied to reproduction and economic systems of production. The figure of the Boss stands as a relay through which the languages of nature and culture (via machinery) can meet. The imbricated rhetoric of production and generation shows the contradictory ways in which political novels explain the people that the Boss (text as well as character) represents and speaks for.

In another extraordinarily popular Tammany text, *Plunkitt of Tammany Hall*, Plunkitt explains that

Tammany Hall is a great big machine, with every part adjusted delicate to do its own particular work. It runs so smooth that you wouldn't think it was a complicated affair, but it is. Every district leader is exactly fitted to the district he runs and he wouldn't exactly fit any other district. (Riordan 1963:45)

Much of the language of *The Boss* is derived from a culture of machines. "Don't get too hot. You'll blow a cylinder head" (Lewis 1967: 62), one character advises another. Or "Big Kennedy's success at the election served to tighten the rivets of his rule" (67). Arguing about the fitness of his ward heelers, the Boss tells us,

My district leaders were the pick of the covey, and every one, for force and talents of executive kind, fit to lead a brigade into battle. Under these were the captains of election precincts; and a rank below the latter come the block captains—one for each city block. Thus were made up those wheels within wheels which, taken together, completed the machine. (Lewis 1967:355)

A phrase like "wheels within wheels" describes the ward heeler's place in the structure, and it resonates against a larger discourse of working-class bodies and machines. The working poor were intimately tied to machines. Immigrants were initially brought to the United States as raw labor for these machines, and machines brutalized them and kept them anonymous. The working-class characters—the mechanics—are represented here not just as cogs in the machine, literally "wheels within wheels," but as the arm of the machine (here, in reverse, we see how machines themselves were anthropomorphized as a way of visualizing, or ordering, the bodies of the immigrants). Because of their intimate relationship with the machines that brutalized them, workers are represented as brutes, animals, and savages. The language of Lewis's text draws a median line through these two seem-ingly polar opposites—on the one hand, the language of machinery and, on the other, the language of the raw material that supplies this machine. The figure of the Boss—both exemplar of the machine and leader of a tribe of men—becomes a figure in whom the twinned discourses of production and reproduction are balanced.

The language of "raw material" and production was not unusual in texts about the working-class and immigrant constituents of Tammany. Josiah Strong says about the immigrant population of New York that "here is a vast amount of valuable raw material out of which admirable Americans can be made" (Strong 1907:65). But while Strong wants to assimilate the immigrant into the category of "American," the Boss sim-ply wishes to gather them as the people who will help him retain power. It is clear that reform texts believe that the populations from which the ward boss produces "the people" are the same discontented immigrants and workers who need to be reformed into good citizens. The novels about Tammany describe the job of the Tammany Boss in relation to a cer-tain amount of physical labor to be done in certain communities. The Boss must be present at social occasions, visit saloons, arrange entertainment, consult with the troubled, and be seen on the streets. In his neighbor-hoods, constituents serve him, and in return, he repays them with the basic necessities of existence—no mean feat. Peter Hales points out that "the [official] political system's failure to cope meant more than loss of representation of the poor and laboring classes. Sewage systems and parks, street paving and city planning, water, gas, and utilities, police ser-vices and justice. All were provided, if at all, last and most reluctantly to the poor" (Hales 1984:165).

Similarly, in her biography of Tammany Boss Charles Murphy, Nancy Weiss tells us that each evening, Murphy would stand beneath a street light waiting for his constituents to come to him for favors. Lewis's Boss conforms to this model, doing

what men call good, too, and spent money and lost sleep in its accomplishment. To the ill he sent doctors and drugs; he found work and wages for idle men; he paid landlords and kept the roofs above the heads of the penniless; where folk were hungry he sent food, and where they were cold came fuel. For all that, it was neither humanity nor any milk of kindness which put him to these labors of grace; it was but his method of politics. (Lewis 1967:39)

It is not simply for love of his constituents that the Boss carries out tasks that should be performed by the city's official structures. It is to tighten his hold on the people he is representing. This comports with the mythology of the Tammany Boss as both a broker for services and a kindly neighborhood parent. This latter image dominates pro-Tammany mythologies. One of the central tropes of Tammany novels is the family, and in his structuring of various modes of power, the ward boss becomes a city father by becoming a patron to various urban dwellers.

In becoming a father to distinct urban dwellers, the Boss must bring together disparate people, must find a way to relate them to one another. The text shows us that the Boss relies on a wide array of models of community to do this. It is interesting that the novel never shows us the Boss exploiting ethnicity, the single model of community that might make sense to the middle-class, reform-minded public. Rather, the Boss chooses models that allow his constituents to move beyond the "natural" relations of ethnic solidarity and identity. One of the first communities on which political novels draw is family. Accordingly, Lewis uses the Boss's constituents to denaturalize family and domesticity as organizing metaphors of identity, just as he denaturalizes the idea of character and subjectivity for his readers through the impersonal figure of the Boss.

Lewis's Boss is like a father to his constituency—he keeps solvent and happy the extended family that constitutes his ward. The characters in this novel are almost entirely male, with only three extremely marginal female characters. The women are primarily off stage for most of the action, and Lewis rarely describes the Boss's home life. The only family bond that seems strong is that between Big John Kennedy (the former Boss) and his own father, Old Mike. Even this bond is not so much deference as shrewdness; Big John yields to Old Mike's word as he does to the power in the ward. All the other "real" families are tangential to the novel's action or are nearly meaningless as social foundations of identity. For example, even though the Boss's family came to America with him from Ireland, they are notably absent. In an aside, he tells us that he has married, and occasionally his only child, a daughter, moves her pallid form from one room to another. The anti-Boss reformist father and his scheming son Morton are at political odds. The Boss recruits this son from the reformers and teaches Morton "lessons" about loyalty and politics as if he were his natural father.

Family is not the only model for community. The structure of Tammany men is organized like the military, and the family, as in the military, becomes cultural and not "natural." The Boss states, "Where a machine and its laws are known, the people when they lift to office one proposed of that machine, thereby direct such officer to submit himself to its direction and conform to its demands" (Lewis 1967:107). Tammany alone stands as the institution that organizes all human relations. It alone locates its members standing in the "home" ward. It is instructive to look at the language the narrator uses to refer to his place in his ward and his affiliation with Tammany. People from outside the ward are invaders who belong to rival tribes (47). "To leave one's own ward, or even the neighborhood where one lived, was to invite attack. In an alien ward, one would be set upon and beaten to rags before one traveled a mile" (50).

Marcus Klein reinforces the novel's discussion of the territorial economy of the street or neighborhood when he writes about immigrant children:

The street had its own demanding cultural criteria. The street was a metaphor for territory. It was something to be possessed and defended, and sometimes extended. Since the urban ghetto was in fact a warren of ghettos, one's own street— meaning one or two city blocks—was likely to have an ethnic definition created by the ethnic differences of the neighboring streets. . . . The street therefore was the place where ethnic warfare was most candid. (1981:30–31)

The "unnatural" reorganization of urban space was a rallying cry for urban reformers like Jacob Riis, who wanted to make streets safe and visible, to map and control them. Riis also railed against business's usurpation of domestic space, arguing that street culture existed because the homes of workers were doubling as places of production. The undermining of the family and the potentially deleterious effect that this might have on the nation's civic health were intimately bound up with the sites of Tammany recruitment. Lewis's Boss contends that

New York has no home. It sits in restaurants and barrooms day and night. It is a city of noisome tenements and narrow flats so small that people file themselves away therein like papers in a pigeonhole. These are not homes: they grant no comfort; men do not seek them until riven by want of sleep. It is for the cramped reasons of flats and tenements that New York is abroad all night. The town lives in the streets. (Lewis 1967:233)

This vision of a town living in the streets is a metaphor for a certain kind of "homelessness" that pertains to the cramped living conditions of individuals and families as well as to the deracination of workers and immigrants. In his function as a ward father, the Boss stands at the head of the culture of the neighborhood and street, drawing together the similarly displaced. The placeless space of Tammany, then, acts as a kind of imaginary region, locating the disparate foreign and criminal elements on a single horizon.⁵

Indeed, it is partly this placeless space that enables Tammany to expose the fictiveness of a unified public and a unified public space in which politics could be debated. Mary Ryan's critique of the public sphere in late-nineteenth-century U.S. culture insists on the flourishing of public spirit and public debate

in distinctive spaces, not primarily in literary and political clubs and in the culture of print but in outdoor assemblages, in open, urban spaces, along the avenues, on street corners, and in public squares. . . . American citizens enacted publicness in an active raucous, contentious, and unbounded style of debate that defied literary standards of rational and critical discourse.

She then says more pointedly that "this urban public found its social base in amorphous groupings of citizens aggregated according to ethnicity, class, race, pet cause, and party affiliation" (Ryan 1994:264).⁶ In the absence of any bounded spaces in the city in which the participation of citizens could be policed or enforced, the public (and its various constituents) seemed to continually rise up and reshape itself. This absence of identifiable physical location is echoed in critical language about the Tammany Boss's city itself. For example, Rufus Shapley's *Solid for Mulhooly* describes the Boss's plans for city improvement:

The Committee on Streets, of which he was a member, was constantly reporting bills to open, pave, and grade streets, some of which no mortal eye had seen, and no mortal foot had ever trodden or would have any occasion to tread for years to come, and many of which appeared only in the city map as spaces between imaginary lines leading from No-where to No-place. (1970:45)

The city is doubly invisible in this citation, since the Boss, as contemporary critics averred, could call into being a constituency out of noncitizens and also seemed to be able to imagine and finance a city that would never exist. Even more exemplary is the rhetoric about the city's unpoliced spaces. The same kinds of official and unofficial reorganizations of streets and neighborhoods enabled by the figure of Tammany finds a parallel in the acknowledgment of constituencies and neighborhoods that enter the public sphere on the basis of their interested identity—on the basis of their needs in a limited public sphere.

Describing the day of a typical ward heeler to his reporter/transcriber, Plunkitt explains,

Ahearn's constituents are about half Irishmen and half Jews. He is as popular with one race as with the other. He eats corned beef and kosher meat with equal nonchalance, and it's all the same to him whether he takes off his hat in the church or pulls it down over his ears in the synagogue. (Riordan 1963:49)

In his history of Tammany in relation to the Democratic Party of New York, James McGuire writes that "the leadership of Tammany Hall was shrewd enough to cultivate these new elements in the rapidly increasing population of New York City. It was sympathetic and helpful to them." It "extended its aid to scores and hundreds of thousands of destitute but eager and helpful newcomers, who naturally remembered with gratitude the kindly hand extended to them in their emergencies." Later he points out that "although intensely American in its principles and doctrines, Tammany Hall has never advocated invidious distinction against foreigners and continuously and zealously opposed Native-Americans, Know-Nothings and all that school of politicians who opposed the admission of naturalized citizens to all the rights of citizenship" (1905:218).

In his biography *Richard Croker*, Alfred Henry Lewis insists that

Tammany from the first has stood for the rights of man rather than the privileges of money. The rights of property are second to the rights of humanity in the teachings of Tammany Hall. This is and was as it should be. Tammany Hall was and is made up in the grand aggregate of its membership of poor folk—those whose craft is of the hands. With ninety thousand names on its tallies the collected private riches of Tammany's whole membership would not reach the single figure of any one of a half dozen fortunes which dwell in this town. (1901:44)

Partisan historian Martin W. Littleton agrees with this emphasis on "pure" democracy, romanticizing Tammany's representation of the people by saying that Tammany "stood like a rock in defense of the great catholic principle of the Jeffersonian Party that government is not the peculiar function of a class, but the right and duty of all the people" (1905:237).[7]

But these are somewhat idealized notions when one returns to the ways in which images and fictions about Tammany described community in the ward and neighborhood. Tammany novels worry the meaning of community, and pro-Tammany novels, such as *The Boss*, present radically progressive ideas about how community could be accounted for. Let us look at the novel's language concerning the actions of the people comprising Tammany's members. An elder ward statesman opines:

Remember this: the public don't care for what it hears, only for what it sees. Never interfere with people's beer; give 'em clean streets; double the number of lamp-posts—th' public's like a fly, it's crazy over lamps—an' have bands playin' in every par-rk. Then kape th' streets free of ba-ad people, tinhorn min, an' such. You don't have to drive 'em out o' town, only off th' streets; th' public don't object to dirt

173

but it wants it kept in th' back alleys. . . . The public will go with ye loike a drunk-ard to th' openin' of a new s'loon. (Lewis 1967:155)

and later argues that

while I believe in rigidly enforcin' every law until it is repealed, I have always held that a law can be tacitly repealed by th' people, whithout waitin' for th' action of some state legislature. . . . To put it this way: If ther's a Sunday closin' law, or a law ag'inst gamblers, or a law ag'inst obstructin' th' streets, an' th' public don't want it enforced, then I hold it's repealed by th' highest authority in th' land, which is th' people, d'ye see. (Lewis 1967:163)

According to the fans of Tammany, it is clearly the disenfranchised who profit by being represented by the Boss, and it is their loyalty that keeps the Boss in power. The first piece of advice that Old Mike offers to the Boss is to remember that the people are interested only in the local conditions of their existence, and the second is to invoke the classical forms and rhetoric of democracy to overturn the laws of the entire city or even, by logical extension, the nation. The first passage imagines the people as complacent dupes, the second as a powerful and organized voice in the course of events.

It is tempting to read Tammany and the Boss as a form of representation—both literary and political—by which the disenfranchised became heard as and for themselves, rather than visible simply as a problem to be solved by philanthropists.

The first citation from *The Boss* works on the unremarked slippage between the categories of "the people" and "the public" with which this chapter began by noting. Such a slippage underscores the mobility of individuals and groups around their perceived interests and dramatizes the potential for citizens of New York to be interpellated by the official institutions of the city against Tammany Hall. The fall of the Tweed ring began with the exposure of graft in the millions of dollars, which shocked not just the middle and upper classes but the constituents of Tammany as well, so that they momentarily moved from being the "people"—represented and representable by Tammany—to being the civic-minded public, scandalized by the offenses against the disinterested public good perpetrated by the parasitic Tammany tiger. In short, the partisan people became the outraged public.

This kind of inability to predict how the "people" could be constituted and governed mimics their curious absence in the histories of Tammany and the novels about Tammany culture. Most political novels, this one included, are only about the Boss, even if he is constructed to be representative of the people. In Priscilla Wald's terms, the stories of the people are "untold narratives," and these untold narratives exist as a visible gap in these novels. What is striking in Lewis's satire *The Boss*—as well as in

Shapley's anti-Tammany, anti-Irish *Solid for Mulhooly,* and even in the hagiographic *The Honorable Peter Stirling*—is the relatively meager discussion of who the constituents are and what they want.

In an extremely negative review of *The Boss,* John Seymour Wood writes:

The boss is a Celtic aborigine, with the treachery, the cunning, the taciturnity, the lawlessness, of an Iroquois. If there is a laugh in Mr. Lewis's new book, it is a satirical laugh at the "reputable" citizen of New York, and the laugh is still on us *citoyens*—since we seem as yet to be unable to tame the Tammany savage and reduce him to law and order. (1904:486–487)

The language of this review suggests that ethnicity is "naturally" tribal and aboriginal. The subtext of the review is the familiar change that some ethnicities, especially the Irish, resembled animals, and that there was a constitutive tension between a tribe and a nation, between the local interests of the "Celt" and the national interests of the citizen.

This reviewer's focus on the "Celt" conforms to the popular idea that the main constituents of Tammany were Irish. Such an idea not only runs counter to most Tammany novels, which try to erase ethnicity as the ground of political alliance, it also pleads for locating the Boss and the people in an easily interpreted system of naturalized relations. In *The Boss* and various other pro-Tammany novels, any ethnicity, including Irishness, is not an essential quality; that is, one chooses to join the family of Tammany, one is not born into it. According to Werner Sollors,

In American social symbolism ethnicity may function as a construct evocative of blood, nature, and descent, whereas national identity may be relegated to the order of law, conduct, and consent. Writers and theorists participate in the delineation of a conflict between contractual and hereditary, self-made and ancestral, definitions of American identity. (1986:151)

Sollors's theory of consent and descent seems to find its logical terminus in the fictions of Tammany Hall, with consent and descent applying instrumentally and in equal measure. Plunkitt's casual remark about the Boss's ability to "be at home" among all ethnic groups is one way of demonstrating that the Boss is a self-made man but that he made himself by appealing to yet traversing codes of ethnicity. Similarly, the ways in which the constituents are interpellated as ethnic yet confederated with others of their class interests does not demonstrate that ethnicity is fictive, or somehow unreal, but that it is only one aspect of how "the people" who vote Tammany might choose to describe themselves.

Martin Shefter writes that

when workers did join with others in an effort to improve their lives, ethnicity was at least as likely as social class *per se* to be the basis of association. It will not do, however, to speak of ethnicity and class as competing principles of identification and organization—the prevailing fashion in the historiography of the period. (Shefter 1986:231)

I am not arguing here that Tammany historically embodied this notion of a completely fictive ethnicity. John Higham writes, for example, that during the funeral procession for Rabbi Jacob Joseph in 1902 on the Lower East Side of New York, Irish workers "pelted the crowd with iron nuts and bolts" and that the predominantly Irish police force injured about two hundred of the Jewish mourners in retaliation for a mass Jewish rebellion against the Tammany ticket of 1901. Ironically, the revolt of the Jewish constituents was meant to protest the brutality of the largely Irish police force (see Higham 1984:95–116). This anecdote reveals the ways in which much of the historical power of Tammany emerged from its stabilization of the category of ethnicity. Instead, my argument is that the novels that brought Tammany and its ethnic constituents to the reading public largely ignored such interethnic warfare in order to present the specter of interethnic cooperation and consolidation as the Tammany machine's primary agenda.

The basis of association itself prompted fictions about Tammany and its collective worries over "the people." The various tropes of family—an argument about ward constituents as based on descent—fall apart in the various texts' presentations of Tammany men as joined in consent in a voluntary association through the figure of Tammany Hall. In *Richard Croker*, for example, Lewis says that what makes Tammany "impregnable" (an interesting term in Tammany's rewriting of the family) is that it "is a political organization one day in the year; it is a charitable-benevolent-fraternal organization three hundred and sixty-five" (1901:158).

It is the fact that Tammany is fraternal, that it can be joined and can recruit, that makes it so alarming to commentators. For instance, if we look back at the humorous discussion in *The Boss* about how people vote in various stages of disguise, we see an image of people instrumentally remaking themselves in an effort to serve a political party. This rhetoric is echoed in all kinds of Tammany novels, in which people become other than what they have been supposed to be. Even in the cynical advice to the Boss about the people's ability to repeal a law, we can see a struggle for meaning between how people's essential identities can be reordered in the fictions of late-nineteenth-century urban culture. As we can see in Lewis's remark that Tammany was composed of "those whose craft was of the hands," Tammany appears as a double of the specter of trade unions that seemed everywhere to be disturbing the laws of industry and capital.[8]

The doubling with Tammany of the voluntary association par excellence—the union—rewrites the crisis over representation at the core of

Tammany novels. Tammany's voluntary "people" are juxtaposed with an official voluntary organization emerging in an organized public space.⁹ Almost every Tammany novel has a section on the emergence of the labor union as a threat to (because it was a mirror image of) the Tammany organization. The narrator of *The Boss* finds his most difficult political fight against the growing power of the union. The Boss says,

When I found myself master of Tammany, my primary thought was to be cautious. I must strengthen myself; I must give myself time to take root . . . the political condition was far from reassuring. The workingman—whom as someone said we all respect and avoid—was through his unions moving to the town's conquest. Nor was I long in coming to the knowledge that behind it marched a majority of the people. Unless checked, or cheated, that labor uprising would succeed; Tammany and its old-time enemies would alike go down. (Lewis 1967:210–211)

About the union, the Boss says portentously, "For Tammany it promised annihilation, since of every five who went with this crusade, four were recruited from the machine" (1967:219). Similarly, Paul Leicester Ford's genteel promachine novel *The Honorable Peter Stirling* (1894) gives us a version of ward Boss Peter Stirling organizing his constituents *against* their class interests in order to quell a violent citywide strike.

This spectral threat resonates with critics of urban conditions like Jacob Riis and Josiah Strong. As I have tried to show by reading the literature produced about the Boss and the machine, the category of "the people" was the Tammany machine's ostensible base of power, but in order to represent "the people" on whom Tammany was built, the novels also had to conflate class and ethnicity. Such a conflation advanced a model of democracy that created its own people and that shocked the public *in* the novels, as well as the public *of* the novels. But the figure of the Tammany Boss also decouples contemporary social debates about ethnicity and class.

In his enormously successful *Our Country, Its Possible Future and Present Crisis*, Josiah Strong identified "perils" to the future of a democratic America. Although the list of chapter headings might seem now somewhat disconnected from one another, the inclusion of "Immigration," "Romanism," "Religion and the Public Schools," "Mormonism," "Socialism," and "The City" have in common their potential to lure the people into obeying governments other than that of the United States. In particular, Strong points out that both Romanism and Tammany Hall recruited from the same pool of individuals and both set up a feudal system of allegiance and obedience that prevented the individual from becoming an American subject.

Immigration is the strength of the Catholic church; and there is a Catholic vote. Immigration is the mother and nurse of American socialism; and there is to be a socialist vote. Immigration tends strongly to the cities and gives them their political complexion. And there is no more serious menace to our civilization than our rabble-ruled cities. (Strong 1963:55)

The crucial slippage here is between "immigrants" and "rabble," a slippage that suggests that immigrants do not, despite what Strong says later, share "an unhappy tendency toward aggregation, . . . thus building states within a state, having different languages, different antecedents, different religions, different ideas and habits, preparing mutual jealousies and perpetuating race antipathies" (Strong 1963:56–57).

The inability to examine how alliances are made across ethnic lines allows Strong to assert that simply assimilating immigrants will break up dangerous allegiances while also arguing that ethnicity is not the entire reason for popular discontent with the ruling powers. Although the novels of machine politics show ward bosses actively working against the union movement, they also invoke the specter of workers, placing these "mechanics" at the center of "the machine" as well as at the center of debates about representation and identity. In highlighting the volatile nature of Tammany's "people" and in arguing that class, rather than ethnicity, formed the basis of their interest in the ward boss, Tammany novels suggest that the products of Plunkitt's "most perfect machine on earth" (Riordan 1963:49) might someday join together to represent themselves in the "more perfect union" in which they live.

Following Raymond Williams's argument about the relations among dominant, emergent, and residual forms, we might see the Tammany novel as foregrounding a struggle over the forms through which people might be understood as citizens. The residual form of government that Tammany represents—a feudal form, as Habermas might say, but a residual "face-to-face" knowable community, as Williams might say—helps configure an emergent bloc of voters, allied through a shared desire for access to the public sphere. That such access itself might have been predicated on a dominant idea of ethnic identity does not mean that it announced ethnicity as the final form of urban identity. Rather, it tells readers that ethnicity merely might have been the first, best point of access. Once inside some version of a public sphere, ethnicity could be embraced or discarded as merely "private." It is the second aspect that is the most compelling. Ascending to "the" or "a" public sphere and finally attaining an unmarked identity means that in the late nineteenth century the public sphere is radically unstable and unevenly developed. Through that uneven development, we might track the unevenly distributed economic and political access of various kinds of subjects.

In this book I have argued that the genre of regionalism is imbricated in the historical and social facts from which it has been traditionally understood as turning away. As earlier chapters demonstrated, the dialect-speaking regional type is an uncanny shadow version of an incompletely understood and assimilated ethnic subject. The process of translating such an ethnic subject into regional fictions and locations allows the genre to keep ethnicity in its "place" and to narrate material and pressing political divisions as variations in local or cultural identities. In closing with Tammany, I contend that the ideological operations of regionalism are not limited to texts normally associated with the genre, such as romantic stories about the chivalrous South or nostalgic stories about preindustrial New England villages. Regional writing adjudicates the role of difference in the creation of an American character. Tammany novels represent "unrepresentable" people, making explicit the conflicts between character and type, native and stranger, home and elsewhere, subtending the representational strategies of regional writing. In creating a region not founded on territory or on quaint cultural traits, but on shared political interests, Tammany novels foreground the divisions among the kinds of people who have access to dominant cultural institutions and practices, revealing that regionalism covers more ground than it has traditionally been assigned. Political novels' critique of the bourgeois sphere of disinterested debate extends to other kinds of analysis in which ideas of culture are substituted for politics or in which individual identity and private interest are recruited to disavow public investment and subject position. Tammany's brokering of identities relies on the relay between *homme* and *citoyen* and it reveals a problem in the construction of the public sphere as a unitary site of debate over the contours and content of the public good.[10]

Notes

Works Cited

Index

Notes

INTRODUCTION

    1. The terms *regionalism* and *local color* have a vexed relationship to each other. Late-nineteenth-century reviews of what I call *regional fiction* did not refer to the texts in question in any consistent way. Rather, such texts were interchangeably called "dialect stories," "local color," or even local-color "sketches." Some analyses of American regional fiction treat the terms as referring to separate (if formally related) kinds of writing. Separating them allowed some critics to distinguish the tone of some stories or to argue that local color and regional writing were differently gendered. Some feminist critics, for example, distinguish between the more obviously "male" caricatured qualities of local color and the empathetic "female" qualities of regionalism. But this description is self-defining; there were many "empathetic" men writing genteel regional fiction. When describing as the texts that I use as "regional," I am following the example of recent scholars working in American literature, many of whom feel as indebted as I do to feminist scholars for recovering crucial regional texts.

    2. For an excellent study of the varying kinds of cultural capital attached to different late-nineteenth-century periodicals, see Nancy Glazener's *Reading for Realism* (1997) and Richard Ohmann's *Selling Culture* (1996).

    3. It is as difficult to pinpoint the direct ancestors of a literary genre as it is to understand a single work by returning to the features of its ostensible genre. Too many literary and cultural components contribute to the formation of any given literary genre or movement. In addition, all genealogies of literary genres are motivated. That is, situating a given genre in relationship to other traditions tells not just the story of how the genre in question came to be but also the story of how a version of the past is organized to explain the present. This is particularly ironic in the case of regional writing, as one of its formal principles is the description of the surviving elements of a local past that can infuse the present with new meaning.

    Having denied knowable paternity, I should point out that scholars have at least given regionalism a family tree. Over the years, many scholars have attempted to situate the development of regionalism in the late nineteenth century, and they have done so in a variety of ways. Some critics argue that late-nineteenth-century genteel regional writing developed out of mid-nineteenth-century tall tales and frontier stories. Crude, exaggerated, and humorous tall tales provided a genre in which the "promise" of American expansionism was packaged for ready consumption by ordinary people. The vernacular stories to which I refer here as the progenitor of genteel regional fiction contain what we might consider folkloric elements. Unlike genteel regionalism, these earlier stories were disseminated in popular venues, such as penny papers and cheap magazines. They were mass-produced and mass-consumed, and their reliance on local vernacular allowed them to use the idea of the folk while also appealing to the a growing mass market. For an excellent genealogy of this kind of development, see Alexander Saxton's *Rise and Fall of the White Republic* (1990), especially pp. 183–203; and Claude Simpson's introduction to his edited volume *The Local Colorists in American Short Stories 1857–1900* (1960).

4. For a compact but thorough study of the economic and social conditions in the late nineteenth century, see Hays, *The Response to Industrialism* (1957). On immigration patterns, see Takaki, *A Different Mirror* (1993); and Higham, *Send These to Me* (1984).

5. For more on the connection between the solidification of the nation and the development of the "folk" and the preservation of folklore, see Anderson, *Imagined Communities* (1991).

6. In reference to the content of Howells's "Editor's Study" columns, Amy Kaplan writes: "Howells develops what can be called an 'aesthetic of the common.' A pivotal term in his vocabulary, the common refers at different times to distinct and often contradictory entities: to the lower classes—'common men and laborers,' to a shared human identity—'our common humanity'; and to ordinary life—'the commonplace.' To resolve the tensions between these meanings, realism works to ensure that social difference can be ultimately effaced by a vision of a common humanity, which mirrors the readers' own commonplace, or everyday life" (1983:21).

7. I will not repeat accounts of the history of regional fiction's critical reception, as that has been done exhaustively and conclusively elsewhere. For excellent surveys, see June Howard's introduction to her edited collection of essays on Sarah Orne Jewett (1994), and Judith Fetterley and Marjorie Pryse's introduction to their collection of women's regional writing (1992).

8. Feminist critics have argued that the content and the publication history of regional stories were particularly welcoming to women authors and argue that we can trace its emergence within a female literary tradition. Excellent sources for such criticism include Ammons, "Going in Circles" (1983); Donovan, *New England Local Color Literature* (1983); Fetterley and Pryse's introduction to *American Women Regionalist 1850–1910* (1992); and Nagel's introduction and collected essays in *Critical Essays on Sarah Orne Jewett* (1984). More recent additions to feminist scholarship on regional writing include Campbell's *Resisting Regionalism* (1997) and Pryse's "Sex, Class, and 'Category Crisis'" (1998).

9. I also want to link my work to contemporary revisions of regional writing. Both Nancy Glazener's *Reading for Realism* (1997) and Michael Davitt Bell's *The Problem of American Realism* (1993) cap their readings of realism with a reconsideration of regional writing.

10. My formulation of regionalism as the "alibi" of realism is drawn from

Baudrillard's "Beyond Use Value" (1981). Traditional critiques of regional writing (by which I also mean to those critiques written by late-nineteenth-century commentators) have read it as a minor branch of the "major" genre of realism. By understanding it as a minor genre, critics have been able to impute unproblematically to its representations of regional life the impossible characteristics of transparency and fidelity. Such traditional commentators have, in other words, taken regionalism at its word, reading it as a genre devoted to the portrayal of fading villages and cultures that find themselves threatened by the relentless expansion of homogenizing capital. This kind of reading reassigns to regionalism the "real" of realism's project. While realism is commonly understood to *construct* subjects, regionalism *preserves* always-naturalized subjects. As Baudrillard argues in reference to use value's relation to exchange value, this means that regionalism is realism's "ideological guarantee" because it promises, however falsely, that the "real" exists somewhere (1981:138).

CHAPTER 1. "I FEARED TO FIND MYSELF A FOREIGNER"

1. There has been a welcome and steady increase in critical reexaminations of regional fiction, and a good deal of it has been of the much adored and much critiqued Jewett text *The Country of the Pointed Firs.* Most of these essays rehearse the history of criticism to which regional texts have been subjected, tracing their status as minor texts protecting subcultures and fading villages through their rediscovery by feminist critics of the 1970s. I have therefore not summarized that literary history here. The most recent essay that traces the reception of regional fiction (using as an example *The Country of the Pointed Firs*) is June Howard's excellent "Sarah Orne Jewett and the Traffic in Words" (1994), the introduction to a volume of essays she edited on that text. This volume of essays also demonstrates the process of critical revision of regional fiction, as Howard has included essays by two critics—Elizabeth Ammons and Sandra Zagarell—who have substantially altered their interpretations of regional fiction. Also of interest for current revisions of regionalism are Bell 1993:167–204; Glazener 1997:189–228; and Sundquist 1988.

2. It is worth pointing out here how indebted reevaluations of regionalism are to current theories of postcolonialism and nationalism, which have demonstrated the uses of the past in constructing a nation. Eric Hobsbawm writes, for example, that "where the supremacy of state nationality and state-language were not an issue, the major nation could cherish and foster the dialects . . . within it" (1990:35), Ernest Gellner argues: "Nationalist ideology suffers from a false consciousness. It claims to defend folk culture even while it invents high culture" (1983:124). Both of these remarks might, with very little amendment, be pressed into the service of a newly politicized reading of regionalism.

3. It may seem that I conflate the role of readers, especially nineteenth- and twentieth-century readers, but reading-as-remembering puts contemporary readers in the same position as nineteenth-century readers. The fictional region and everything that it represents about our pristine and, most important, purportedly common past, are equally distanced from us. In fact, our historical position may even intensify the nostalgic effect of regional fiction because we are so much more

innocent of the material and social history that produced it but so much more inundated with its effects. In a larger sense, too, it is crucial to remember that to some extent, scholars who approach the genre of regionalism have been complicit in the design of the regional writer. It is not difficult to see that regionalism's minor status has kept it intact and protected from the seeming depredations of critical theory.

4. In "The Metropolis and Mental Life," for example, Georg Simmel observes about social relations in the city: "[The] mental attitude of metropolitans toward one another we may designate, from a formal point of view, as reserve. If so many inner reactions were responses to the continuous external contacts with innumerable people as are those in the small town, where one knows almost everyone, one would be completely atomized internally and come to an unimaginable psychic state" (1950:415).

5. I have tried to resist the tendency to conflate Sarah Orne Jewett with the narrator of *The Country of the Pointed Firs*. But I think that I may be excused for this single footnote devoted to exploiting the biographical similarities between the two. The scene of the Bowden family reunion provokes a conflicted response toward the regional community in the heart of the narrator, and it also marks the first moment in which she overtly compares her city life and acquaintances with her country life and acquaintances. Jewett herself seems to have been torn by the same conflicted responses as she balanced her regional life in South Berwick and her glamorous life in Boston, which she shared with her longtime companion Annie Fields. She yearned for the city and for Fields but felt that South Berwick was the best place to write. We also know that her letters to her friends were filled with the doings and sayings of the regional folk in her town, which she sent to the city as if they were vacation snapshots. At the same time, she was protective of the rhythms of regional life and wrote in a letter that her first collection of short stories and sketches, *Deephaven*, was "to teach the world that country people were not the awkward, ignorant set those persons seemed to think. I wanted the world to know their grand, simple lives" (Cary 1967:16). It is not difficult to see how Jewett herself implicates herself in that economy of stranger and native.

6. It strikes me that it is also one of the effects that allowed regionalism to be read by some male critics and, for different reasons, some female critics, as a female, rather than a feminized genre, which tells the smaller, private stories that make up the vast national history.

7. The stories to which I refer are "A New England Nun," "A Church Mouse," "A Gatherer of Simples," "A Village Singer," and "A Poetess."

CHAPTER 2. THE REGION OF THE REPRESSED AND THE RETURN OF THE REGION

1. The texts of New England women's regional writing that focus on women not only highlight the local nature of the work performed in the community, but they also argue that such work is gendered labor. Male labor is either performed by men who have left the region and are not present in the text (the son in Jewett's "A White Heron" or the returned lover in Mary Wilkins Freeman's "A New-England Nun," for example, whose appearance in the text coincides with the end

of his labor elsewhere) or who have been superseded, as with the shipbuilders of Dunnet Landing in *CofPF*.

2;. In his chapter "The Shadowed Country," Raymond Williams writes, "Rises and falls on the market . . . which differentially affected agriculture as a mode of capitalist production, worked their final effect through a whole social and economic structure in which the classical problems of rural England—ownership of the land, the means of production, the possession of and function of capital for investment, and the persistent problems of wages, housing and education—were also the predominant problems of the society as a whole. . . . What came out, dramatically, in leaving the land, was how the land itself had hitherto been distributed" (1973:188). The link between the problems of the country and their relation to what regionalism figured as properly urban problems is, in some sense, the project of Garland's writing, as well as Frederic's demystification of the regional subject's self-knowledge.

3. In a remarkably useful and prescient essay, Lewis O. Saum wrote that "literary critics have claimed both too much and too little for the son of the middle border" (1972:36). Saum points out that there is evidence that Garland's commitment to the realism he seemed to champion was always somewhat questionable. He argues that the social-protest elements in *Main-Travelled Roads*, for example, have been overplayed, thereby obscuring the idealistic strain of many of the stories toward human potential for justice. Warren French expresses his suspicion of the literary value of Garland's early work more bluntly: "Even during Garland's most dynamically creative period, he was never more than a stylish journalist" (1970:287).

4. Brown writes, "Reading Garland's fiction and criticism as efforts to imagine the relation between social change, on the one hand, and cultural production and reception, on the other, can help us both to account for his subsequent institutional status, and to think through the way 'populism' has been thought as a cultural possibility" (1994:92).

5. For an excellent discussion of the conflicted notions of value regionalism generates in the literary and political spheres, see Bruce Levy's " 'The Country of Corner Lots,' " (1995).

6. "Again I was disturbed by the feeling that in some way my own career was disloyal, something built upon the privations of my sister as well as upon those of my mother" (Garland 1962:400).

7. Many of Garland's stories are peopled with foreigners from the city who have moved to the Midwest to farm or with immigrants who have come directly to the Midwest. For the most part, these characters are generally Swedes and Germans and are depicted in neither an admiring nor an alarmed way. In general, such people are characterized individually, which allows Garland to avoid the larger issues of their nature in order to focus on the pressures a depression economy and farming exert on them.

8. "Up the Coolly" has been an especially popular story for Garland critics. Recent rereadings of it can be found in Jordan 1993 and in Pizer's reconsideration of Garland (1991:53–67). Bonney MacDonald analyzes both of the stories I focus on in this chapter. McDonald's essay takes up the thematic question of how the two stories allegorize an idealization of an economically desperate land and asks

how such idealizations lead to an imaginative "second 'closing of the frontier' " (1993:229). My essay also notes the idealizing tendencies of the texts but concentrates on the imbrication of literary-aesthetic and reformist-political economies. Of real interest to me, though, is the fact that each of us generated similar kinds of readings of the stories, although to different ends. This testifies to a welcome and an important turn in literary criticism to the political and cultural meanings of the "local."

9. It should be clear that my essay regards Howard as the uncomfortable site not just of regional writing but also of the perils of trying to assume both a local identity and an urban identity. Howard's role as the site of Garland's anxiety about authorship and local identity is clear, for example, in Garland's phrase "I am a Western man" in *Crumbling Idols*, which unconsciously repeats Howard's pride in still considering himself a "Western man," a conceit that the text ironizes and finally destroys. It is particularly interesting, therefore, that Garland's seeming critique of Howard's "false" sympathy is belied by the injunction in *Crumbling Idols* for the regional writer to write with a "full heart" (1952:61). My citation of *Crumbling Idols* is not meant to suggest that it contains anything like a coherent philosophy. Rather, it is to stress that one of the ways in which Garland deflects examination of his own complicity in the entangled forms of value he is critiquing is by trying to establish and naturalize the criteria for membership in local communities.

10. For a good recent (and popular) history of populism, see Stock 1996, esp. 54–86; and also Hays 1957:27–43, 116–139. My reading of the suspicion about the relationship between Grant's ability to speak well and his financial success is drawn from Nancy Glazener, who writes, "Free-flowing speech often seems to be an urban prerogative, part of an implied urban economy of excess, luxury, and deceit that might be exemplified by the language of advertisements and con men, even by easy money. This might seem to be a contradictory attitude, given that rural-identified reformers were working to expand the money supply" (1997:220). Glazener goes on to argue that this "contradictory attitude" represents a general producerist suspicion toward consumer culture. My own argument differs from her invigorating critique in that I do not see the economy of regional fiction—even that written by women and set in the world of the domestic—as underwritten in any way by a desire to replace exchange value with use value. Rather, I think that the narratives of regionalism that I am discussing already recognize their complicity with market values in the East and can only barely suppress that complicity by figuring public chaos as private deviance.

11. Bill Brown writes that for Garland, "a cultural agenda is proclaimed to be the very raison d'être for the economic agenda. Rather than believing that 'culture' will help to effect socio-economic change, he presumes that only such change can effect a transformation of culture." He cites Garland's January 1891 *Arena* essay "A New Declaration of Rights": "It is because into the life of the farmer the single tax would bring music, painting, song and theatre, that I advocate it with such persistent enthusiasm" (Brown 1994:93).

12. In *Crumbling Idols*, Garland champions localism, but as Edward E. Hale Jr. notes in "Signs Life in Literature," "Literature in America may never come to anything without plenty of local color and provincialism (to use Mr. Garland's

expressions), but it will never be a great literature so long as it has nothing besides," going on to say that "everybody writes 'local' stories nowadays; it is as natural as whooping-cough. There is no need of encouragement: to tell the truth, a little restraint would do no harm" (1982:56).

13. In perorations about the identity of the local-color writer and his subject matter in *Crumbling Idols*, Garland writes, "Take, for a single example, the history of the lumbering district of the Northern Lakes . . . this life has had only superficial representation in the sketches of the tourist or reporter; its inner heart has not been uttered" (1952:15); "I am using local color to mean something more than a forced study of the picturesque scenery of a State. *Local color in a novel means that it has such quality of texture and back-ground that it could not have been written in any other place or by any one else than a native*" (1952:53–54; italics in the original).

14. Thomas LeClair notes the same strategy in *Theron Ware*, writing that "the psychological condition Frederic explores in *The Damnation* is the complex relationship between being seen and seeing, between the person as object of perception and the person as perceiver of self and others" (1975:95).

15. This insistence that the region be stripped of nostalgia, which I discussed in the first section of this chapter, is even more pronounced in Frederic's novel *Seth's Brother's Wife*, in which a wealthy New York City man recognizes that his only chance to win a seat in the Senate depends on his running in a relatively sparsely populated region of New York. In order to capture the votes he needs, the politician moves to the country and immediately begins to cultivate the appropriate rustic accent, values, and friends.

16. There is some precedent in the novel for the kind of self-revelation through the eyes of other people that Theron experiences. Describing Celia Madden's stepmother, the narrator makes a seemingly unaccountable detour to describe this woman's characteristics. "Incredibly narrow-minded, ignorant, suspicious, vain, and sour-tempered, she must have driven a less equable and well-rooted man than Jeremiah Madden to drink or flight" (Frederic 1960:92). Interestingly, as with Theron's self-revelation, Mrs. Madden's also comes at the hands of Celia: "There was a note of unreality nowadays in [her friends'] professions of wonder. . . . Worst of all, something of the meaning of this managed to penetrate her own mind. She caught now and again a dim glimpse of herself as others must have been seeing her for years,—as a stupid, ugly, boastful, and bad-tempered old nuisance. And it was always as if she saw this in a mirror held up by Celia" (94).

17. In an argument about the novel as a dramatization of "one archetype of the American consciousness . . . to recognize that amid the intellectual disorder of that time, something may have changed in the *relationship* of the individual self to such turmoil" (1992:55), Bruce Michelson writes that Theron's trip to New York demonstrates a comic ineptitude, as he is "unaware that intellectual posing has an etiquette, and that there are laws against acting fin de siecle in the streets of American towns. The twist is that Ware remains 'sincere,' assuming as he does that creeds should be worn on the sleeve and be significant to professional and domestic life" (61). See also Carrie Bramen's excellent analysis of the racialized thematics of Theron's visit to the city.

CHAPTER 3. THE HISTORY OF A HISTORYLESS PEOPLE

1. In his introduction to *Bret Harte's California*, Scharnhorst deliberately ties together the economic and cultural aspects of regionalism by describing Harte's early writing as "like cartloads of raw ore ready to be milled. They are obviously not finished coin, though they display an abundance of 'color.' In several cases, especially in some of his early articles. . . . Harte seems to be merely prospecting. At their best, however, his letters from California contain nuggets of topical comment and local history quarried from the mother lode" (1990:1).

2. In a later story, Atherton exploits this ethnic/temporal divide even more assertively and clearly. In "Talbot of Ursula," the last in her collection of short stories entitled *The Bell in the Fog and Other Stories* (1905), Atherton tells the tale of Talbot, a wealthy American who goes to the deathbed of an old Spanish friend with whom he was once in love. "The Senora had gone and Delfina Carillo lay there . . . the ugly browns had gone . . . her skin was white, and her cheeks flamed with colour. Her eyes looked enormous, and her mouth had regained its curves and mobility." Talbot's response to the "return" of his old love: "After that first terrible but ecstatic moment of recognition, he was conscious of a poignant regret for the loss of his brown old friend" (1905:298).

3. In her autobiography, *Adventures of a Novelist* (1932), Atherton describes reading an article in a periodical that convinced her that stories about "old" California would be extremely profitable, that such writing was "a mine of wealth waiting for some bright genius to pan it out." Atherton writes: "I read no more. Forked lightning was crackling in my skull. It illumined a dazzling vista. Bret Harte had barely touched upon that period and its nuggets were mine." Although she knew nothing of the ethnic background of her native state, she began collecting material, inspired by "vague rumors, scattered pictures by Bret Harte" (1932:186). For more complete material on Atherton's shrewd reading of the literary market for local-color writing, see Leider 1991.

4. Nostalgia for the romance of the Spanish mission period is well documented, most famously through Helen Hunt Jackson's 1884 novel *Ramona*, which was written, like Harte's letters, from Hunt's experiences as a professional tourist. Carey McWilliams writes that such romanticizing, especially of Native American culture "was second-hand and consisted, for the greater part, of odds-and-ends of gossip, folk tales, and Mission-inspired allegories of one kind or another." Jackson "had originally been sent to Southern California by *Century* magazine to write some stories about the Missions, which, according to the illustrator who accompanied her, were to be 'enveloped in the mystery and poetry of romance.' . . . These crumbling ruins, with their walled gardens and broken bells, their vast cemeteries and caved-in wells, exerted a potent romantic influence on Mrs. Jackson's highly susceptible nature" (1971:59). Jackson, a New Englander, would certainly have been familiar with the conventions of regional writing in the East, and in her somewhat haphazard although earnest collection of gossip and folklore, she advances the most commercial aspects of local color writing.

5. This text is a reissue of a collection of stories that Atherton had published under the title *Before the Gringo Came*.

6. Also in regard to time, the simultaneity about which I write has resonance

not just with a theoretical time of the nation but also with Gellner's practical and acute observation that nationalism as an era comes into being partly because nations industrialize at different speeds and times (Gellner 1983:52).

7. Hobsbawm also tells us that there was already a Chinese restaurant in San Francisco by the 1840s. This might be seen not simply as a sign of how large the city of San Francisco became in a very short period of time but also that it had already developed the neighborhoods that would prove so dangerous to the heroine of this novel.

8. This was also Strong's fear in *Our Country*. He writes, "There is among our population of alien birth an unhappy tendency toward aggregation, which concentrates the strain upon portions of our social and political fabric. Certain quarters of many of the cities, are, in language, customs and costumes, essentially foreign. Many colonies have bought up lands and so set themselves apart from Americanizing influences . . . thus building up states within a state, having different languages, different antecedents, different religions, different ideas and habits, preparing mutual jealousies, and perpetuating race antipathies" (1963:56, 57).

CHAPTER 4. "THE SHADOW OF THE ETHIOPIAN"

1. It would be wrong to ascribe this effect simply to Cable's novel. Richard Brodhead points out that the genre of regionalism "effected a revision of the traditional terms of literary access, a major extension of the literary franchise" and argues further that regionalism's "public function was not just to mourn lost cultures but to purvey a certain story of contemporary cultures and of the relations among them: to tell local cultures into a history of their supersession by a modern order now risen to national dominance" (1993:118, 121). Eric Sundquist also argues for the ideological complexity of regionalism's relationship to culture: "Increasingly evident in the realism of both city and country, is an anthropological dimension in which new 'regions' are opened to fictional or journalistic exploration and analysis. . . . Manifest Destiny, peaking in imperial adventurism at the turn of the century, along with a sudden rise in anxiety about immigration, is not unrelated to the developments of capitalism" (1988:503).

2. Ladd goes on to write that Cable and his editors argued about "whether the romance plot dealing chiefly with the white characters would be foregrounded, or the historical context dealing with issues of race and genealogy stemming from the legacies of colonialism and slavery; how prominent a role black and mulatto characters would play; and how much discursive editorializing about race and slavery could be permitted" (1996:50).

3. This resonates with V. N. Volosinov's observation in *Marxism and the Philosophy of Language* that "any current curse word can become a word of praise, any current truth must inevitably sound to many other people as the greatest lie. This *inner dialectic* quality of the sign comes out fully in the open only in times of social crises or revolutionary changes" (1973:23). Gavin Jones uses the characters of Aurora and Clotilde to point out that when white characters address one another in private in a French-inflected-by-slave dialect, they are participating in a "wider cross-cultural transmission of the creative materials of African America" (1997:250).

4. This story is also at the center of the book in a more literal way. Cable initially wrote a story of a captured African King called "Bibi," but the story was rejected by the *Atlantic Monthly* because it was potentially upsetting to readers. The challenge to slavery that "Bibi" represented seems to have found its way into the chronicle of Bras-Coupé (see Michael Kreyling's introduction to the 1988 Penguin edition of *The Grandissimes*).

It also is interesting that the story appears to have had a life of its own in the culture of New Orleans as well. Arlin Turner, Cable's biographer, speculates that he had heard a version of it in New Orleans from a black porter. Furthermore, Lafcadio Hearn transcribed "The Original Bras-Coupé" as he had heard it from another Creole scholar for the *New Orleans Item* in October 1880. Louis Moreau Gottschalk, a creole musician, claimed to have heard a version from his grandmother and included it in his 1881 autobiography (Turner 1956:94–95). Barbara Ladd also offers a complete genealogy of the story's existence in Louisiana culture, placing it against fears about the Haitian revolution, as well as against stories of Louisiana slaves (see Ladd 1996:60–68).

5. In "The Freedman's Case in Equity," Cable returns to the example of Native American versus African origins in regard to the falseness of the category of "race instinct": "We subordinate instinct to society's best interests as apprehended in the light of reason. If there is such a thing, it behaves with strange malignity toward the remnants of African blood in individuals principally of our own races, and with a singular indulgence to the descendants of—for example—Pocahontas" (1885:35).

6. Jerah Johnson writes that the Choctaw were the favored tribe with whom the Louisiana French wished to ally themselves and argues that a pattern of recognizable French–Indian relations could be discerned in Louisiana that paralleled those of Canada, where the assimilationist ideal and state-encouraged intermarriages were commonly accepted colonial strategies until the beginning of the eighteenth century (see esp. 1992:23–38).

CHAPTER 5. DISORIENTING REGIONALISM

1. John Kasson notes that the genre of urban local color and the practice of slumming already were common by the mid-nineteenth century. Such rhetorical conventions as the rewriting of authorial perspective as policing or detection (embodied in the narrator's ability to take both "the bird's-eye view" and a street-level view in the city) in Jacob Riis's narrative were well-used conventions (see esp. Kasson 1990:78–109; also Trachtenberg's analysis of the similarities between literary and pictorial conventions, 1982a:138–154).

2. Wilson further argues that the stress on the local as a way for a rising reporter to distinguish himself led to the sensationalization of the news and the emergence of "stunts" which then were covered by the same reporter who engineered them.

3. See, for example, Marjorie Pryse and Judith Fetterly, Nancy Glazener, Josephine Donovan, Donna Campbell, June Howard, Michael Davitt Bell, Nancy Glazener, Sandra Zagarell, and Elizabeth Ammons.

4. Writing about Stephen Crane's parodic style in *Maggie: A Girl of the Streets*,

Michael Davitt Bell contends that "what seems to be at issue here is the authority of the narrator's ironic language. From the very outset of *Maggie* the reader is obliged to wonder which, if any, of the book's rival languages, the language of the narrator or the language of the street, is authorized by the author, 'Stephen Crane' " (1993:137). Although Bell's study is of realism more generally, it also takes up the related genre of regionalism. I have used some of his arguments about naturalism, following his argument that the study of genre seems less interesting than the study of strategies that link texts to one another. Thus, I do not read Crane as a regionalist any more than I read him as a naturalist. Instead, I wish to show that the strategies of narrating and naming others might be read "regionally."

5. Alan Trachtenberg analyzes "An Experiment in Misery" and "An Experiment in Luxury" in his essay "Experiments in Another Country: Stephen Crane's City Sketches" (1982a). His reading explores Crane's participation in the genre of the urban sketch popularized by the "mysteries of the city" genre but distinguishes Crane's narratives from those of his predecessors by underscoring Crane's negotiation of "newspapers' need to transform random street experience into *someone's* experience. The [newspaper's] convention provided Crane with an opportunity to cultivate an authentic style as a vehicle of personal vision. The danger was that pressure to distinguish his vision, to make his signature recognizable, would lead to stylization" (1982a:141). Trachtenberg's preoccupation with perspective and point of view is consonant with most of the criticism of late-nineteenth-century photographic journalism, but more important, his focus on literary or authorial style reveals how closely literary devices like point of view are implicated in the more obviously political project of containing the other half while protecting readers from "an exchange of subjectivities" with them (1982a:144).

Although I am indebted, in this chapter, to Trachtenberg's classic essay, I make a fundamentally different argument. I do not believe that the hyperstylization of urban local color (a hyperstylization that Michael Davitt Bell also stresses in *The Problem of American Realism*) works to "free" the reader's "point of view from any limiting perspective" (1993:147). I believe that the opposite effect is achieved. The hyperstylization of urban local color producing and produced by the moralistic work of reformers like Jacob Riis and celebrity reporters like Stephen Crane is drawn from the literary conventions of pastoral regionalism. Like the highly visual narratives of urban local color, this hyperstylization relies on the primacy of authentic experience, on the description of the folkways of the proximate other, on the transformative possibilities of contact with strangers, and on the illumination of pictorial conventions drawn from a culture saturated by photographs and images. The stories do not free the reader but illuminate a way of reading that repeats and reinstalls regionalism's project of creating cultural difference out of political difference.

6. Stallman and Hagemann (1966) note that this piece has been reprinted from the *New York Press*, April 22, 1894.

7. The full name of the sketch as it appeared in 1896 in Philadelphia Press is "Stephen Crane in Minetta Lane, one of Gotham's most notorious thoroughfares. The novelist tells what he saw and heard on a street where the inhabitants have been famous for evil deeds. Where the burglar and the shoplifter, and the murderer live side by side. The novel resort of Mammy Ross and others of her kind."

8. Beaumont Newhall points out in *The History of Photography* (1964) that the first edition of Riis's text was not printed with the full photographic documentation we have available now and that not until the 1940s did the full text appear in its present form. Although *HtOHL* was printed with some photographic plates, most of the illustrations were crudely reproduced and supplemented by woodcuts based on photographs. The edition available to the general public does not seem to me to undercut the general point about Riis's use of the technology of seeing photographically and organizing his subjects around such a visual archive. Rather, it supports the ways in which Riis naturalizes a certain kind of visual archive when he describes the ethnic groups and the layout of the city as a whole, since his reliance on such an archive is already present as a narrative strategy even when the photographs were unavailable.

9. Riis's argument about the safety of slumming is repeated in his autobiography almost verbatim, but here he adds: "I have often been asked if such slumming is not full of peril. No, not if you are there on business. Mere sightseeing at such unseasonable hours might easily be. But the man who is sober and minds his own business—which presupposes that he has business to mind there—runs no risk anywhere in New York, by night or by day. . . . [T]he nickname 'Doc' had somehow stuck to me, and I was supposed by many to be a physician connected with the Health Department. Doctors are never molested in the slum. It does not know but that its turn to need them is coming soon" (1901:153). This subtle shift between "mere sightseeing" and "business" does not simply underscore the motives for a tour of the slums; it manages to introduce an unremarked element of "looking back" into Riis's argument, as it explains how the slum decides who will be allowed to pass through it unmolested.

10. Amanda Anderson has also commented on the role of the Chinese in *HtOHL*. See her unpublished 1986 essay, "Resistance and Immunity in Riis's Chinatown: Photography and Philanthropy."

11. The Chinese Six Companies was not a myth, although Riis's inflamed rhetoric played on the worst fears of Americans who believed in the prevalence of secret societies. As important to the Six Companies as the adjudication of internal conflict was its negotiation on behalf of the Chinese with members of the white business community and other public officials (see Takaki 1989:117–119; also Wu 1982:71–127).

12. In attempting to explain this position, Riis says only that "I shall not in this place have to enter into a protracted argument to prove that the home is the pivot of all and why it is so. We *know* that it is so, that it has been so in all ages; that the home-loving peoples have been strong peoples in all time, those that have left a lasting impression on the world. Stable government is but the protection the law throws around the home, and the law itself is the outgrowth of the effort to preserve it" (1903:18).

13. These numbers are from Higham 1963, 1984; and Saxton 1995. For a chronology of Chinese activity in the United States and the local and federal laws enacted against them, as well as the full text of the Geary law, see Tung 1974; also Takaki 1989:79–131.

14. Describing a tramp he wished to photograph, Riis writes that "he was willing to be photographed for ten cents; but, before I could train my camera on

him, his mind had evolved possibilities not to be neglected. He was smoking a clay pipe that had, perhaps, cost a cent, but I suppose it was an effort to hold it between his teeth while I made ready, for he made a demand for twenty-five cents if he was to be photographed in character, pipe and all" (1903:109).

CHAPTER 6. REPRESENTATION AND TAMMANY HALL

1. In their essay "Why Did Political Machines Disappear?" Harvey Boulay and Alan DiGaetano argue that "the political machine was an ingenious answer to the question of who would control the local state in a period of rapid social and economic change. Mass-based but with ties to social and economic elites, it provided a useful meeting point for the volatile elements of the late nineteenth- and early twentieth-century American city" (1985:26).

2. Here I draw on Priscilla Wald's *Constituting Americans* (1995). Her vision of the uncanny helps define individual subjectivity in the nineteenth century, but I use it instead to discuss a group modeled in certain ways on the very nation on which it seemed to be a parasite. See in particular Wald's incisive introduction, in which she writes that "national narratives of identity seek to harness the anxiety surrounding questions of personhood, but what they leave out resurfaces when the experiences of individuals conspicuously fail to conform to the definition of personhood offered in the narrative" (1995:10).

3. Clearly, not all Tammany novels are identical, although many of them have similar plot structures, and as I argue, all of them meditate in some fashion on the representability of "the people" that Tammany serves. What differentiates them into two loose camps is where the narrator stands on Tammany itself. I have chosen to look at Alfred Henry Lewis's *The Boss* (1903) not because it is the "best written" or the most accurate. Indeed, its extravagantly partisan spirit is somewhat suspect, lying somewhere between the pro-Tammany texts like Francis Churchill William's *J. Devlin, Boss* (1901) and Rufus Shapley's rabidly anti-Irish and anti-Tammany *Solid for Mulhooly: A Political Satire* (1889). In addition, Lewis's novel is valuable as a source because it can be contextualized by his historical work on Tammany. Other novels worth consulting in this genre are Brand Whitlock's 1902 *The 13th District*, Paul Leicester Ford's 1894 *The Honorable Peter Stirling*, and Wyllis Niles's 1872 *Five Hundred Majority*.

4. As a historical corollary to this, Gustavus Myers writes in his *History of Tammany Hall* (1917) that the bosses made citizens where there were none before by setting up naturalization offices at which immigrants could get full citizenship rights. This process usually ended when the "immigration officer" took the new American to the polls. In a discussion of one of Boss Tweed's campaigns, Myers estimates that 25,000 to 30,000 citizens were naturalized in a six-week period in 1868, no fewer than 85 percent of whom voted the Tammany ticket (1968:217).

5. According to Jackson Lears, "in the speed with which labor organizations grouped, disbanded and regrouped elsewhere, one can see the impact of a rootless proletariat, wandering over entire regions in search of work. That floating population, as demographic historians have recently shown, constituted a huge proportion of the nineteenth-century workforce" (1981:29).

6. Ryan's argument is that the bourgeois public sphere in the nineteenth-

century United States was never even proximate to a Habermasian ideal of a bourgeois public sphere but that it was a "variegated, decentered, and democratic array of public spaces" (1994:264), which allows us to see "public life . . . cultivated in many democratic spaces where obstinate differences in power, material status, and hence interest can find expression. The proliferation of democratic publics . . . posed a major counterforce to the escalating dominance of the state and capitalism in the nineteenth-century United States" (1994:286). Ryan's argument is useful to my own analysis of Tammany Hall as a vested public sphere, as opposed to the official civic public sphere, which under the Progressive reform movement wished to align itself more closely with the state. I use her analysis to explain how any vested identity could find its way into a public sphere or could find a public sphere in which the interests of a particular identity could be articulated to those of another and so create a temporary fantasy of a particular public good.

7. Whether or not Tammany actually stood as the friend and ally of the immigrant is still a matter much under debate. Although it is not the purpose of this chapter to adjudicate the facts about the historical function of Tammany, books like Thomas Henderson's *Tammany Hall and the New Immigrants* (1976), Alexander Callow's *The City Boss in America* (1976), Scott Greer's *Ethnics, Machines, and the American Urban Future* (1981), and Seymour J. Mandelbaum's *Boss Tweed's New York* (1965) take up various aspects of this debate.

8. Martin Shefter writes in his historical assessment of Tammany that "the labor union and the political machine institutionalized an accommodation between these warring forces" (1986:199).

9. Here I rely on Raymond Williams's famous formulation of dominant, residual, and emergent literatures in *Marxism and Literature* (1977). He writes, "By 'residual' I mean something different from the 'archaic,' though in practice these are often very difficult to distinguish. Any culture includes available elements of its past, but their place in the contemporary cultural process is profoundly variable. I would call the 'archaic' that which is wholly recognized as an element of the past, to be observed, to be examined, or even on occasion to be consciously 'revived,' in a deliberately specializing way. What I mean by the 'residual' is very different. The residual, by definition, has been effectively formed in the past, but it is still active in the cultural process, not only and often not at all as an element of the past, but as an effective element of the present. Thus certain experiences, meanings, and values which cannot be expressed or substantially verified in terms of the dominant, are nevertheless lived and practised on the basis of the residual—cultural as well as social—of some previous social and cultural institution or formation" (1977:122). The coexistence of the terms in Williams's formulation correspond to this chapter's argument about the use of archaic forms to provide an access point to dominant culture for potentially emergent voices.

10. George Chauncey follows this logic in *Gay New York* (1994). Linking urban reformers' attempts to police working-class culture generally with the effects of such reform on specific minority groups denominated by ethnicity, race, gender, and sexuality, Chauncey argues that resistance to social policing enabled a reorganization of the city and the uses of "official" public spaces, such as parks and streets—creating, in other words, the secret city that Jacob Riis had so feared. "What sociologists and reformers called the social *disorganization* of the city might

more properly be regarded as a social *reorganization*. By the more pejorative term, investigators actually denoted the multiplication of social possibilities that the massing of diverse peoples made possible. 'Disorganization' also evoked the declining strength of the family, the neighborhood, the parish, and other institutions of social control, which seemed, in retrospect at least, to have enforced older patterns of social order in smaller communities. But it ignored, or was incapable of acknowledging, the fact that new forms of social order were emerging in their place" (1994:133).

Works Cited

Ammons, Elizabeth E. 1983. "Going in Circles: The Female Geography of Jewett's *Country of the Pointed Firs.*" *Studies in the Literary Imagination* 16 (fall): 83–92.

Anderson, Benedict. 1991. *Imagined Communities: Reflections on the Origin and Spread of Nationalism.* Rev. ed. London: Verso.

Anderson, Amanda. 1986. "Resistance and Immunity in Riis's Chinatown: Photography and Philanthropy." Unpublished paper, John Hopkins University.

Atherton, Gertrude. 1902. *The Splendid Idle Forties: Stories of Old California.* New York: Macmillan.

Atherton, Gertrude. 1905. *The Bell in the Fog and Other Stories.* New York: Harper and Brothers.

Atherton, Gertrude. 1914. *California: An Intimate History.* New York: Harper and Brothers.

Atherton, Gertrude. 1932. *Adventures of a Novelist.* New York: Liveright.

Atherton, Gertrude. 1968. *The Californians.* Ridgewood, N.J.: Gregg Press.

Balibar, Etienne, and Emmanuel Wallerstein. 1991. *Race, Nation, Class: Ambiguous Identities.* New York: Verso.

Barthes, Roland. 1974. *S/Z: An Essay.* Trans. Richard Miller. New York: Noonday Press.

Barthes, Roland. 1981. *Camera Lucida: Reflections on Photography.* Trans. Richard Howard. New York: Hill & Wang.

Baudrillard, Jean. 1981. *For a Critique of the Political Economy of the Sign.* Trans. Charles Levin. St. Louis: Telos Press.

Bell, Michael Davitt. 1993. *The Problem of American Realism: Studies in the Cultural History of a Literary Idea.* Chicago: University of Chicago Press.

Belsey, Catherine. 1980. *Critical Practice.* New York: Methuen.

Bhabha, Homi. 1990. "DissemiNation: Time, Narrative, and the Margins of the Modern Nation." In *Nations and Narration,* ed. Homi K. Bhabha. London: Routledge.

Bhabha, Homi. 1994. *The Location of Culture.* New York: Routledge.

Boelhower, William. 1987. *Through a Glass Darkly: Ethnic Semiosis in American Literature.* New York: Oxford University Press.

Boulay, Harvey, and Alan DiGaetano. 1985. "Why Did Political Machines Disappear?" *Journal of Urban History* 12 (November): 25–49.

Bowlby, Rachel. 1985. *Just Looking: Consumer Culture in Dreiser, Gissing, and Zola.* New York: Methuen.

Bramen, Carrie Tirado. 1997. "The Americanization of Theron Ware." *Novel* 31 (fall): 63–86.

Brodhead, Richard. 1993. *Cultures of Letters: Scenes of Reading and Writing in Nineteenth-Century America.* Chicago: University of Chicago Press.

Brown, William. 1994. "The Popular, the Populist, and the Populace—Locating Hamlin Garland in the Politics of Culture." *Arizona Quarterly* 50 (autumn): 89–110.

Cable, George Washington. 1879. *Old Creole Days.* New York: Charles Scribner's Sons.

Cable, George Washington. 1885. *"The Silent South" Together with "The Freedman's Case in Equity and the Convict Lease System."* New York: Charles Scribner's Sons.

Cable, George Washington. 1988. *The Grandissimes: A Story of Creole Life.* New York: Penguin Books.

Callow, Alexander B., ed. 1976. *The City Boss in America: An Interpretive Reader.* New York: Oxford University Press.

Campbell, Donna. 1997. *Resisting Regionalism: Gender and Naturalism in American Fiction, 1885–1915.* Athens: Ohio University Press.

Cary, Richard. 1967. *Letters of Sarah Orne Jewett.* Waterville, Maine: Colby College Press.

Cawelti, John. 1965. *Apostles of the Self-Made Man.* Chicago: University of Chicago Press.

Certeau, Michel de. 1986. *Heterologies: Discourse on the Other.* Minneapolis: University of Minnesota Press.

Chauncey, George. 1994. *Gay New York: Gender, Urban Culture, and the Making of the Gay Male World 1890–1940.* New York: Basic Books.

Clay, Charles M. 1980. "George W. Cable." In *Critical Essays on George W. Cable,* ed. Arlin Turner. Boston: G. K. Hall.

Crane, Stephen. 1986. *Maggie: A Girl of the Streets and Other Stories.* New York: Bantam Books.

Donovan, Josephine. 1983. *New England Local Color Literature: A Woman's Tradition.* New York: Frederick Ungar.

Eagleton, Terry. 1985. *Criticism and Ideology: A Study in Marxist Literary History.* London: Verso.

Eagleton, Terry. 1990. "Nationalism: Irony and Commitment." In *Nationalism, Colonialism, and Literature,* ed. Seamus Deane. Minneapolis: University of Minnesota Press.

Fetterley, Judith. 1994. "'Not in the Least American': Nineteenth-Century Literary Regionalism." *College English* 56 (December): 877–895.

Fetterley, Judith, and Marjorie Pryse, eds. 1992. *American Women Regionalists 1850–1910.* New York: Norton.

Fine, David. 1977. *The City, the Immigrant and American Fiction, 1880–1920.* Metuchen, N.J.: Scarecrow.

Fisher, Philip. 1985. *Hard Facts: Setting and Form in the American Novel*. New York: Oxford University Press.

Ford, Paul Leicester. 1967. *The Honorable Peter Stirling*. 1894. Reprint, Ridgewood, N.J.: Gregg Press.

Frakes, George E., and Curtis B. Solberg, eds. 1971. *Minorities in California History*. New York: Random House.

Frederic, Harold. 1960. *The Damnation of Theron Ware*. Cambridge, Mass.: Belknap Press.

Freeman, Mary Wilkins. 1983. *Selected Stories of Mary E. Wilkins Freeman*. Ed. Marjorie Pryse. New York: Norton.

French, Warren. 1970. "What Shall We Do with Hamlin Garland?" *American Literary Realism* 3: 283–289.

Garland, Hamlin. 1914. *A Son of the Middle Border*. New York: Macmillan.

Garland, Hamlin. 1952. *Crumbling Idols: Twelve Essays on Art and Literature*. Gainesville, Fla.: Scholars' Facsimiles and Reprints.

Garland, Hamlin. 1962. *Main-Travelled Roads*. New York: New American Library.

Garner, William Robert. 1970. *Letters from California, 1846–1847*. Ed. Donald Munro Craig. Berkeley: University of California Press.

Gellner, Ernest. 1983. *Nations and Nationalism*. Oxford: Blackwell.

Gibson, Otis. 1978. *The Chinese in America*. New York: Arno Press.

Gillman, Susan. 1994. "Regionalism and Nationalism in Jewett's *Country of the Pointed Firs*." In *New Essays on* The Country of the Pointed Firs, ed. June Howard. Cambridge: Cambridge University Press.

Glazener, Nancy. 1997. *Reading for Realism: A History of a U.S. Literary Institution, 1850–1910*. Durham, N.C.: Duke University Press.

Greenwood, Roberta S. 1992. "Testing the Myths of the Gold Rush." In *Historical Archaeology of Nineteenth-Century California, Papers Presented at a Clark Library Seminar*. Los Angeles: William Andrews Clark Memorial Library at the University of California, Los Angeles.

Greer, Scott A., ed. 1981. *Ethnics, Machines, and the American Urban Future*. Cambridge, Mass.: Schenkman.

Hale, Edward E., Jr. 1980. "Mr. Cable and the Creoles." In *Critical Essays on George W. Cable*, ed. Arlin Turner. Boston: G. K. Hall.

Hale, Edward E., Jr. 1982. "Signs of Life in Literature." In *Critical Essays on Hamlin Garland*, ed. James Nagel. Boston: G. K. Hall.

Hales, Peter. 1984. *Silver Cities: The Photography of American Urbanization, 1839–1915*. Philadelphia: Temple University Press.

Hall, Gwendolyn Midlo. 1992. "The Formation of Anglo-Creole Culture." In *Creole New Orleans: Race and Americanization*, ed. Arnold R. Hirsch and Joseph Logsdon. Baton Rouge: Louisiana State University Press.

Hays, Samuel P. 1957. *The Response to Industrialism, 1885–1914*. Chicago: University of Chicago Press.

Hearn, Lafcadio. 1923. "A Creole Courtyard." In *The Writings of Lafcadio Hearn*. 16 vols. Boston: Houghton Mifflin.

Hearn, Lafcadio. 1924. "Review of the Grandissimes." In *Creole Sketches*, ed. Charles Woodward Hutson. Boston: Houghton Mifflin.

Henderson, Thomas. 1976. *Tammany Hall and the New Immigrants: The Progressive Years.* New York: Aron Press.

Higham, John. 1963. *Strangers in the Land: Patterns of American Nativism, 1860–1925.* New York: Atheneum.

Higham, John. 1984. *Send These to Me: Immigrants in Urban America.* Rev. ed. Baltimore: Johns Hopkins University Press.

Hobsbawm, Eric. 1979. *The Age of Capital, 1848–1875.* New York: New American Library.

Hobsbawm, Eric. 1990. *Nations and Nationalism since 1780: Programme, Myth, Reality.* Cambridge: Cambridge University Press.

Howard, June. 1986. *Form and Content in American Literary Naturalism.* Chapel Hill: University of North Carolina Press.

Howard, June, ed. 1994. *New Essays on* The Country of the Pointed Firs. Cambridge: Cambridge University Press.

Howells, William Dean. 1983. "Editor's Study Columns." In *Editor's Study,* ed. James W. Simpson. Troy, N.Y.: Whitson Publishing.

Jameson, Frederic. 1989. "Nostalgia for the Present." *South Atlantic Quarterly* 88 (spring): 517–537.

Jewett, Sarah Orne. 1981. *The Country of the Pointed Firs and Other Stories.* Ed. Mary Ellen Chase. New York: Norton.

Jewett, Sarah Orne. 1993. *Deephaven.* South Berwick, Maine: Old Berwick Historical Society.

Johnson, Jerah. 1992. "Colonial New Orleans: A Fragment of the Eighteenth-Century French Ethos." In *Creole New Orleans: Race and Americanization,* ed. Arnold R. Hirsch and Joseph Logsdon. Baton Rouge: Louisiana State University Press.

Jones, Gavin. 1997. "Signifying Songs: The Double Meaning of Black Dialect in the Work of George Washington Cable." *American Literary History* 9 (summer): 244–267.

Jordan, David. 1993. "Representing Regionalism." *Canadian Review of American Studies* 23 (winter): 101–114.

Kaplan, Amy. 1988. *The Social Construction of American Realism.* Chicago: University of Chicago Press.

Kasson, John F. 1990. *Rudeness and Civility: Manners in Nineteenth-Century Urban America.* New York: Noonday Press.

Keller, Morton. 1968. *The Art and Politics of Thomas Nast.* New York: Oxford University Press.

Klein, Marcus. 1981. *Foreigners: The Making of American Literature, 1900–1940.* Chicago: University of Chicago Press.

Ladd, Barbara. 1996. *Nationalism and the Color Line in George W. Cable, Mark Twain, and William Faulkner.* Baton Rouge: Louisiana State University Press.

Lears, T. J. Jackson. 1981. *No Place of Grace: Antimodernism and the Transformation of American Culture, 1880–1920.* New York: Pantheon Books.

LeClair, Thomas. 1975. "The Ascendant Eye: A Reading of *The Damnation of Theron Ware.*" *Studies in American Fiction* 3: 95–102.

Leider, Emily Wortis. 1991. *California's Daughter: Gertrude Atherton and Her Times.* Stanford, Calif.: Stanford University Press.

Levy, Bruce. 1995. "'The Country of Corner Lots:' *The Mystery of Metropolisville*, the Single Tax, and the Logic of Provincial Realism." Unpublished essay, Southern Methodist University.

Lewis, Alfred Henry. 1901. *Richard Croker*. New York: Life Publishing.

Lewis, Alfred Henry. 1903. *The Boss, and How He Came to Rule New York*. 1967. Reprint, Ridgewood, N.J.: Gregg Press.

Littleton, Mark W. 1905. "Historical Sketch of the Democracy of King's County." In *The Democratic Party of the State of New York: A History of the Origin, Growth and Achievements of the Democratic Party of the State of New York, Including a History of Tammany Hall in Its Relation to State Politics*, vol. 2, ed. James K. McGuire. New York: United States History Company.

Lott, Eric. 1993. *Love and Theft: Blackface Minstrelsy and the American Working Class*. New York: Oxford University Press.

MacDonald, Bonney. 1993. "Eastern Imaginings of the West in Hamlin Garland's 'Up the Coolly' and 'God's Ravens.'" *Western American Literature* 28 (November): 209–230.

Mandelbaum, Seymour J. 1965. *Boss Tweed's New York*. New York: Wiley.

Marcus, George. 1990. "What Did He Reckon Would Become of the Other Half If He Killed His Half? Doubled, Divided and Crossed Selves in *Pudd'nhead Wilson*, or Mark Twain as Cultural Critic in His Own Times and Ours." In *Mark Twain's Pudd'nhead Wilson: Race, Conflict, and Culture*, ed. Susan Gillman and Forest G. Robinson. Durham, N.C.: Duke University Press.

McGuire, James K., ed. 1905. *The Democratic Party of the State of New York: A History of the Origin, Growth and Achievements of the Democratic Party of the State of New York, Including a History of Tammany Hall in Its Relation to State Politics*. Vol. 2. New York: United States History Company.

McWilliams, Carey. 1971. "Southern California: Ersatz Mythology." In *Minorities in California History*, ed. George E. Frakes and Curtis B. Solberg. New York: Random House.

Michelson, Bruce. 1992. "Theron Ware in the Wilderness of Ideas." *American Literary Realism* 25 (1): 54–73.

Miller, Zane L. 1981. "Bosses, Machines, and the Urban Political Process." In *Ethnics, Machines, and the American Urban Future*, ed. Scott Greer. Cambridge, Mass.: Schenkman.

Myers, Gustavus. 1917. *The History of Tammany Hall*. 2d ed. 1968. Reprint, New York: B. Franklin.

Nagel, Gwen L. 1984. *Critical Essays on Sarah Orne Jewett*. Boston: G. K. Hall.

Nagel, James, ed. 1982. *Critical Essays on Hamlin Garland*. Boston: G. K. Hall.

Nairn, Tom. 1977. *The Break-up of Britain: Crisis and Neo-Nationalism*. London: Verso.

Newhall, Beaumont. 1964. *The History of Photography, from 1839 to the Present Day*. Rev. ed. New York: Museum of Modern Art.

Newhall, Beaumont. 1976. *The Daguerreotype in America*. 3d ed. New York: Dover.

Niles, Wyllis. 1872. *Five Hundred Majority: A Tale for the Times*. New York: Putnam.

"Novel Notes." 1898. *The Bookman* 8 (November): 254.

Ohmann, Richard. 1996. *Selling Culture: Magazines, Markets, and Class at the Turn of the Century*. London: Verso.

Omrcanin, Margaret Stewart. 1973. *The Novel and Political Insurgency*. Philadelphia: Dorrance.

Pitt, Leonard. 1970. *The Decline of the Californios: A Social History of the Spanish-Speaking Californians, 1846–1890*. Berkeley: University of California Press.

Pizer, Donald. 1991. "Hamlin Garland's Main-Travelled Roads Revisited." *South Dakota Review* 29: 53–67.

Pryse, Marjorie. 1998. "Sex, Class, and 'Category Crisis': Reading Jewett's Transitivity." *American Literature* 70 (September): 517–549.

Renza, Louis. 1984. *"A White Heron" and the Question of Minor Literature*. Madison: University of Wisconsin Press.

Riis, Jacob. 1901. *The Making of an American*. New York: Macmillan.

Riis, Jacob. 1903. *The Peril and Preservation of the Home, Being the William L. Bull Lectures for the Year 1903*. Philadelphia: George W. Jacobs.

Riis, Jacob. 1971. *How the Other Half Lives: Studies among the Tenements of New York*. New York: Dover.

Riordan, William. 1963. *Plunkitt of Tammany Hall: Very Plain Talks on Very Practical Politics*. New York: Dutton.

Ryan, Mary. 1994. "Gender and Public Access." In *Habermas and the Public Sphere*, ed. Craig Calhoun. Cambridge, Mass.: MIT Press.

Saum, Lewis O. 1972. "Hamlin Garland and Reform." *South Dakota Review* 10: 36–62.

Saxton, Alexander. 1990. *The Rise and Fall of the White Republic: Class Politics and Mass Culture in Nineteenth-Century America*. New York: Verso.

Saxton, Alexander. 1995. *The Indispensable Enemy: Labor and the Anti-Chinese Movement in California*. Berkeley: University of California Press.

Scharnhorst, Gary, ed. 1990. *Bret Harte's California: Letters to the* Springfield Republican *and* Christian Register, *1866–67*. Albuquerque: University of New Mexico Press.

Seltzer, Mark. 1992. *Bodies and Machines*. New York: Routledge.

Shapley, Rufus. 1889. *Solid for Mulhooly: A Political Satire*. 1970. Reprint, New York: Arno Press.

Shefter, Martin. 1986. "Trade Unions and Political Machines: The Organization and Disorganization of the American Working Class in the Late Nineteenth Century." In *Working-Class Formation: Nineteenth-Century Patterns in Western Europe and the United States*, ed. Ira Katznelson and Aristide R. Zolberg. Princeton, N.J.: Princeton University Press.

Simmel, Georg. 1950. "The Metropolis and Mental Life." In *The Sociology of Georg Simmel*, trans. and ed. Kurt H. Wolff. New York: Free Press.

Simpson, Claude, ed. 1960. *The Local Colorists: American Short Stories, 1857–1900*. New York: Harper.

Sollors, Werner. 1986. *Beyond Ethnicity: Consent and Descent in American Culture*. New York: Oxford University Press.

Stallman, R. W. 1972. *Stephen Crane: A Critical Bibliography*. Ames: Iowa State University Press.

Stallman, R. W., and E. R. Hagemann, eds. 1966. *The New York City Sketches of Stephen Crane and Related Pieces*. New York: New York University Press.

Stange, Maren. 1989. *Symbols of Ideal Life: Social Documentary Photography in America, 1890–1959*. Cambridge: Cambridge University Press.

Steffens, Lincoln. 1901. *The Shame of the Cities*. New York: Peter Smith.

Stewart, Susan. 1984. *On Longing: Narratives of the Miniature, the Gigantic, the Souvenir, the Collection*. Baltimore: Johns Hopkins University Press.

Stewart, Susan. 1991. *Crimes of Writing: Problems in the Containment of Representation*. New York: Oxford University Press.

Stock, Catherine McNicol. 1996. *Rural Radicals: Righteous Rage in the American Grain*. Ithaca, N.Y.: Cornell University Press.

Strong, Josiah. 1907. *The Challenge of the City*. New York: Eaton and Mains.

Strong, Josiah. 1963. *Our Country: Its Possible Future and Its Present Crisis, Revised Edition Based on the Census of 1890*. Ed. Jurgen Herbst. Cambridge, Mass.: Belknap Press.

Sundquist, Eric. 1988. "Realism and Regionalism." In *Columbia Literary History of the United States*, ed. Emory Elliott. New York: Columbia University Press.

Swann, Charles. 1987. "*The Grandissimes*: A Story-Shaped World." *Literature and History* 13 (autumn): 257–277.

Takaki, Ronald. 1989. *Strangers from a Different Shore: A History of Asian-Americans*. New York: Penguin Books.

Takaki, Ronald. 1993. *A Different Mirror: A History of Multicultural America*. Boston: Little, Brown.

"Topics of the Time." 1902. *The Century Magazine* 63 (February): 635–636.

Trachtenberg, Alan. 1982a. "Experiments in Another Country: Stephen Crane's City Sketches." In *American Realism: New Essays*, ed. Eric Sundquist. Baltimore: Johns Hopkins University Press.

Trachtenberg, Alan. 1982b. *The Incorporation of America: Culture and Society in the Gilded Age*. New York: Hill & Wang.

Tregle, Joseph G., Jr. 1992. "Creoles and Americans." In *Creole New Orleans: Race and Americanization*, ed. Arnold R. Hirsch and Joseph Logsdon. Baton Rouge: Louisiana State University Press.

Tung, William L. 1974. *The Chinese in America, 1820–1973: A Chronology and Fact Book*. Dobbs Ferry, N.Y.: Oceana Publications.

Turner, Arlin. 1956. *George Washington Cable: A Biography*. Durham, N.C.: Duke University Press.

Twigg, Reginald. 1992. "The Performative Dimension of Surveillance: Jacob Riis' *How the Other Half Lives*." *Text and Performance Quarterly* 12: 305–328.

Volosinov, V. N. 1973. *Marxism and the Philosophy of Language*. Trans. Ladislav Matejka and I. R. Titunik. Cambridge, Mass.: Harvard University Press.

Wald, Priscilla. 1993. "Terms of Assimilation: Legislating Subjectivity in the Emerging Nation." In *Cultures of United States Imperialism*, ed. Amy Kaplan and Donald Pease. Durham, N.C.: Duke University Press.

Wald, Priscilla. 1995. *Constituting Americans: Cultural Anxiety and Narrative Form*. Durham, N.C.: Duke University Press.

Warner, Michael. 1994. "The Mass Public and the Mass Subject." In *Habermas and the Public Sphere*, ed. Craig Calhoun. Cambridge, Mass.: MIT Press.

Whitlock, Brand. 1902. *The 13th District: A Story of a Candidate.* 1968. Reprint, Ridgewood, N.J.: Gregg Press.

Wiess, Nancy Joan. 1968. *Charles Francis Murphy, 1858–1924: Respectability and Responsibility in Tammany Politics.* Northampton, Mass.: Smith College.

Williams, Francis Churchill. 1901. *J. Devlin, Boss: A Romance of American Politics.* Boston: Lothrop.

Williams, Raymond. 1973. *The Country and the City.* New York: Oxford University Press.

Williams, Raymond. 1977. *Marxism and Literature.* New York: Oxford University Press.

Wilson, Christopher P. 1985. *The Labor of Words: Literary Professionalism in the Progressive Era.* Athens: University of Georgia Press.

Wood, John Seymour. 1904. "Alfred Henry Lewis." *The Bookman* 18 (January).

Wu, William F. 1982. *The Yellow Peril: Chinese Americans in American Fiction, 1850–1940.* Hamden, Conn.: Archon Books.

Zagarell, Sandra A. 1994. "*Country*'s Portrayal of Community and the Exclusion of Difference." In *New Essays on* The Country of the Pointed Firs, ed. June Howard. Cambridge: Cambridge University Press.

Ziff, Larzer. 1979. *The American 1890s: Life and Times of a Lost Generation.* Lincoln: University of Nebraska Press.

Index

access point, 99, 127, 157, 178
aesthetics: in Garland's works, 42, 56, 57–58; in Harte's works, 79; in Riis's works, 141
Africa/African, 113, 114, 117
alienation: in Atherton's works, 91; in Cable's works, 122; and characteristics of regional fiction, 17, 36; in Frederic's works, 66, 67, 70; in Jewett's works, 22, 23, 37; and link between real property and regionalism, 121; and urbanism, 5–6; and what difference regional writing makes, 5–6, 15. *See also* estrangement; isolation; marginalization
American Scene, The (James), 127
Ammons, Elizabeth, 12
anthropology, 19, 23, 61, 129, 138
Arena magazine, 50
artificiality, in Garland's works, 49
assimilation: in Atherton's works, 74, 89, 90, 95; in Cable's works, 99, 113, 114, 117, 121, 122; and characteristics of regional fiction, 179; in Frederic's works, 66; in Jewett's works, 28, 29, 40; in Riis's works, 138, 139, 140, 143, 146, 147, 149, 150, 161; Strong's views about, 169, 178; and Tammany, 169, 178; and travel writings about California, 76–77; and urban/slumming literature, 125, 132; and what difference regional writing makes, 7, 16
Atherton, Gertrude, 7, 127; *The Bell and the Fog* by, 87–88; *California: An Intimate History* by, 89; *The Californians* by, 14, 15, 73–75, 76, 79, 80–97; James's influence on, 87–88; "The Pearls

of Loreto" by, 90; *The Splendid Idle Forties* by, 89, 90
Atlantic Monthly, 4, 50
audience. *See* readers
authenticity: in Atherton's works, 74–75, 84, 86, 87, 91; Bell's views about, 131; in Cable's works, 100, 104–5, 118; in Crane's works, 128, 129; in Frederic's works, 66, 71; in Garland's works, 44; in Jewett's works, 18; nineteenth-century preoccupation with, 35; and pastoral regionalism, 125; and problems in regional fiction, 72; in urban/slumming literature, 125, 126, 128, 129
authority: and access to authorship, 127; in Lewis's works, 167; in Riis's works, 132, 138, 140, 147; in slumming fiction, 127
autobiography. *See Son of the Middle Border, A* (Garland)

Balcony Stories (King), 105
Balibar, Etienne, 20, 101, 119
Barthes, Roland, 20, 22
Bell, Michael Davitt, 14, 129, 131
Bell and the Fog, The (Atherton), 87–88
Belsey, Catherine, 120–21
Bhabha, Homi, 89, 110, 111, 122
Bible, 62, 65, 66, 67
blacks: in Cable's works, 99, 107, 115–16, 120, 121, 122–23; Chinese compared with, 148; and link between real property and regionalism, 121; and New Orleans history, 101, 102; stereotypes of, 32. *See also* Creoles; race; slavery; *specific character*
Bloom, Robert (fictional character), 55–56

155; function of, 11; private sphere in fiction in, 20; and what difference regional writing makes, 4–5, 11, 12; Wilson's study of changes in, 126–27. *See also specific editor or periodical*

perspective: "bird's eye view," 134; in Jewett's works, 27; in Riis's works, 133–34

Philosophe, Palmyre la (fictional character), 103, 109, 110, 113, 115–16, 119–20

photographs: and memory, 20; in Riis's works, 133, 136–37, 138, 141–43, 145–46, 150–51, 152, 154; in urban/slumming literature, 131, 133

pioneer spirit, 45

Plunkitt of Tammany Hall (Riordan), 168, 172–73, 175, 178

politicians/politics, in Frederic's works, 71–72. *See also* machine novels; Tammany; *specific author or work*

poor, 155, 156, 169

popular culture, 41–42

Populism, 41–42, 49–50, 54, 55, 57

primitiveness, in Frederic's works, 60

private sphere: in Atherton's works, 74, 75; in Cable's works, 100, 101, 105, 106, 107; and characteristics of regional fiction, 17, 20, 36, 37, 157; in Frederic's works, 64; in Freeman's works, 37; in Jewett's works, 34–35; in Riis's works, 141, 143, 144, 146–47, 154, 161; in Saxton's works, 161–62; in slumming literature, 126; and Tammany, 159, 161–62, 163, 178, 179

professionalism, literary, 127

Progress and Poverty (George), 47

Progressivism, 10, 132, 135, 144, 151, 155, 159, 160, 161, 173

Pryse, Marjorie, 12

psychic dislocation, 5

public sphere: in Atherton's works, 74; in Cable's works, 101, 105, 106, 107; in Jewett's works, 35; in Lewis's works, 161, 173–74; in Riis's works, 144, 146, 154, 161; Ryan's views about, 172; in Saxton's works, 161–62; and Tammany, 157, 158–59, 161–62, 163, 172, 173–74, 177, 178, 179; and urban fiction, 155. *See also* private sphere

"Question of Success, The" (Garland), 57

race: in Atherton's works, 74, 76, 79, 81, 82, 83, 88, 96, 97; in Cable's works, 99, 100, 102, 103, 105, 107, 110–14, 116–22; and characteristics of regional fiction, 158; and Chinese mixing with white women, 148; in Frederic's works, 64–65; inferiority of, 122; in Jewett's works, 31–32, 34; and New Orleans history, 102; in Riis's works, 133, 135, 149; stereotypes of, 133; and travel writings about California, 80; and what difference regional writing makes, 4, 16. *See also* blacks; Chinese; Jews

railroads, 44, 45, 147, 148

readers: of Cable's works, 121; and characteristics of regional fiction, 18, 19, 20, 158; and Crane's works, 128; and epilogues of nineteenth-century novels, 121; and Frederic's works, 59; and Garland's works, 43, 51, 53; and Jewett's works, 21, 35; and Lewis's works, 165; and pastoral regionalism, 125; and regional fiction as responsive to market, 19; and Riis's works, 125, 132, 133, 136–37, 138, 153; as strangers, 136; and Tammany, 163, 165; and urban fiction, 125; and what difference regional writing makes, 3, 4–5, 14, 15–16

realism: in Atherton's works, 74, 75, 79, 80, 83, 87, 88, 89, 90, 91, 97; in Cable's works, 104, 105; Eagleton's views about, 88; and ethnicity, 122; in Garland's works, 41, 44, 47, 57; Howells as standard bearer of, 7; and identity, 104; of James, 87–88, 91; in Lewis's works, 166; and narrator, 138; and regional fiction as genre, 5, 13–14, 124; and Tammany, 165, 166; and what difference regional writing makes, 5, 7, 9, 13–14

real property, regionalism's link with, 121

recollection. *See* memory

Reconstruction, 99, 100, 102, 121, 122

reform: in Crane's works, 129; in Garland's works, 41, 49; in Riis's works, 125–26, 132, 133, 135, 139, 143, 144, 151, 152, 155, 171; and Tammany, 156, 159, 169, 170, 171; and urban/slumming literature, 125, 126, 132, 155

regional fiction: as access point, 99, 127; binaries in, 15; characteristics of, 3, 6, 17–20, 35–37, 38–39, 124–27, 157–58,

social problems: and characteristics of regional literature, 35–36; and pastoral regionalism, 124; rural life as antidote to nineteenth-century, 36

society, "reserve force" of, 27, 28

Solberg, Curtis B., 82

Solid for Mulhooly: A Political Satire (Shapley), 162–64, 172, 175

Sollors, Werner, 88, 175

Son of the Middle Border, A (Garland), 40, 42–50

Soulsby, Candace (fictional character), 67, 69–71

South, resurrection of, 102. *See also* New Orleans, Louisiana

Spain/Spanish, 79, 101, 102. *See also* California; *Californians, The* (Atherton)

spatialization: and characteristics of regional fiction, 20, 36; in Jewett's works, 26, 35; in Lewis's works, 167, 172; and pastoral regionalism, 125; and placeless space, 172; in Riis's works, 132, 134, 138, 143, 146, 147, 149, 153, 171; and Tammany, 167, 171, 172; and urban fiction, 125

speculation, 43, 49, 51, 56, 102, 128

spirit world, in Jewett's works, 19, 23, 24, 25, 33

Splendid Idle Forties, The (Atherton), 89, 90

Stallman, R. W., 131

Stange, Maren, 136, 137–38, 150–51

Steffens, Lincoln, 155, 162

"Stephen Crane in Minetta Lane, One of Gotham's Most Notorious Thoroughfares" (Crane), 130–31

stereotypes: in Atherton's works, 84, 85, 89; of blacks, 32; in Cable's works, 117; ethnic, 139; of greed, 140; in Jewett's works, 32; of Jews, 141; racial, 133; in Riis's works, 133, 139, 140, 141

Stewart, Susan, 12, 35, 64

storytelling. *See* folklore/folktales; tall tales

strangers: and characteristics of regional fiction, 18, 20, 36, 38; and class issues, 36; and culturally barren regions, 39–40; in Frederic's works, 41, 67; in Garland's works, 41, 49, 51, 56; in Jewett's works, 18–19, 20–34, 38, 39–40; narrators as, 18–19, 20–29; natives as, 43; in pastoral regionalism, 125; readers as, 136; in Riis's works, 133, 136, 137, 141, 144,

146, 147, 148, 149; and Tammany, 179; in urban fiction, 125; and what difference regional writing makes, 15. *See also* immigrants/immigration

Strong, Josiah, 96–97, 155–56, 165, 169, 177–78

subjectivity: in Atherton's works, 74, 75, 76, 88, 91; in Cable's works, 105, 119, 121; and epilogues of nineteenth-century novels, 121; in James's works, 88; in Jewett's works, 35–36, 37; in Lewis's works, 170

Sue, Eugene, 126

Sundquist, Eric, 14

surveillance, technique of in Riis's works, 136, 137

Swann, Charles, 103, 113

Takaki, Ronald, 147, 148, 149

tall tales, 159–60, 166

Tammany: as access point, 157; actual, 155; as association, 155, 156; characteristics of, 155–56, 179; and characteristics of regional fiction, 16, 158; criticisms of, 155, 162–64; as cultural site, 156; doubling of, 176–77; feudal image of, 159, 178; as fictional figure, 156; fraternal nature of, 176; history of, 162–63, 173; and labor unions, 176–77, 178; machine analogy about, 168–69; mythical nature of, 155, 162–64, 170; Nast's satire about, 158–59, 164; role in regional fiction of, 16, 179; "wigwams" of, 155, 162. *See also specific author or work*

temporality: in Atherton's works, 79, 83, 91; in Cable's works, 110; in Frederic's works, 59, 60–61, 65; in Garland's works, 45, 48; in Jewett's works, 27–28, 38, 40; and local color, 125; and pastoral regionalism, 125; in Riis's works, 125–26, 132; and travel writings/letters about California, 76, 78, 79; and urban fiction, 125

tenement: Riis's blueprint for model, 152–53; "The Ship" as, 136–37

theatre, in Frederic's works, 70–71

Tilley, Elijah (fictional character), 21, 23, 29, 33

timelessness, in Jewett's works, 27–28, 33

Todd, Almira (fictional character), 21, 22, 26, 27, 28, 29–31, 32–34